Thomas Heider

Goal-based Interaction with Smart Environments

Thomas Heider

Goal-based Interaction with Smart Environments

A Unified Distributed System Architecture

Südwestdeutscher Verlag für Hochschulschriften

Impressum/Imprint (nur für Deutschland/ only for Germany)
Bibliografische Information der Deutschen Nationalbibliothek: Die Deutsche Nationalbibliothek verzeichnet diese Publikation in der Deutschen Nationalbibliografie; detaillierte bibliografische Daten sind im Internet über http://dnb.d-nb.de abrufbar.

Alle in diesem Buch genannten Marken und Produktnamen unterliegen warenzeichen-, marken- oder patentrechtlichem Schutz bzw. sind Warenzeichen oder eingetragene Warenzeichen der jeweiligen Inhaber. Die Wiedergabe von Marken, Produktnamen, Gebrauchsnamen, Handelsnamen, Warenbezeichnungen u.s.w. in diesem Werk berechtigt auch ohne besondere Kennzeichnung nicht zu der Annahme, dass solche Namen im Sinne der Warenzeichen- und Markenschutzgesetzgebung als frei zu betrachten wären und daher von jedermann benutzt werden dürften.

Verlag: Südwestdeutscher Verlag für Hochschulschriften Aktiengesellschaft & Co. KG
Dudweiler Landstr. 99, 66123 Saarbrücken, Deutschland
Telefon +49 681 37 20 271-1, Telefax +49 681 37 20 271-0
Email: info@svh-verlag.de
Zugl.: Rostock, Universität, Diss., 2009

Herstellung in Deutschland:
Schaltungsdienst Lange o.H.G., Berlin
Books on Demand GmbH, Norderstedt
Reha GmbH, Saarbrücken
Amazon Distribution GmbH, Leipzig
ISBN: 978-3-8381-1528-3

Imprint (only for USA, GB)
Bibliographic information published by the Deutsche Nationalbibliothek: The Deutsche Nationalbibliothek lists this publication in the Deutsche Nationalbibliografie; detailed bibliographic data are available in the Internet at http://dnb.d-nb.de.

Any brand names and product names mentioned in this book are subject to trademark, brand or patent protection and are trademarks or registered trademarks of their respective holders. The use of brand names, product names, common names, trade names, product descriptions etc. even without a particular marking in this works is in no way to be construed to mean that such names may be regarded as unrestricted in respect of trademark and brand protection legislation and could thus be used by anyone.

Publisher: Südwestdeutscher Verlag für Hochschulschriften Aktiengesellschaft & Co. KG
Dudweiler Landstr. 99, 66123 Saarbrücken, Germany
Phone +49 681 37 20 271-1, Fax +49 681 37 20 271-0
Email: info@svh-verlag.de

Printed in the U.S.A.
Printed in the U.K. by (see last page)
ISBN: 978-3-8381-1528-3

Copyright © 2010 by the author and Südwestdeutscher Verlag für Hochschulschriften Aktiengesellschaft & Co. KG and licensors
All rights reserved. Saarbrücken 2010

Abstract

The vision of Ambient Intelligence is based on the ubiquity of information technology, the presence of computation, communication, and sensorial capabilities in an unlimited abundance of everyday appliances and environments.

It is now a significant challenge to let ambient intelligence effortlessly emerge from the devices that surround the user in his environment. Future ambient intelligent infrastructures (*e.g.*, Smart Environments) must be able to configure themselves from the available components in order to be effective in the real world. They require software technologies that enable ad-hoc ensembles of devices to spontaneously form a coherent group of cooperating components. This is specifically a challenge, if the individual components are heterogeneous in nature and have to engage in complex activity sequences in order to achieve a user goal. Typical examples of such ensembles are smart environments.

It will be argued that enabling an ensemble of devices to spontaneously and coherently act on behalf of the user, requires software technologies that support unsupervised spontaneous cooperation. This thesis will illustrate why a goal based approach is reasonable and how explicit goals can be used to find device spanning strategies that assist the user.

In order to solve the challenges noted above, an overall concept and architecture based on goal based interaction will be illustrated. Furthermore different concepts of cooperation strategies will be introduced and finally an evaluation will prove the validity of the approach.

Kurzfassung

Die Vision von Ambient Intelligence basiert auf ubiquitären Informationstechnologien in Alltagsgeräten und Umgebungen, wobei Rechnerkapazität, Kommunikation und sensorische Fähigkeiten in einer unlimitierten Form vorhanden sind.

Eine der zentralen Herausforderungen ist es dafür zu sorgen, dass Ambient Intelligence aus den Geräten die den Nutzer umgeben mühelos enstehen kann. Zukünftige Ambient Intelligence Infrastrukturen (z.B. Intelligente Umgebungen) müssen in der Lage sein, sich aus den vorhandenen Komponenten selbst zu konfigurieren, um in der realen Welt effektiv zu sein. Dies erfordert Softwaretechnologien, die es einem ad-hoc Ensemble von Geräten ermöglichen, spontan eine Gruppe von kooperierenden Komponenten zu bilden. Dies ist besonders deshalb eine Herausforderung, da die individuellen Komponenten sehr heterogen sind und sich an komplexen Aktivitäts-Sequenzen beteiligen müssen, um die Nutzerziele zu erreichen. Ein typisches Beispiel für solche Ensembles sind sogenannte Smart Environments.

Um Geräte-Ensembles zu befähigen, spontan und kohärent im Interesse des Nutzers zu agieren, werden Technologien benötigt die unüberwachte spontane Kooperation unterstützen. Die Dissertation wird darstellen, warum ein zielbasierter Ansatz erfolgversprechend ist, und wie explizite Ziele verwendet werden können, um systemübergreifende Strategien zu generieren.

Um die zuvor erwähnten Herausforderungen zu lösen, wird ein Gesamtkonzept und eine Architektur vorgestellt, die auf zielbasierter Interaktion basiert. Weiterhin werden verschiedene Konzepte zur Generierung von Kooperationsstrategien erläutert. Eine abschließende Evaluierung zeigt die Gültigkeit des Ansatzes.

Contents

1	**Introduction**	**1**
1.1	Thematic Context & Motivation	1
1.2	Ambient Intelligent Environments	5
	1.2.1 Application Scenarios	6
	1.2.2 User Requirements	10
1.3	Building AmI Systems	12
	1.3.1 Some Challenges	13
	1.3.2 System Requirements	16
1.4	Approach	16
	1.4.1 Paradigm	17
	1.4.2 Architectural Integration	18
	1.4.3 Operational Integration	19
	1.4.4 Proof of Realizability & Usefulness	20
	1.4.5 Generalization	21
1.5	Contribution & Results of the Thesis	21
1.6	Chronology of the presented work	22
1.7	Outline	23
2	**Goal-based Interaction**	**25**
2.1	The Application Domain	25
2.2	Function-based vs. Goal-based	26
2.3	Dynamic Extension	28
2.4	Explicit Goals	29
	2.4.1 Goals in Smart Environments	30
	2.4.2 Goal classification	34
	2.4.3 Goal Example: Direct Goals	36
	2.4.4 Goal Example: Indirect Goals	36
2.5	Goal-based Interaction – Conclusion	37

		2.5.1	Intention Analysis	38
		2.5.2	Strategy Generation	39
	2.6	GbI and Computer-based Assistance		39
		2.6.1	The Mental Model	41
	2.7	Chapter Summary		42

3 Related Work – Smart Environments   45

- 3.1 Device cooperation / user assistance in smart environments 46
  - 3.1.1 Custom-tailored by the designer 46
  - 3.1.2 Device cooperation by Plan Recognition 48
  - 3.1.3 Learning by observing the user 50
  - 3.1.4 Device cooperation by Matchmaking 51
  - 3.1.5 Device cooperation – Projects focusing on middleware 54
  - 3.1.6 Strategies for cooperation from other research areas 55
- 3.2 Software infrastructures for distributed systems 57
- 3.3 Summary 59
  - 3.3.1 Verdict on operational integration 60
  - 3.3.2 Verdict on architectonic integration 60

4 Architecture Framework   63

- 4.1 Introduction 63
- 4.2 Middleware challenges 65
- 4.3 The EMBASSI architecture 68
  - 4.3.1 The Multi-Modal-Interaction (MMI) levels 68
  - 4.3.2 The assistance levels 69
  - 4.3.3 Additional notes on the generic architecture 70
- 4.4 The middleware model SODA-POP 72
  - 4.4.1 Component types 73
  - 4.4.2 Channels & systems 74
  - 4.4.3 Subscriptions 75
  - 4.4.4 Message handling 76
- 4.5 Related work 78
- 4.6 Summary and outlook 80
  - 4.6.1 What has been achieved so far 80
  - 4.6.2 Additional considerations 81
  - 4.6.3 Enhancement of SODA-POP with an agent selection algorithm 82
- 4.7 Ensemble Communication Framework – ECo 83

5 AI Planning as Source of the Assistance Strategy — 87
- 5.1 Introduction 87
- 5.2 Architecture overview 88
- 5.3 Planning as assistance 90
  - 5.3.1 Concrete example 91
- 5.4 Why Planning as Inference? 92
  - 5.4.1 Reasoning Methods in AI 92
  - 5.4.2 Planning vs. Service Matching 93
- 5.5 The planning domain model 93
  - 5.5.1 Representing Plans 94
  - 5.5.2 Choosing a planning language 96
  - 5.5.3 PDDL 98
  - 5.5.4 Choosing a Planning System 105
  - 5.5.5 What about HTN planning? 107
- 5.6 The Scheduling Coordination Algorithm 108
- 5.7 The joint ontology 110
- 5.8 Prototype 110
  - 5.8.1 System extension 111
  - 5.8.2 Operating sequence example 113
- 5.9 Limits of the AI planning approach as assistance method 115
- 5.10 Distributed vs. Centralized Strategy Generation 115
- 5.11 Chapter summary 117

6 Optimization as Source of the Assistance Strategy — 119
- 6.1 Introduction 119
- 6.2 Smart Meeting Rooms 120
- 6.3 Managing Multi-Display Environments 121
- 6.4 The Need for Automatic Display Mapping 123
  - 6.4.1 User Requirements 124
- 6.5 Defining Optimal Display Mapping 125
  - 6.5.1 q_s – Spatial Quality 127
  - 6.5.2 q_t – Temporal Continuity 129
  - 6.5.3 q_p – Semantic Proximity 130
  - 6.5.4 Discussion of q 130
  - 6.5.5 Using q 131
- 6.6 Distributed Optimization in ad-hoc Ensembles 132

		6.6.1	Related Work	134
		6.6.2	The Search Space	134
		6.6.3	The Display Mapping Problem as a Special Case of the Quadratic Assignment Problem	137
		6.6.4	Distributed Optimization – The Approach	138
		6.6.5	GRASP	139
		6.6.6	Distributing GRASP (DGRASP)	141
		6.6.7	Running DGRASP	146
	6.7	Evaluation of DGRASP		146
		6.7.1	Environment Simulator	151
		6.7.2	Section Summary	151
	6.8	Combining DGRASP and Planning		153
		6.8.1	Goal Refinement - Goal Deliberation	153
		6.8.2	SODA-POP's Selection Mechanism	154
	6.9	Evaluation of q		155
		6.9.1	Overview	157
		6.9.2	Calibration Experiment	158
		6.9.3	Evaluation Experiment – Setup	160
		6.9.4	Results	163
		6.9.5	Section Summary	170
	6.10	Excursus: Goal function as Benchmark:		170
	6.11	Chapter Summary		171

7 Conclusion — 173

7.1	Final example	174
7.2	Summary of the results	175
7.3	Outlook	177
7.4	Acknowledgements	178
References		179

A AI Planning Documents — i

A.1	Example operator file	i
A.2	Environment Ontology extract	iii
A.3	Dynamic Strategy Planning	vi

B Test rooms for optimization algorithms — xi

List of Figures

1.1	Smart Environment Server Room	3
1.2	SmartKom System Architecture	4
1.3	MMIS Smart Appliance Lab	8
1.4	Final meeting agenda	9
1.5	Dynamic Ensembles	12
1.6	Achieving the same effect with different ensembles	14
1.7	Goal based Interaction	17
1.8	Sketch: Devices, Basic Topology, and Ensemble Creation	19
2.1	The ecological interface	27
2.2	Principle of goal based interaction	38
2.3	Different User Interfaces and the corresponding Mental Model	41
2.4	Multidimensional Classification of Human-Environment-Interaction	43
4.1	Generic EMBASSI architecture	69
4.2	EMBASSI architecture – Home Control Instance	71
4.3	Basic message handling process in SODA-POP	77
4.4	MMIS Smart Appliance Lab, schematic view	84
4.5	ECo Architecture of MMIS Smart Appliance Lab	85
5.1	Goal based ensemble control: Example	92
5.2	PDDL domain structure	99
5.3	PDDL domain file	100
5.4	PDDL problem file	101
5.5	Planning and Scheduling Procedure	108
5.6	Planning Procedure	114
6.1	Examples of multiple display environments	121
6.2	Multiple display environment: Smart Appliance Lab at Rostock University	123

6.3	Mapping documents to displays	126
6.4	Visibility & Projectability	127
6.5	MMIS-Lab Steerable Projector	129
6.6	Ensemble creation	132
6.7	Visualization of the search space	134
6.8	Simple examples for discussion of the search space	136
6.9	Finding solutions for multiple devices	141
6.10	Multiple machines: search in parallel	142
6.11	Multiple machines: Split search space	142
6.12	Distributed optimization with multiple devices: Approach	142
6.13	Implementation Approach	145
6.14	Test rooms number 4 and 5	149
6.15	Environment Simulation System	151
6.16	Experimental setup	158
6.17	Calibration experiment	159
6.18	Problem documents	160
6.19	GUI for document importance and document-display assignment	161
6.20	Boxplots of solution time vs. mode	163
6.21	Boxplots of interaction count vs. mode	165
6.22	Boxplots of user satisfaction vs. mode	166
A.1	Ensemble Creation: new device added	vi
A.2	Ensemble Creation: joining the topology	vii
A.3	Ensemble Creation: self description	viii
A.4	Ensemble Creation: strategy generation	ix
B.1	Keys for the testroom pictures	xi
B.2	Testroom 1	xii
B.3	Testroom 2	xii
B.4	Testroom 3	xiii
B.5	Testroom 4	xiii
B.6	Testroom 5	xiv
B.7	Testroom 6	xv
B.8	Testroom 7	xv
B.9	Testroom 8	xvi
B.10	Testroom 9	xvi
B.11	Testroom 10	xvii

List of Tables

1.1	Ambient Intelligence Components	13
3.1	Smart Environment Projects	60
5.1	IPC 2002 Planning Competition results	106
6.1	Distributed GRASP messages	147
6.2	DGRASP solution quality	149
6.3	Average computing time in ms	150
6.4	Average number of communications	150
6.5	Questionnaire summary	167

Chapter 1

Introduction

> *We are in the midst of a major change in how we relate to technology ...*
> *As technology became more powerful and complex, we became*
> *less able to understand how it worked.*
> Donald A. Norman, The Design of Future Things, 2007

1.1 Thematic Context & Motivation

Modern technical infrastructures and personal computational appliances provide a multitude of opportunities for simplifying and streamlining the everyday life. However, many of the systems available today – such as the typical feature-loaded audio and video components, or complex instrumented meeting rooms – are not always efficiently usable for the average person. But, in an environment where features abound, easy access to these features more and more becomes the key quality criterion for the user.

Consequently, the desire for intelligent[1] systems will continue, where people are surrounded by intelligent intuitive interfaces that are embedded in all kinds of objects and environments. These systems must be capable of recognising and responding to the presence of different individuals in a seamless, unobtrusive and often invisible way.

Concepts like "Ubiquitous Computing" [2], "Pervasive Computing" [3], and "Ambient Intelligence" [4, 5] paraphrase the vision of a world in which we are surrounded by smart, intuitively

---
[1] "Intelligent" or "smart" could – in the context of this topic – also be substituted by "reasonable behavior". The meaning of this notion is that the systems show a meaningful behavior because they understand the goals of the user instead of relying only on sensor data or direct interaction. (see *e.g.* [1])

operated devices that help us to organize, structure, and master our everyday life. They share the notion of a smart, personal environment which characterizes a new paradigm for the interaction between a person and his everyday surroundings: Smart environments enable these surroundings to become aware of the human that interacts with them, his goals and needs. So it is possible to assist the human proactively in performing his activities and reaching his goals. – If my car stereo tunes in to exactly the station I just listened to at the breakfast table, then this is a simple example for such an aware, proactive environment; just as the mobile phone that automatically redirects calls to my voice mail in case I am in a meeting, or the bathroom mirror that reminds me of taking my medications.

To date, it is the user's responsibility to manage his personal environment, to operate and control the various appliances and devices available for his support. But, the more technology is available and the more options there are, the greater is the challenge not to get lost in an abundance of possibilities. Failing to address this challenge adequately simply results in technology becoming inoperable, effectively useless. The goal of Smart Environments is to take over this mechanic and monotonous control task from the user and manage appliance activities on his behalf. Technical foundation of Smart Environments is ubiquitous computing technology: the diffusion of information technology into all appliances and objects of the everyday life, based on miniaturized and low cost hardware. In the near future, a multitude of such "information appliances" and "smart artifacts" will populate everyone's personal environment. In order to make the vision of smart environments come true, a coherent teamwork between the environment's appliances has to be established that enables a co-operative, proactive support of the user.

A rather popular scenario illustrating this application area is the smart conference room (or smart living room, for consumer-oriented projects) that automatically adapts to the activities of its current occupants [6, 7]. Such a room might, for instance, automatically switch the projector to the current speaker's presentation as she approaches the lectern, and subdue the room lights – turning them up again for the discussion. Of course, we expect the environment to automatically fetch the presentation from the speaker's notebook. And the speaker should be able to use her own wireless presentation controller to move through her slides – although she might just as well choose to pick up the lectern's presentation controller.

Such a scenario doesn't sound too difficult, it can readily be constructed from common hardware available today, and, using pressure sensors and RFID tagging, doesn't even require expensive cameras and difficult image analysis to detect who is currently at the lectern. Setting up the application software for this scenario that drives the environment's devices in response

Introduction

Figure 1.1: Smart Environment Server Room (Source: *Aware Home* project, Georgia Tech)

to sensor signals doesn't present a major hurdle either. So it seems as if smart environments are rather well understood, as far as underlying information technology is concerned. But this only applies as long as the device ensembles that make up the environment are anticipated by the developers. Today's smart environments in the various research labs are usually built from devices and components whose functionality is known to the developer. So, all possible interactions between devices can be considered in advance and suitable adaptation strategies for coping with changing ensembles can be defined. When looking at the underlying software infrastructure, we see that the interaction between the different devices, the "intelligence", has been carefully handcrafted by the software engineers, who have built this scenario. This means: significant changes to the ensemble require a manual modification of the smart environment's control application.

In the examples of Fig. 1.1 and Fig. 1.2 it is apparent that a static architecture is not practical. In Fig. 1.1 we see the server room of the *Aware Home* project [8] at the Georgia Tech university and in Fig. 1.2 the architecture of the BMBF project *SmartKom* [9]. In these system architectures, you need a system integration engineer to add new components to the system.

This is obviously out of the question for real world applications, where people continuously buy new devices for embellishing their home. And it is a severe cost factor for institutional operators of professional media infrastructures such as conference rooms and smart offices. Things can be even more challenging: imagine a typical ad hoc meeting, where some people meet at a perfectly average room. All attendants bring notebook computers, at least one brings a projector, and the room has some light controls. Of course, all devices will be accessible by wireless networks. So it would be possible for this chance ensemble to provide the same assistance as a deliberate smart conference room. Enabling the devices to configure themselves into

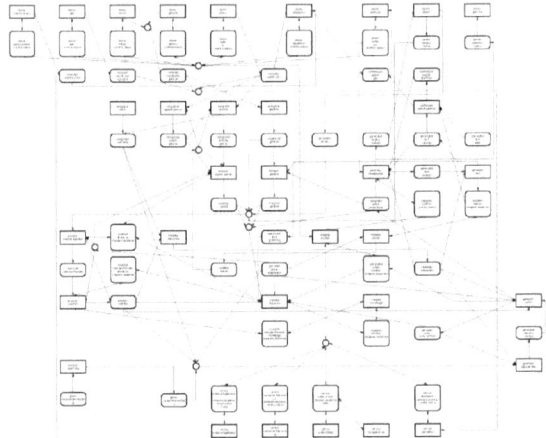

Figure 1.2: SmartKom System Architecture (Source: *SmartKom* project)

a coherently acting ensemble requires more than setting up a control application in advance. Here, we need software infrastructures that allow true self-organization of ad hoc appliance ensembles, with the ability to afford non-trivial changes to the ensemble.

It will become even more clear that a manual / static system configuration will be impossible in the near future, if we look at the concepts of "The Internet of Things" [10] or "Smart Dust". These concepts are an expansion of ubiquitous computing, where all appliances and devices are equipped with network connectivity and authentication. Hereby a new dimension will be added to the world of information and communication: in addition to *anytime, any place* connectivity for *anyone*, there will be the be connectivity for *anything*. In the not so distant future, the personal environment of the average user may be populated by hundreds or thousands of dynamic objects that are able to communicate and have computing power. In such a scenario, it is not possible to use a static system architecture that has to be maintained manually.

The consequence is that Smart Environments will have to be composed from individual components ("smart appliances") that have to assemble themselves into a coherently acting ensemble. This requires software technologies that enable appliances to cooperate spontaneously on behalf of the user's needs.

Things will become even more complicated when looking at the visions of "The Invisible Computer" from Don Norman [11] or "The Disappearing Computing" from the FET-IST [12]. A part of these visions is that computers will disappear from the setting, become invisible, and vanish from the perception of the users. This creates a new set of issues concerning the inter-

Introduction

action with computers embedded in everyday objects:

- How do you interact with smart things you are not aware of?
- How do you control devices you do not perceive?
- How to do this in a dynamic environment?

Answering these questions requires systems that provide specific properties – I will discuss the resulting system requirements in Section 1.3.

1.2 Ambient Intelligent Environments

What are Smart Environments[2]? – In their book "Smart Environments: Technology, Protocols and Applications", Cook and Das define a smart environment as "one that is able to acquire and apply knowledge about an environment and also to adapt to its inhabitants in order to improve their experience in that environment" [13]. This definition seems fair enough. However, it has the drawback of defining Smart Environments by a specific implementation strategy (explicit knowledge, learning), rather than just by the behavior visible to the user. I will therefore use a less implementation-specific definition:

> Smart Environments are *physical spaces* that are able to *react* to the activities of users, in a way that *assists* the users in achieving *their objectives* in this environment.

The central characteristic that justifies the adjective "smart" is the environment's capability to select its actions based on the user's objectives – and not just on the current sensor data. The notion of objectives implies that the environment has to have a certain level of understanding of the user's view of the world. The concept of assistance describes the benefit of smart environments for the user: They off-load work from the user. Today, the type of work off-loaded are primarily memory and control tasks. This results in a reduction of the characteristic cognitive "glitches" (and their consequences) associated with these tasks: forgetting to turn off the oven, forgetting one's point in a speech while fidgeting with the projector's remote control, wasting energy because of forgetting (or being too occupied) to turn off the bathroom heat, not doing

---

[2] I use the notions Smart Environment and Ambient Intelligent Environment as synonyms. If we constrain Ambient Intelligence to assistive environments (rooms) and if we use Ubiquitous Computing as the technical foundation of Smart Environments, then there is no difference.

video conference because of not wanting to take the pain of having to memorize a two hundred page operation manual; etc.

What could you possibly really mean with ubiquitous? Like everywhere, like ambient, like pervasive, geo-spatial, calm, tangible, physical, everywhere, like smart dust? How precisely do you plan to get all ubiquitous?

Bruce Sterling, UbiComp 2006 keynote

Regardless of the name of the concept, be it ambient intelligence, ubiquitous computing, or pervasive computing, they all refer to a digital environment that proactively, but sensibly, supports people in their daily lives. The vision of what has to be accomplished for the user is relatively similar in all concepts. The next sentence is borrowed from the journal of "Pervasive and Mobile Computing", but could have originated from all the other concepts in that area too:

> "The goal of pervasive computing is to create ambient intelligence where network devices embedded in the environment provide unobtrusive connectivity and services all the time, thus improving human experience and quality of life without explicit awareness of the underlying communications and computing technologies. In this environment, the world around us (e.g., key chains, coffee mugs, computers, appliances, cars, homes, offices, cities, and the human body) is interconnected as pervasive network of intelligent devices that cooperatively and autonomously collect, process and transport information, in order to adapt to the associated context and activity." [14]

1.2.1 Application Scenarios

Potential scenarios for Ambient Intelligence are so manifold, as the underlying technology is expected to be ubiquitous. Thus you will find countless scenario descriptions in the literature (see *e.g.* "Scenarios for ambient intelligence in 2010" [15]), especially in the work of the state of the art smart environment projects (*e.g.* see Section 3).

The design of Ambient Intelligence applications realized by the different projects relies on the vision of their particular application domain. The usual approaches cover indoor or outdoor assistance, are envisioned to react immediately or just to record a scene to be processed later on.

Introduction

Some focus on optimizing the environment without direct interaction, others rely on explicit interaction with the user.

Typical instances of Smart Environments are Smart Living Rooms and Smart Meeting Rooms. I will use scenarios from both these instances to prove that my unified distributed system architecture for goal-based interaction is an appropriate approach. In Chapter 2 I will analyze which kinds of goals are common in such environments and have to be supported. The implementation of a Smart Living Room scenario will be shown in Chapter 5 and a scenario from the domain of Smart Meeting Rooms will be presented in Chapter 6.

To get an idea about Smart Environments and what the general user requirements are, we need first to have a look at some visionary story lines.

Smart Living Room Scenario

The following is a representative scenario, adapted from an internal document of the EMBASSI project [16]:

"It is 7 a.m. in the morning. The home assistant wakes me with my favorite music and reminds me of a first important appointment at 8 a.m.. On my way to the bathroom I tell the system to make coffee and to open the shutter. The music follows to the bathroom and continuous seamlessly. During the preparation of the breakfast, I let the system show me the appointments and to do's for today on the kitchen radio. Via speech interaction I initiate a call to a business partner. It is known to the system that I like to use the available loudspeakers and microphone in the kitchen, instead of the telephone device. After the telephone conversation, the music automatically starts playing again – my new audio system has integrated itself automatically and smoothly into the existent device ensemble. The functions and features of the new audio system were communicated to all ensemble devices of my residence. The TV now uses the surround sound feature for music TV and movies. Also the operator assistance uses all available I/O devices of the system, *e.g.* for speech interaction or avatar display.

I glance through today's TV program in the electronic program guide and want the afternoon football game to be recorded. I tell the system to record the game with the video recorder.[3] The system makes me aware that the video tape is almost full and suggests the hard drive as alternative storage, which I acknowledge. Although I still sometimes use the standard operator functions of the classical I/O-devices, the intelligent assistance of the system is very helpful."

---
[3] A reason for specifying this could be that the user intended to have a transportable media.

Figure 1.3: MMIS Smart Appliance Lab

Smart Meeting Room Scenario

Consider a Smart Meeting Room environment designed to feature user tracking and environment monitoring as well as occupancy schedule and meeting agenda retrieval. The room is equipped with sensing devices (*e.g.*, RF-positioning sensors, motion sensors, luminosity sensors, cameras) and actuators (*e.g.*, steerable projectors, motor screens, motor window blinds) that form an ad hoc ensemble together with mobile devices including notebooks and mobile projectors. The climate control delivers a comfortable air condition in the case of a used room and tries to save energy in case of an empty room. The Smart Appliance Lab of the department Mobile Multimedia Information Systems of the Rostock University is an example of such a room (see Fig. 1.3).

In such a room, situated *e.g.* in a company's IT department, a meeting of a software design group could be scheduled. Therefore, project manager Maria announces the meeting using the internal calendar management system of this company. With her announcement she provides an outline of a preliminary agenda. Maybe the meeting is structured like in the agenda of Fig. 1.4 where engineer Carmen is first to present her insights about the user requirements for the new product. Afterwards, software architect Annette presents the system architecture and after that it is the turn of project manager Maria to present. Later on a discussion on those presentations is scheduled. Invitations to the meeting are sent to both colleagues. They confirm the announcement and prepare their presentations. In parallel, the calendar management system of the company informs the Smart Meeting Room that this meeting is appointed and the persons Carmen, Annette and Maria will probably show up at the scheduled time to process

Introduction

Smart Appliance Lab
- ☐ Software Architecture Meeting
  - ☐ 11:00 Presentation of the User Requirements by Carmen (Document: UR2.ppt)
  - ☐ 11.15 Presentation of the System Architecture by Annette (Document: SA1.ppt)
  - ☐ 11:30 Presentation of the Project Planning by Maria (Document: Plan2008.ppt)
  - ☐ 11:45 Discussion

Figure 1.4: Final meeting agenda

the agreed agenda.

Shortly before the scheduled meeting time, Carmen and Annette enter the Smart Meeting Room. Since all employees and visitors of the company have to wear identifiable RF-badges, the room immediately knows who is walking in. Luminosity sensors measure available light so that the appliance ensemble in the room can decide if it needs to adjust the ambient brightness (e.g., turn on lamps, lift motor blinds). The calendar management system indicates that a meeting is about to begin. Hence, the ensemble goes into a meeting stand-by configuration where screens and projectors are prepared to provide their assistance. As Maria has indicated to the system that she wants a record of the meeting, the camera will follow the speakers and will automatically zoom and focus at details.

As project manager Maria walks in, the occupants walk to their seats and open their brought-in notebooks. The notebooks add themselves dynamically to the ensemble and make the presentations of their owners available to the room. Then, the meeting starts and deviating from the preliminary agenda, Annette goes to the presentation stage to give her talk. But the environment recognizes this deviation, infers that the team decided to bring forward the presentation of Annette and puts her presentation on the screen, just before she enters the presentation stage. The light automatically adjusts so that there is an appropriate light level in the room and a low light level in the area of the display. As Annette likes to give her talks a little informal character, she starts to walk around. The steerable projector is following her with the projection so that the presentation is displayed next to the speaker[4], the lights adjusts accordingly.

After Annette's presentation, the team turns back to the agenda and Carmen presents. Finally, project manager Maria walks to a display and is giving her presentation. To support a smooth transition between the presentations, the system proactively provides the respective presentations. During the following discussion, light may adjust again and the display appliances are going to stand-by modus, just in case an occupant wants to show something additionally. In

---

[4]It is a subject for debate if this is a useful feature. However, during presentations of our Lab we had always positive feedback from the audience.

the end of the meeting, the attendees grab their mobile appliances and leave the room. Now the remaining appliance ensemble in the room can go to energy saving or re-calibration mode.

This scenario emphasizes the need for unobtrusive assistance in complex technical environments. It identifies two important research aspects of ambient intelligence, namely implicit interaction and automatic strategy generation in dynamic ad hoc ensembles.

1.2.2 User Requirements

Before we look further at the technology, we first must get an understanding of the user requirements. Eliciting requirements for AmI systems, like for any novel technology, is not easy because of high uncertainties. The biggest problem is that you cannot just interview the user, because people have problems to state in advance what they want. The developers have to make an educated guess about the scenarios of the future, and evoke the user requirements from that.

Röcker et al. [17] for example made a big effort to figure out the user requirements for a future intelligent home. They conducted an empirical cross-cultural study at six different sites in five European countries in the context of the EU IST-IP project Amigo, Ambient Intelligence for the Networked Home Environment [18]. To elicit feedback from the target user population, they used a scenario-driven approach. The user study consisted of three different parts: a quantitative evaluation of fictitious scenarios, a structured focus group discussion addressing different scenario topics, and an open-ended discussion about people's expectations of ambient intelligence technologies in their home and life. As the result of their studies, they found the following requirements have a high priority for all users:

1. "The user must always remain in control of the system and never the other way around.

2. The system must be secure, safe and protect the privacy of all users.

3. The system must provide an added value over existing systems.

4. The system should never unnecessarily replace direct interaction between people.

5. The home comfort should always be maintained and not be subversive [sic] to the system.

6. The system should provide concurrently the appropriate information to the right persons for the appropriate occasion at different locations.

Introduction

7. The system should reduce the time needed for household chores and where possible do most of the cleaning jobs.

8. The system should integrate and combine functionality of appliances.

9. The system should be energy saving.

10. The system should be cost saving.

11. The system should support the activities organizing and planning for multiple persons at home, between homes and between home and work.

12. The system should protect against abuse, intrusions, loss of data, house system hackers.

13. The system should provide controllable access and respect individual preferences and authorities.

14. The system should take context/environment conditions into account and be aware at any time of the local situation.

15. The system should take implicit social rules of behavior into account.

16. The system should protect people's privacy at all times." [17]

Whether these user requirements are correct and complete, will have to be proven in the future, when real life systems are available and can be evaluated. However, these requirements should be a good basis for the development of appropriate and useful appliances in the context of ambient intelligence.

To guide my own research, I narrowed the user requirements down to the three following, more general items. These requirements are at the current state of research the most important to be considered. Although other requirements, like security oder privacy issues are consequential too, at the present time it is more important to prove that ambient intelligence is **realizable**, **appropriate**, and **useful**. If that proof is done, future research must integrate the other user requirements. These requirements are derived from the above presented user scenarios.

1. The system must have an understanding of the user goals and act accordingly. That means, the system must allow the user to state or express the desired effect or the system must infer the intention of the user automatically. (This user requirement (UR) is related to the Amigo requirements (AR) 1, 13, and 15.)

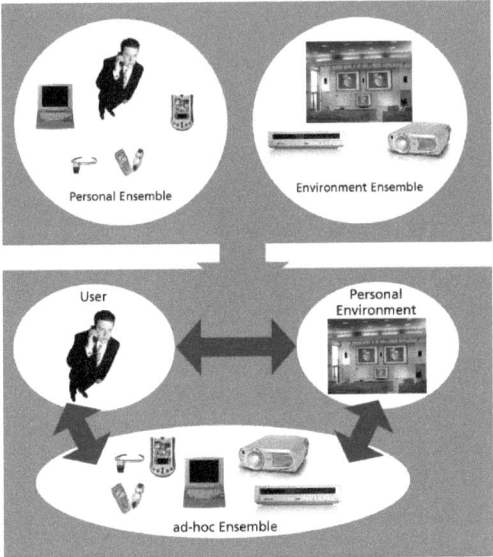

Figure 1.5: Dynamic Ensembles

2. Based on the goal of the user, the system should deliberately perform the necessary actions that lead to the desired goal. (UR is related to AR 6, 7, 8, 11, 13, and 14.)

3. If new devices or components are added to the system, no system engineer should be needed. The new appliances should integrate themselves dynamically and coherent into the system. This requirement is not only important for the reason of convenience, but also for the cost factor of the system. (UR is related to AR 8 and 10.)

1.3 Building AmI Systems

The vision of Ambient Intelligence is based on the ubiquity of information technology, the presence of computation, communication, and sensorial capabilities in an unlimited abundance of everyday appliances and environments.

It is now a significant challenge to let ambient intelligence effortlessly emerge from the devices that surround the user in his environment. A user's personal device ensemble and the device ensemble of the environment must create a coherent ad-hoc ensemble (see Fig. 1.5 and user requirement No. 3). Future ambient intelligent infrastructures must be able to configure

Introduction

Ambient (technology)	**Intelligence** (assistance for the user)
• Smart materials	• Media management
• MEMS tech. & sensor tech.	• Media handling
• Embedded Systems	• Natural interaction
• Ubiquitous Communications	• Computational intelligence
• I/O device technology	• Contextual awareness
• Adaptive software	• Emotional computing

Table 1.1: Ambient Intelligence Components [19]

themselves from the available components in order to be effective in the real world. They require software technologies that enable ad-hoc ensembles of devices to spontaneously form a coherent group of cooperating components. This is specifically a challenge if the individual components are heterogeneous in nature and have to engage in complex activity sequences in order to achieve a user goal.

The question is now how to build such ensemble environments. An attempt to identify the required components for such a system was made by the IST Advisory Group of the European Commission [19] (see Table 1.1).

Of course there are some more research areas that will influence the development of Ambient Intelligence. However, the development of the individual components is currently not the pressing problem. The question is which mechanisms can be found to enable the seamless integration of components and their convergence into ambient intelligent systems. We need architectures, methods and tools that are capable of combining technologies into AmI systems.

1.3.1 Some Challenges

A Smart Environment must identify the user's intention and, in response, it needs to be able to generate multi-appliance strategies for a coherent ensemble reaction. It is now interesting to look at the means current projects employ for performing these obligations. Typical examples are for instance Microsoft's EasyLiving [6] and MavHome from UTA [7]. For further examples have a look at Chapter 3.

The intelligent agents of MavHome for example predict the inhabitant's next action in order to automate selected repetitive tasks for the inhabitant. This prediction is based only on previously-seen inhabitant interaction with various devices. In order to do this prediction the

Chapter 1

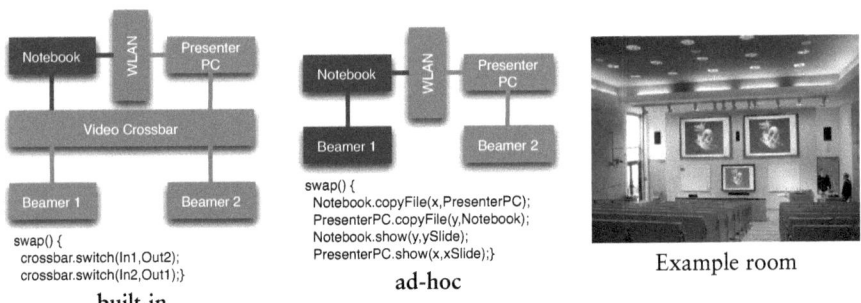

built-in   **ad-hoc**   Example room

Figure 1.6: Achieving the same effect with different ensembles

researchers of MavHome have saturated the house with sensors and characterize inhabitant-device interaction as a Markov chain of events. They utilize an *Active-LeZi* algorithm to do the prediction. To learn strategies they use a reinforcement learning agent.

The EasyLiving Geometric Model (EZLGM) provides a general geometric service for ubiquitous computing, focusing on in-home or in-office tasks in which there are input/output, perception and computing devices supporting multiple users. EZLGM provides a mechanism for both determining the devices that can be used for a user interaction and aiding in the selection of appropriate devices. The EasyLiving system has 'behavior rules' that cause things to happen automatically when certain relationships are satisfied in the world model. If we look at a variety of well-known Smart Environments projects (see Chapter 3) we can see that there are two basic approaches to strategy generation:

(a) learn from user – by observing the user's interaction with the infrastructure, as is done by MavHome

(b) learn from system designer – by receiving a set of behavioral rules, as has been done for EasyLiving

Unfortunately, both approaches are not viable any more as soon as we look at dynamic ensembles.

Why the system designer cannot provide the strategies: Consider the example outlined in Figure 1.6, which shows the built-in infrastructure of two hypothetical conference rooms (greenish boxes). The room on the left provides two projectors and a video crossbar, enabling a rather straightforward way for swapping two presentations. On the right, the conference room just contains a single projector; the second one has been presumably provided by an attendee. (In both sketches, the reddish boxes denote components that have been added dynamically.)

Clearly, both conference rooms require two significantly different strategies for realizing the user's goal of swapping two presentations. And, while in the built-in case one maybe could expect the room designer to provide a suitable macro, this is not realistic for the ad-hoc situation: No designer of a smart room can be expected to anticipate every possible ad-hoc extension of the built in infrastructure and to provide control strategies for every possible activity that could be performed with the ad hoc extended ensemble. Therefore, approaches such as EasyLiving are not viable for the case where the environment's capabilities are provided by a dynamic ensemble.

Why the system cannot learn the strategies from the user: The approach taken by MavHome, to learn strategies from the user, is not an option either: If a substantial set of devices is *invisible* to the user, they can obviously not become part of a control strategy the user might develop. Therefore, a system can not learn from the user how and when to use these devices.

Since in dynamic ensembles neither system designer, nor system user have an overview over the complete ensemble and its potential, there is no human being that could provide strategies to this ensemble.

Either the user has to be made aware of the available devices and their potential (pushing the responsibility back to the user), or the ensemble *itself* must become able to develop strategies on its own, based on the user's objectives. With respect to this, it should be noted that the systems developed in the above projects have *no* explicit notion of the user's objectives: They learn *procedures* from the user (or receive them from the system designer), but they have no concept of the *effect* of these procedures with respect to the user's objectives.

The consequences for the creation of intelligent ad hoc environments are:

- *Disappearing Computer:* The system cannot learn the strategies from the user.
- *Computers are everywhere - dynamic ensembles:* The system designer cannot predict the ensemble and therefore cannot provide predefined system strategies.
- *Result:* Strategies have to be generated dynamically by the ensemble.

1.3.2 System Requirements

These are the resulting system requirements:

1. Smart Environments will have to be composed from individual components that have to assemble themselves into a coherently acting ensemble.

2. In order to allow for environments to be smart as well as dynamic, we need appliances that cooperate spontaneously and that are able to autonomously generate strategies for assisting the user.

System requirement No. 1 correlates directly with user requirement No. 3. In the section before, I described already that it would be a severe cost factor to rely on a static system architecture that has to be build and maintained manually. So this requirement should be clearly motivated.

System requirement No. 2 correlates directly with user requirement No. 2. The user wants to be relieved of the responsibility to directly control the appliances. But where can the strategy come from? I will try to answer this in the next sections.

1.4 Approach

The main goal of this thesis is the development of a concept for creating Smart Environments from ad hoc ensembles. Therefore we need an overall system concept for controlling intelligent ad hoc environments. As motivated before, and in conformance with the system requirements, we need software infrastructures that allow for true self-organization of ad hoc appliance ensembles, with the ability to afford non-trivial changes to the ensemble.

Besides providing the middleware facilities for service discovery and communication, such a software infrastructure also has to identify the set of fundamental interfaces that characterize the standard event processing topology to be followed in all possible ensembles. This standard topology is the foundation for an appliance to be able to smoothly integrate itself into different ensembles: In a conference room, the user's notebook may automatically connect to a projector and deliver the user's presentation, while it will hook up to the home entertainment system and deliver a movie playlist when arriving back home.

When dealing with these challenges indicated above, we can distinguish two different aspects here:

Introduction

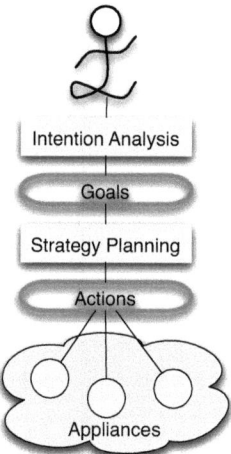

Figure 1.7: Goal based Interaction

Architectonic Integration – refers to the integration of the device into the communication patterns of the ensemble. For instance, a user interface from one appliance can be used to control another device or even the whole ensemble, through the attachment of the input component to the ensemble's interaction event bus.

Operational Integration – describes the aspect of making (new) functionality provided by the device (or emerging from the extended ensemble) available to the user. For instance, a scanner and a printer can together provide the same functionality as a dedicated copy machine. This can be termed the task of *ensemble strategy generation*.

Obviously, both aspects eventually have to be accounted for by a "Smart Environment Software Architecture" and both are part of this thesis. I will show how to cope with the problems of *invisible computer* and *dynamic infrastructures* and how we can allow a smart ensemble to cooperate spontaneously on behalf of the user's needs.

1.4.1 Paradigm

Before we begin to discuss the relevant architectural demands, we need a fundamental paradigm as foundation. As I will explain in Section 2.2 in more detail, I rely on goal-based interaction (GbI) as the foundation of the architectural concept of this thesis.

In today's technical infrastructures, the users are forced to execute *functions* or to learn action sequences to get a desired *effect* from the infrastructure. But of course, a user is not really interested in a function or the action sequence he needs to execute. It is the function's *effect* which is important to the user. As I have stated in user requirement No. 1, the user wants to express his goals or have the system to recognize his intention and have the *ensemble* fill in the strategy leading to this goal.

Goal-based interaction (*c.f.* Fig. 1.7) requires two functionalities: *Intention Analysis*, translating user interactions and context information into concrete *goals*, and *Strategy Planning*, which maps goals to (sequences of) device operations. The data flow of GbI will specify the set of fundamental interfaces that characterize the standard event processing topology to be followed by the devices in the ensemble and to be shared through public busses.

1.4.2 Architectural Integration

When developing a middleware concept, it is important to consider the objects that are to be supported by this middleware. For appliance ensembles, this means we have to look mainly at *physical devices*, which have at least *one* connection to the physical environment they are placed in: they observe user input, or they are able to change the environment (e.g. by increasing the light level, by rendering a medium, etc.), or both. When looking at the event processing in such devices, we may observe a specific *event processing pipeline* (application topology), as outlined in Fig. 1.8: Devices have a User Interface component that translates physical user interactions to events, the Control Application is responsible for determining the appropriate action to be performed in response to this event, and finally the Actuators are physically executing these actions. It seems reasonable to assume that *all* devices employ a similar event processing pipeline (even if certain stages are implemented trivially, being just a wire connecting the switch to the light bulb).

It would then be interesting to extend the *interfaces* between the individual processing stages across multiple devices, as outlined in the right side of Fig. 1.8. This would allow a dialogue component of one device to see the input events of other devices, or it would enable a particularly clever control application to drive the actuators provided by other devices. By turning the private interfaces between the processing stages in a device into public *channels*, we observe that the event processing pipeline is implemented cooperatively by the device ensemble on a per-stage level. In order to make ensemble dynamics transparent to message senders, these spread interfaces clearly need to support a kind of *content-based routing* mechanism that is also able to handle the competition between listeners for messages. Each pipeline stage is then realized

Introduction

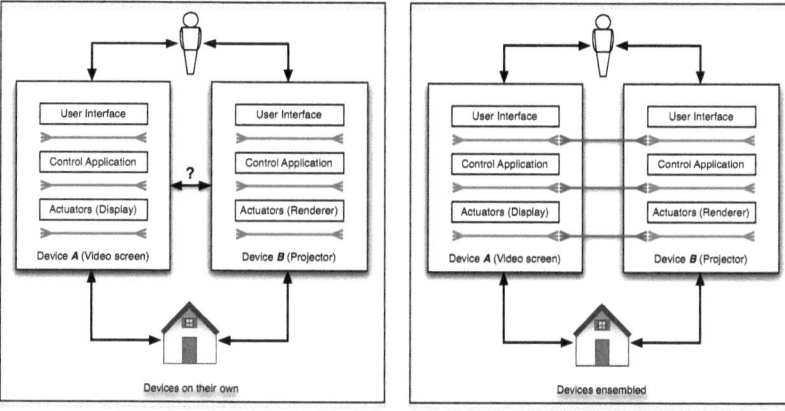

Figure 1.8: Sketch: Devices, Basic Topology, and Ensemble Creation

through the cooperation of the respective local functionalities contributed by the members of the current ensemble.

With respect to the information processing inside appliances as outlined here, the two functionalities required for Goal-Based interaction – *Intention Analysis* and *Strategy Planning* – can be interpreted as components of the Control Application.

So, my proposal for solving the challenge of *architectonic integration* is to provide a middleware concept that provides the essential communication patterns of such data-flow based multi-component architectures. Note that the *channels* outlined in Fig. 1.8 are not the complete story. Much more elaborate data processing pipelines are outlined in Section 4. Therefore, the point of such a middleware concept is not to fix a *specific* data flow topology, but rather to allow *arbitrary* such topologies to be created ad hoc from the components provided by the devices in an ensemble.

1.4.3 Operational Integration

In the system requirement subsection 1 motivated in detail the need for the ability of ad hoc device ensembles to autonomously generate strategies for assisting the user. This demand can now be met by the utilization of goal-based interaction. GbI is able to account for operational integration, while considering the pitfalls outlined in the system requirements (Section 1.3.2).

In order for a system to *autonomously* generate strategies for achieving certain goals, we need a mechanism to *explicitly* represent goals, which allows the system to reason about goals and different ways for achieving them. Specifically, we need a *declarative* representation of goals. The application area of Smart Environments is concerned with achieving effects of interest to the user in his current environment – therefore, an explicit representation of user goals is basically given by a suitable state model of the environment. This model serves as a mechanism for explicitly representing user objectives.

These system goals can then be used by an inference system for deriving strategies for reaching user goals, which consider the capabilities of all currently available devices.

My research has shown that we have to distinguish between two types of goals:

Environment state vector: This type of goals is represented by state vectors that are to be made true in the given environment. This is based on an explicit modeling of the *semantics* of device operations as "precondition / effect" rules, which are defined over an environment ontology. Chapter 5 will outline how we can use artificial intelligence (AI) planning methods to accomplish the given goals.

Definition of optimal ensemble behavior: This type of goals is the definition[5] of an optimal ensemble behavior by a goal function. This function must then be jointly optimized by the ensemble. In Chapter 6 I will describe how the distributed GRASP (DGRASP) algorithm I developed is able to approximate the best solution for the optimization of the goal function.

As soon as we rely on the concept of explicit declarative goals, it serves *two* purposes:

(a) It allows goal-based interaction for the user, i.e., the user can state his goals[6] rather than selecting functions. Alternatively the system can infer the user goal with an intention analysis, which leads to a descriptive goal.

(b) It is the foundation for the autonomous computation of control strategies by the ensemble, even with ad hoc added new devices.

1.4.4 Proof of Realizability & Usefulness

The so far outlined concepts were implemented within demonstrators as prototypes. With those demonstrators it was shown, that the proposed concepts were working and provided the

---
[5]This definition of course must be made by the developers in advance. Therefore we need usability experts which elucidate optimal ensemble behavior for given situations.
[6]Goals can be stated via speech interaction, gestures, or with the use of user interfaces.

claimed functionality.

To prove the appropriateness and usefulness of the developed system, an evaluation is necessary. But valid evaluation metrics for smart environments are not available. The question is, what evaluation methods and metrics give us an accurate picture. I chose to compare my automatic approach with a manual approach.

1.4.5 Generalization

The presented approaches were implemented in dedicated scenarios and projects. Nevertheless I will show that these approaches are generalizable and are useful in other settings and context.

1.5 Contribution & Results of the Thesis

The last Section 1.4 gives a good overview of what I consider to be the results of my thesis. Itemized the results of this dissertation thesis are:

- Review of state of the art Intelligent Environments and proof that assistance strategies have to be generated dynamically. (Main publication: [20])

- The development of an overall architectural concept for the creation of ad hoc Smart Environments from dynamic device ensembles founded on Goal based Interaction. (Main publication: [21])

- A concrete architecture for goal based interaction and the middleware model SODA-POP that provides the essential communication patterns of a data-flow based multi-component architecture. (Main publication: [21])

- The identification of different kinds of goals that are necessary to support automatic assistance in the application domain of Smart Environments. (Main publication: [22])

- A concept of using artificial intelligence planning technologies for the dynamic generation of sequential plans for the realization of goal based interaction and the specification of the limits of that technology. (Main publications: [23, 24])

- The development of the distributed algorithm DGRASP, based on the GRASP framework, that is able to approximate the global optimum of an optimization task through local interactions of dynamic device ensembles. (Main publication: [25])

- The Display Mapping problem as proof of concept for the utilization of explicit criteria for globally optimal ensemble behavior. (Main publications: [26, 27])

- Technical results of this work were re-used, further developed, or served as a starting point of the projects DYNAMITE – "Dynamic Adaptive Multimodal IT Ensembles" [28, 29] and PERSONA – "PERceptive Spaces prOmoting iNdependent Aging " [30, 31], the Dissertation of Michael Hellenschmidt [32], and the DFG post graduate programme MUSAMA – "Multimodal Smart Appliance Ensembles for Mobile Applications" [33].

This thesis will show that enabling an ensemble of devices to spontaneously act and cooperate coherently requires software technologies that support unsupervised spontaneous cooperation. It will be illustrated why a goal based approach is reasonable and how explicit declarative goals can be used to find system comprehensive strategies.

1.6 Chronology of the presented work

2001 – 2003 The overall architectural concept of my thesis came up when I was a member of the EMBASSI project. At that time, I was involved in the development of the EMBASSI architecture (see Section 5.2). Both the EMBASSI architecture and my concept influenced each other. To achieve the dynamic extensibility of the EMBASSI architecture, I developed – based on a rough sketch by my advisor – the SODA-POP middleware [21] that provides the essential communication patterns of a data-flow based multi-component architecture.

In the context of EMBASSI, I also developed the concept of using artificial intelligence planning technologies for the dynamic generation of sequential plans in 2002 [23, 24].

2005 – 2006 In 2005 I realized that the description of goals as environment states is not always sufficient. In some cases, a definition of an optimal environment behavior is needed, whereby the the desired environment state is unknown. It showed that such goals can be defined as goal functions which define an optimal ensemble behavior. To maximize the goal functions, which leads to the desired environment state, I developed the distributed algorithm DGRASP [25]. DGRASP is based on the GRASP framework, and is able to approximate the global optimum of an optimization task through local interactions of dynamic device ensembles.

2007 – 2008 The Display Mapping problem is an example of the concept of using explicit criteria for global optimal ensemble behavior [26, 27]. To prove the usefulness of that approach, I conducted a user study and got promising results.

1.7 Outline

Chapter 2 will show that we need a paradigm shift, that is, the transition from function-oriented interaction with devices to goal-oriented interaction with systems. Goal-based interaction requires two functionalities: Intention Analysis and Strategy Generation. The latter will be a main focus, the first will not be part of this thesis.

Chapter 3 deals with the state of the art. Here I will analyze how other approaches and projects deal with the desiderata of Smart Environments and what benefits and shortcomings we can learn from the state of the art.

Chapter 4 introduces an architectural concept, based on goal based interaction, that will be the foundation for creating intelligent systems from dynamic ensembles. It outlines the architecture of a multi-agent system that supports multimodal interaction with technical infrastructures of everyday life, that are composed from dynamic ensembles. Furthermore, it will outline the underlying middleware mechanisms, the SODA-POP model, that provides the essential communication patterns for data-flow based multi-component architectures.

Chapter 5 presents the resulting requirements for the integration of an AI planning system into the backbone architecture of Chapter 4. It will show how the different individual components provide a semantic self-description, and thus the environment is, with the help of a strategy planner, able to act like as a coherent united system, even with (completely) new devices integrated in an ad hoc fashion.

Chapter 6 will deal with the concept of goals as a definition of an optimal ensemble behavior, regarding the mapping of tasks to the available resources. This allows to compare different mappings with respect to their optimality. These types of goals tend to be typical optimization problems that have to be jointly approximated by the ensemble. As an example, the Display Mapping problem will be introduced and a new distributed optimization algorithm (DGRASP) will be presented. Finally, an evaluation of the developed system will show the usefulness of this approach.

Chapter 2

Goal-based Interaction

> *The challenge is to create a new kind of relationship of people to computers, one in which the computer would have to take the lead in becoming vastly better at getting out of the way, allowing people to just go about their lives.*
>
> Mark Weiser, 1993

In the introduction I have illustrated that we have to cope with *disappearing computer* and *dynamic ensembles* as a major challenge for future systems. I argued that as a consequence, we need appliances that cooperate spontaneously and are able to generate strategies that accomplish the goal of the user. In this chapter I will discuss how the paradigm of goal-based interaction is able to provide a solution for these challenges.

2.1 The Application Domain

A human being's daily activities – professional or private – are based on a broad range of interactions with numerous external objects: controlling the TV at home, driving a car, buying a ticket from a vending machine, visiting an exhibition, discussing project plans with colleagues, setting up a multimedia presentation in the conference room, editing documents, delegating travel planning to a secretary, and so on. These objects make up the user's personal environment.

As computers are becoming more and more ubiquitous, moving from the desktop into the infrastructure of our everyday life, they begin to influence the way we interact with this environment – the (physical) entities that we operate upon in order to achieve our daily goals.

The most important aspect of future human-computer interaction is therefore the way computers support us in efficiently managing our personal environment. This might be called the *ecological* level[1] of user-interface design.

At the ecological level, we look at future developments from the perspective of helping a user in achieving his individual goals and purposes by providing computer-based assistance. The vision is to have the computer acting as a *mediator* between the user and his personal environment (Fig. 2.1).

In addition, in order to minimize the cognitive (and sensomotorical) gap between human / computer interaction on the one side and human / environment interaction on the other side, *natural* (anthropomorphic) *interaction* should be supported through multimodal user interfaces, which integrate *e.g.*, classical GUI, speech interaction and gesture-based interaction. In order to support this kind of interaction, we need a paradigm shift:

- Transition from a function-oriented interaction with devices to a goal-oriented interaction with systems.

2.2 Function-based vs. Goal-based

When people are using their technical infrastructure they have certain goals they want to achieve; a certain satisfaction they want to experience. This goal-based nature of users is agreed upon in the field of cognitive psychology. But today's engineered environments force us to think of interaction in terms of the individual "functions" that the numerous devices provide: functions such as "on", "off", "play", "record", etc.. When interacting with devices, we select, parameterize, and then execute functions these devices provide. Upon execution, they cause an effect: a broadcast is recorded on videotape, the light is turned brighter, and so on.

Of course, different devices have different functions, similar functions in different devices behave differently, and staying on top of all features is not altogether easy. So, interaction with devices is usually not intuitive and straightforward – as anybody trying to coax an unfamiliar projector into adjusting its contrast or programming a new VCR will probably acknowledge. Such activities can get very much in the way and interfere massively with a user's foreground task, such as giving a lecture or enjoying a show on TV.

---

[1] "Ecology is the scientific study of interactions of organisms with one another and with the physical and chemical environment." So this notion captures the essence of the above discussion quite well.

Goal-based Interaction

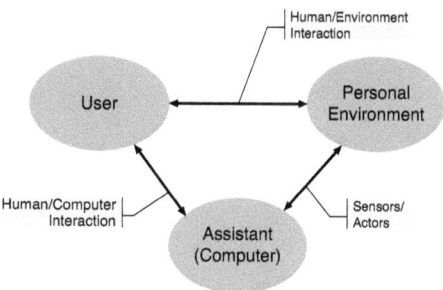

Figure 2.1: The ecological interface

The proliferation of computational capabilities and the advent of ad-hoc ensembles will not make things easier. On the contrary: interesting devices in an ad-hoc ensemble may be completely invisible to a user, such as a rear-projection facility in an unfamiliar conference venue. Now how is a user expected to interact with components and devices he is not even aware of (even if he knew how to operate them)?

But then a user is not really interested in the function he needs to execute on a device – it is rather the function's effect which is important.

This observation immediately leads to the basic idea of goal-based interaction. Rather than requiring the user to invent a sequence of actions that will produce a desired effect ("goal") based on the given devices and their capabilities, we should allow the user to specify just the goal ("I want to see 'Star Wars' now!") and have the ensemble fill in the sequence of actions leading to this goal. Goals allow services to be named by their semantics - i.e., by the effect they have on the user's environment - thereby evading the problems of syntactical service addressing.

Once we abstract from the individual devices and their functions, we arrive at a system-oriented view where the user perceives the *complete* set of (networked) devices as a single system of interoperating components that helps him in reaching his specific goals. Once we abstract from (device) actions and have the system communicate with the user in terms of (user) goals, we also have effectively changed the domain of discourse from the system's view of the world to the user's view of the world.

In order to support this kind of interaction, we need a system that is able to reason about the effects a device operation has with respect to the environment state as perceived by the user.

2.3 Dynamic Extension

Dynamic configuration, the ad hoc extension of a system by new appliances and components, is another important architectural goal.

Imagine a new appliance – *e.g.*, a projector – is plugged into a dynamic system and the user wants to see a slideshow of his last vacation pictures. How should the system handle the new device when trying to fulfill the user goal? Of course, the system components that are responsible for producing solution strategies for the "slide show" goal need to know that the new device provides functions that change the environment variable *setOfPeceivableMedia*. Furthermore, if the environment variable *perceivableMediumQuality* would be higher if the system uses the video projector instead of the TV, then the system could automaticly use the video projector and the user goal is fullfilled in the best possible way[2].

This means, in order to solve the problem of dynamic system extension by new appliances, without simply fixing the set of allowable functions and environment variables, we need to find a way for making the state-changing semantics of appliance functions explicitly visible to the system. As in the previous section, we must enable the system to reason about the effects available actions will have on the environment.

Why can't we just use a service oriented approach? After all, services such as *Universal Plug and Play* (UPnP) allow us to dynamically discover devices that provide a specific functionality – and even to rediscover alternative service providers once a certain device becomes unavailable. So is the problem raised above not already solved? An example from the conference room domain is already outlined in Section 1.3. Let us consider another abstract example. Assume we need a service s named `moveFromAtoB`. And suddenly, this service has become unavailable. But there are other services, for instance p, named `moveFromAtoQ`, and q, named `moveFromQtoB`. So, to a human reader it might seem as if we could compensate for the missing service `moveFromAtoB` by combining the existing services `moveFromAtoQ` and `moveFromQtoB`, sucht that $s = q \circ p$. But this ad hoc combination of services is a feat, service discovery mechanisms are not designed for.[3] The "intelligence" for service decomposition then needs to be provided by the requesting agent - rendering it private property and not a general capability of ensembles[4].

---

[2]What "in the best possible way" means exactly has to be worked out by usability engineers with dedicated studies.

[3]Recent efforts from the area of Semantic Web services are trying to address this problem with a similar approach that I present in Chapter 5.

[4]Advanced multi-agent infrastructures such as the Open Agent Architecture [34] indeed look at providing mechanisms for service decomposition at the infrastructure level rather than at the individual

Now consider another situation: Imagine, there are services named `moveFromAtoQ` and `moveFromQtoB`, but nobody so far has thought about a service named `moveFromAtoB` (whose *meaning* can be defined by the composition of p and q, which are denoted by the name `moveFromAtoQ` and `moveFromQtoB`, respecitvely). That is: the service s is available in principle, but we don't have a name to ask for it! In any ensemble, where p and q are available, s emerges naturally. But without a suitable name, we are not able to access it using conventional service discovery mechanisms that operate syntactically, on the *names* (more general: type signatures) of services. In order to cope with the discovery of emergent services as well as with service decomposition in general, we need a stronger mechanism for discovering and combining services, a mechanism that is based on the *semantics* of services rather than on their names.

Note that a similar consideration holds when looking at the interpretation of user utterances and user goals. Imagine adding a device to the home entertainment infrastructure that supports a whole new set of user goals – such as a printer, which makes it possible to create hardcopies of video stills. Here, the concept of a "hardcopy" is completely new to the system, and the dialogue managers need to be told what kinds of user sentences do refer to this concept and what kinds of goals they do represent. Here too we need a mechanism for reasoning about goals.

2.4 Explicit Goals

What are goals? A goal is an objective that the assistive system should achieve. A goal formulation thus refer to intended properties.

Goals can be defined as two aspects: **declarative**, where a goal is a description g of the state of the world which is sought ($Env \vDash g$)[5]; and **procedural** where a goal is a set of procedures which are executed (in an attempt) to achieve the goal.

For example, systems in the standard BDI concept (Belief Desire Intention) [35, 36] treat goals as events which trigger plans:

Beliefs: Information about the environment.

Desires: Objectives (goals) to be accomplished, possibly with each objective's associated priority/payoff.

---
agent level.

[5] $Env \vDash g$ means Env (Environment state) entails g (goal state), that is in every model in which Env is true, g is also true.

Intentions: The currently chosen course of action.

Plans: Means of achieving certain future world states. Here, plans are an abstract specification of both the means for achieving certain desires and the options available to the agent. Each plan has (I) a body describing the primitive actions or sub-goals that have to be achieved for plan execution to be successful; (II) an invocation condition which specifies the triggering event, and (III) a context condition which specifies the situation in which the plan is applicable.

However, by excluding the declarative aspect of goals, BDI systems lose the ability to reason about goals [37]. So, the procedural description of goals is not an option for our application domain. In order for a system to *autonomously* generate strategies for achieving certain goals, we need a mechanism to *explicitly* represent goals, which allows the system to reason about goals and different ways for achieving them. Specifically, we need a *declarative* representation of goals. The application area Smart Environment is concerned with achieving effects of interest to the user in his current environment – therefore, an explicit representation of user goals is basically given by a suitable state model for the environment. Goals are then represented by state vectors that are to be made true in the given environment.

How to represent goals depends on the inference system that is chosen to compute the respective plan and the specification language the inference system can handle. I will outline this topic more detailed in Chapter 5. Primarily it is important to look at the kind of goals that are relevant for the application domain of Smart Environments.

2.4.1 Goals in Smart Environments

What kind of goals must be supported by an assistive system for typical Smart Environments? To analyze this I cite below some of the scenarios looked at by previous projects.

- A quite early development, the *Reactive Video-Conferencing Room* [38] is an example for streamlining the interaction with complex video conferencing systems based on pre-defined reaction patterns, which are triggered by sensors dispersed throughout the environment:

  "Just before noon, Nicole arrives at the university and enters the lab. The room lights turn on automatically and an audio message greets her. [...] An electronic calendar that has been awaiting her arrival then activates the presentation equipment and initiates a video connection with the conference room automatically. Nicole begins her presentation by placing a diagram under the document camera. The remote participants immediately receive a view of this diagram, along with a small 'picture-in-picture' of the presenter [...]" [38]

- The *Intelligent Classroom* [39] aims at supporting a lecturer through anticipating his activities and adjusting the room's infrastructure in a suitable way, as outlined by the following scenario description:

  "The classroom observes the speaker walk away from the podium and over to the chalkboard [...], once he has reached the chalkboard and stopped, the Classroom adjusts the lights and sets the camera to show the portion of the chalkboard he is likely to write on." [39]

- The objective of Microsoft's *EasyLiving* project [40] is to simplify the control of home infotainment infrastructures by automatically selecting devices based on the spatial relations between user and device location:

  "Tom is at home. He enters the living room sits down at a PC in the corner. He surfs through a selection of MP3's, and adds them to a playlist. He gets up and sits down on the couch. His session follows him to the large wall screen across from the couch. This screen is selected because it is available and in Tom's field of view." [40]

- Michael Mozer's *Neural Network House* [41] tried to learn how to optimize both energy consumption and inhabitant satisfaction with respect to lighting and heating control:

  "We call the system ACHE, which stands for adaptive control of home environments. ACHE monitors the environment, observes the actions taken by occupants (e.g., adjusting the thermostat; turning on a particular configuration of lights), and attempts to infer patterns in the environment that predict these actions.

  ACHE has two objectives. One is anticipation of inhabitants' needs. Lighting, air temperature, and ventilation should be maintained to the inhabitants' comfort; hot water should be available on demand. When inhabitants manually adjust environmental setpoints, it is an indication that their needs have not been satisfied and will serve as a training signal for ACHE. If ACHE can learn to anticipate needs, manual control of the environment will be avoided. The second objective of ACHE is energy conservation. Lights should be set to the minimum intensity required; hot water should be maintained at the minimum temperature needed to satisfy the demand; [...]" [41]

- Using a conceptually similar approach, the *MavHome*[6] project [13] aims at additionally off-loading routine appliance operation tasks from the user:

  "At 6:45am, MavHome turns up the heat because it has learned that the home needs 15 minutes to warm to optimal waking temperature. The alarm sounds at 7:00, after which the bedroom light and kitchen coffee maker turn on. Bob steps into the bathroom and turns on the light. MavHome records this interaction, displays the morning news on the bathroom video screen, and turns on the shower." [13]

- In the spirit of earlier work at MIT on intelligent environments [42], the *AIRE* sub-project of MIT's *Oxygen* initiative emphasizes multimodal interaction with the environment, as outlined by the following scenario

  "[...] 'Alright, then,' Alice asserts, 'let's get this going. Computer—start the meeting.' Back in the conference room, the meeting agenda is projected onto a wall, and the first agenda item is highlighted: David's Presentation on «Adapting Traditional Games in Intelligent Environments: iBoggle.»

  [...] At this point, your computer beeps to remind you that you only have two minutes left in the presentation. You skip ahead to your last slide and summarize your major points. 'Thank you, David, for the presentation,' Alice remarks. 'Computer, move on to the next agenda item.' On the agenda display, which is back to the front of the navigation panel, 'David's Presentation' is checked off. The next agenda item, 'Set up the New Product Focus Group,' is now highlighted. [...]" [43]

  At a similar conceptual level, the EMBASSI Project [44] aimed at providing speech and gesture interaction with everyday appliances.

- The *Anthropomorphized Product Shelf* [45] enables objects in the environment to engage in multimodal interaction with the user. The goal is to simplify getting background information on goods in shopping scenarios.

---

[6]MavHome stands for **M**anaging **A**n **I**ntelligent **V**ersatile **Home**.

Goal-based Interaction

- The *iCat* home dialogue system [46] looks at strategies for exploiting social intelligence as a means for manipulating the user's perception of system quality and the user's acceptance.

- Stanford's *iRoom* [47] concentrates on providing *direct manipulative* interaction metaphors for smart environments. For instance, using a 2D floor plan of the iRoom, users can control devices by selecting them from the floor plan visualization on a PDA.

This list is by no means intended to be comprehensive. Links to additional literature can be found at the AAAI web page on smart rooms [48]. Further projects will be outlined in the state of the art analysis in Chapter 3.

It is interesting to note that the projects outlined above can be grouped into three distinct classes, based on their preferred primary *interaction metaphor*[7]:

- Implicit interaction: Reactive Video-Conference Room, Intelligent Classroom, EasyLiving, Neural Network House, MavHome.

- Explicit interaction that addresses an environment proxy: AIRE (proxy: "Computer"), iCat (proxy: "dialogical robot"), iRoom (proxy: PDA).

- Explicit interaction with individual appliances / objects: Anthropomorphised Product Shelf.

The environments are ordered based on an *increasing visibility* of the objects to be controlled by the user and on *increasing interaction requirements* on behalf of the user.

If we analyze the described scenarios we can see that there are some commonalities. To identify the goals that typically have to be supported, we can divide the main aspects of the scenarios coarsely in (I) where they take place; (II) what has to be provided, and (III) how can it be accomplished.

- Where?

    Smart Living Rooms: In living rooms we have mostly single user situations. If there are more than one user, the users have normally the same goal. There are seldom resource conflicts. (E.g., EasyLiving, ACHE, MavHome)

---
[7] I will elaborate interaction metaphors more detailed in Section 2.6.

Smart Meeting Rooms: In meeting rooms we have mostly team situations with restricted recourses. The users have often diverging interests and are competing about resources.[8] Often the users are not aware of the available functionalities and the exact goals of the other team members. (E.g., Reactive Video-Conference Room, Intelligent Classroom, AIRE)

- What?

Provision of Information: Many scenarios deal with the presentation of some media or the provision of communication. This can be the automatic play-back of a movie, the display of important information, or the establishing of a video call.

Environment control: The second important requirement for a Smart Environment is to adjust an appropriate environment for the user. This can be *e.g.* illumination, indoor climate, or audio level.

- How?

Communication pipeline: The provision of information or communication requires a communication pipeline. For example the display of information involves the finding of the media, the transportation from the source to the target (rendering device) and may be the conversion of the media.

Location based: If we look at the described scenarios, it is obvious that the location of devices and users and their spatial relation are one of the most important contextual information. Whether it will be used to infer the intention of the users or to find an appropriate solution strategy, location information is vital for Smart Environments.

So, the provision of information and the establishment of an adequate environment seems to be the most important aspects of Smart Environments. If we look at the research efforts on Ubiquitous Computing we can find that these aspects play a major role there too.[9]

This observations lead us to the kind of goals that have to be supported in Smart Environments.

2.4.2 Goal classification

Goals can be of different types. Several classification axes have been proposed in the literature (see *e.g.* [50] for an overview). Functional goals underlie objectives that the system is expected

---

[8]Resource conflicts cannot be found in the presented scenarios, but are a logical assumption.
[9]Even in theoretical models: Milners *bigraphical reactive systems* [49] provide a formal model for describing ubiquitous systems based explicitly on spatial topologies and communication topologies.

Goal-based Interaction

to deliver whereas non-functional goals refer to expected system qualities, *e.g.* security, safety, performance, usability, flexibility, customizability, or interoperability.

A distinction often made in the literature is between *soft goals*, whose satisfaction cannot be established in a clear-cut sense [51], and *hard goals* whose satisfaction can be established through verification techniques [52]. Soft goals are especially useful for comparing alternative goal refinements and chosing one that contributes the "best" to them.

Another classification axis is based on types of temporal behavior stated by the goal. Dardenne et al. [52] used the following patterns for the classification of goals:

Goal type	Pattern
Achieve:	$P \Rightarrow \Diamond Q$ (Achieve the goal at some point in the future.)
Cease:	$P \Rightarrow \Diamond \neg Q$ (Undo a goal at some point in the future.)
Maintain:	$P \Rightarrow \pounds Q$ (Maintain a goal for some time.)
Avoid:	$P \Rightarrow \pounds \neg Q$ (Prevent a goal from becoming true.)
Optimize:	Maximize (objective function) or Minimize (objective function)

Achieve and Cease goals generate behaviours, Maintain and Avoid goals restrict behaviors, and Optimize goals compare behaviors [52]. Achieve and Optimize goals are the most important ones for our application domain. Cease, Maintain, and Avoid are basically refinements of the goal type Achieve.

Achieve goals (I call them *direct goals*, or *goals as environment state*) are goals where the system has concrete knowledge of the intention of the user and the environment state that has to be achieved. For this goals the system needs to create a plan that leads to this state.

Optimize goals (I call them *indirect goals*, or *goals as definition of optimal ensemble behavior*) are goals where the system has no exact knowledge of the environment state that would fulfill the intention of the user. For this type of goal it is possible that even the users have no idea what would be the best support by the system. This is common in multi user environments, unknown environments, or environments with limited resources. For that, we need system designer and usability experts to define general indirect goals for specific situations that define an optimal behavior of the environment for that specific situation. These goal definitions will provide a number of possible system behaviors and the ensemble has to choose which behavior will be the best for a given situation. For this, the system can use optimization algorithms, hence the name "optimize goal".

Following, I give two examples for the explicit definition of goals and the accompanying plans to reach these goals.

2.4.3 Goal Example: Direct Goals

Direct Goals – Goals as environment state

Description: Basis for the use of AI planning technologies for creating sequential strategies. The use of these types of goals will be discussed in Chapter 5.

Example Scenario: The user is located in his living room and wants to watch the movie "Terminator" in an appropriate environment setting.

Environment: Smart Living Room

Main objective: Provision of media and environment control

Goal: $render(\mathbf{AVEvent_{Terminator}})^{10} = \mathbf{AVEvent_{Terminator}} \in renderedMedia \land \mathbf{AVEvent_{Terminator}} \in perceivableMedia \land ambientBrightness = \mathbf{low} \land ambientTemperature = \mathbf{comfortable}$

Plan:
1. Find the media source containing media event "Terminator".
2. Turn on the Display.
3. Turn on the media player – e.g., a HDD recorder.
4. Position the media source to the start of the media event.
5. Make sure the air condition is set to a comfortable temperature.
6. Find out the ambient noise level and set the volume to a suitable level.
7. Set ambient light to a suitable brightness.
8. Set the Display input to HDD recorder.
9. Start the rendering of the media event.

2.4.4 Goal Example: Indirect Goals

Indirekt Goals – Goals as definition of optimal ensemble behavior

Description: Implicit persistent goals are those that are identified a priori by the system developers. These implicit goals will be triggered by the situation through the intention analysis and must then be achieved by the appliance ensemble. These types of goals are the basis for resource optimization and will be illustrated in Chapter 6.

---

[10] The user would utter the goal "I want to watch Terminator!", the Dialogue Manager translates this user goal into the system goal *render* and a goal description, defined by usability experts, specifies the concrete aspects of the goal.

Goal-based Interaction

Example Scenario: A number of users come together in a meeting room with multiple displays for a discussion and want to be able to see their important documents as good as possible.[11]

Environment: Smart Meeting Room

Main objective: Provision of information

Goal: $DisplayMapping = \exists \textbf{Document} \in perceivableMedia$[12]
Metric:

$$maximize \sum_{\substack{user \in User \\ doc \in Document}} importance(doc, user) * \max visibility(display, user)$$

Plan:
1. Open motor screen 1.
2. Bring the document A to display on video projector 1. (Subgoal 1)
   (a) Find document A and copy it to computer X.
   (b) Start display application on computer X.
   (c) Switch the crossbar: $input$ to computer X, $output$ to projector 1.
   (d) Turn on projector 1.
   (e) Set the projector input to VGA (connected to crossbar).
3. Open motor screen 3.
4. Pan streerable projector 2 to motor screen 3.
5. Bring the document C to display on steerable projector 2. (Subgoal 2)
   (a) Find document C and copy it to computer Y.
   (b) Start display application on computer Y.
   (c) Switch the crossbar: $input$ to computer Y, $output$ to projector 2.
   (d) Turn on projector 2.
   (e) Set the projector input to VGA (connected to crossbar).

2.5 Goal-based Interaction – Conclusion

Once the concept of explicit declarative goals is made available, it serves *two* purposes:

(a) it allows goal-based interaction for the user

---

[11] Even if every single user would express her personal goal directly, the system would have to translate the single direct goals into an over-all implicit goal, because of resource conflicts.

[12] This goal definition implies that there has to be at least one document that is a perceivable media, *i.e.*, a document must be displayed and must be visible for a user. What and how many documents should be displayed at which display is defined by the metric (goal function).

Chapter 2

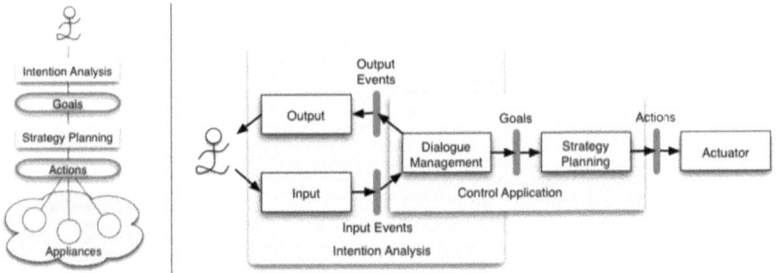

Figure 2.2: Principle of goal based interaction

(b) it is the foundation for the autonomous computation of control strategies by the ensemble.

So, we are no longer restricted to strategies that are either learned from the user or from the system designer – the ensemble itself is leveraged to unsupervised spontaneous cooperation.

Goal-based interaction requires two functionalities: **Intention Analysis**[13], translating user interactions and context information into concrete *goals*, and **Strategy Planning**, which maps goals to (sequences of) device operations (Fig. 2.2).

2.5.1 Intention Analysis

To enable smart environments to help users with their real world problems and tasks in offices, schools, or home environments, these environments need to acquire knowledge about users and their environments. To do so, sensors observe the states of both the users and the environment. These states are interpreted by a model to infer or predict a user's needs resulting in a strategy that enhances the user's experience of the environment.

The architecture of goal-based interaction requires that the processing of the user input / environment state is separated from the execution of system operations by introducing an interface between the intention analysis and the appliances that are controlled by the assistance layers. These explicit separation (two-stage approach) is not existent in most of the surveyed projects of Chapter 3. Nevertheless, Table 3.1 of Section 3.3 contains a list with the identified methods of selected projects.

---

[13]In the project *EMBASSI*[44] we used for example speech recognition to translate user interaction into system goals.

Goal-based Interaction

Intention recognition is a whole research field itself and is not part of this thesis. However, in the prototypes of the project EMBASSI and the Smart Appliance Lab of the Rostock university we used intention recognition components that were developed by my colleagues. Examples for intention analysis are dialogue management and team intention behavior recognition.

In EMBASSI we used a dialogue management system that featured declarative modeling of the system's evolving state and a fine-grained, well-structured ontological hierarchy of semantic concepts that were formalized using Description Logics[14] [54].

In our Smart Appliance Lab we used a team intention model based on a hierarchical dynamic Bayesian network (DBN) for inferring the current task and activity of a team of users online. This model enabled filtering and prediction of intended group activities with the support of a-priori knowledge about the group situation [55].

2.5.2 Strategy Generation

The synthesis of strategies, based on explicit goals that are provided by the intention analysis, is one of the major parts of this thesis and will be discussed in detail in the Chapters 5 and 6.

2.6 GbI and Computer-based Assistance

There are different options to simplify the interaction with technology for the user. Options are, e.g., to downgrade the functionality, the simplification of the user interface, or the provision of computer-based assistance. Of course, in the age of ubiquitous computing only the latter is really an option. Also, if we look at the conditions of ambient intelligence, it is no longer a pure human-computer interaction. Actually it is more a human-environment interaction.

In the interaction among the user and his environment, we can distinguish between two major approaches: *implicit* and *explicit* interaction. "Explicit" interaction refers to direct commands, e.g. via speech input or using a dedicated user interface. "Implicit" interaction refers to the reaction of the system by observing the user. In this case, only the implicit[15] actions of the user – his behavior – will be used to trigger the response of the environment. Implicit interaction offers two types of assistance, *reactive* and *pro-active*. In the case of reactive assistance, the system analyses the context and situation, and reacts promptly on the basis of the current needs

---

[14]Introduction to Description Logics: [53].
[15]The actions are only implicit in relation to the computing-based assistance system.

of the user. When using proactive assistance, the system infers not only the current goals of the user, but also future needs. To deal with those needs, the required actions will be performed in advance.

But there are also more complex classifications of assistive systems. One is the taxonomy of decision support by Sheridan [56] that were developed not for assistance systems, but to characterize degrees of automation. It gives a good example of how fine grained a taxonomy for assistive systems can be. Sheridan identified ten different degrees of function allocation, when decision on intervention within a process has to be made:

1. Human does the whole job up to the point of turning it over to the computer to implement.
2. Computer helps by determining the options.
3. Computer helps determine the options and suggests one, which human need not follow.
4. Computer selects action and human may or may not do it.
5. Computer selects action and implements if human approves.
6. Computer selects action, informs human in plenty of time to stop it.
7. Computer does the whole job and necessarily tells human what it did.
8. Computer does the whole job and tells human what it did if requested.
9. Computer does the whole job and tells human what it did if the computer decides he should be told.
10. Computer does the whole job if it decides it should be done, and if so tells human, if it decided he should be told.

This taxonomy covers three relevant attributes of assistance: the allocation of functions in the decision process, the initiative for assistance (explicit or implicit, reactive or pro-active), and the information of the user by the computer. But it has also its limitations. It refers only to decision-making and action implementation, but not to different action stages and it makes no explicit differentiation between the three attributes , function allocation, initiative, and feedback. Some researchers have extended this taxonomy to overcome these shortcomings. Wandke [57] for example distinguishes six stages of human action with machines that can be assisted by technical components:

Goal-based Interaction

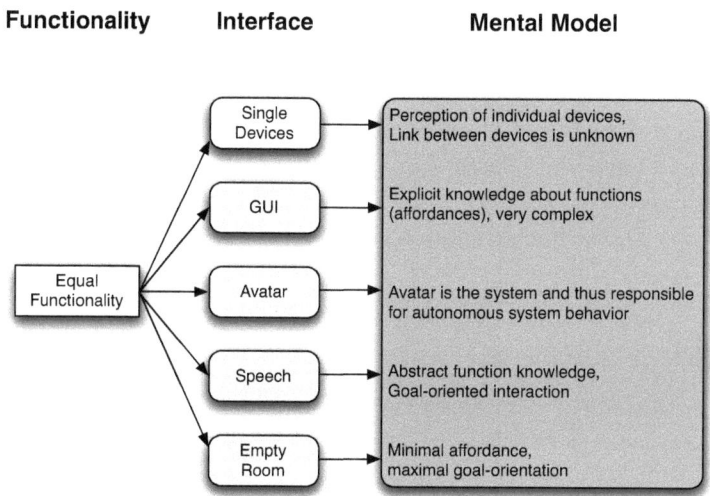

Figure 2.3: Different User Interfaces and the corresponding Mental Model, Source: [59]

1. Motivation, activation and goal setting.

2. Perception.

3. Information integration, generating situation awareness.

4. Decision making, action selection.

5. Action execution.

6. Processing feedback of action results.

This taxonomy definition can be a prerequisite for communication between researchers and technologists in the field and can also be helpful for designing concrete assistance systems. In the EMBASSI project for example, Nitschke and Wandke [58] developed a software tool to guide engineers in the development of assistance in the application areas home entertainment, driving, and public access systems.

2.6.1 The Mental Model

The vision of a networked world in which we are surrounded by numerous appliances and devices raises a new key challenge to usability research, that is, how to bring to mind the achievement potential of the networked system. How does the user know which goals the system is able to accomplish, which complex models the system knows? It is not enough to provide manifold facilities in principle and not to make this transparent to the user. A known solution concept is the usage of metaphors from the natural world of experience of the user. The advantage of smart environment scenarios, like smart living rooms oder smart meeting rooms is that the user is situated in an environment that already supplies a hint of possible goals. In a living room for example, with audio and video devices, most users have a good idea of what to expect.

For the development of assistant systems, it is now important to know, how the user perceives the environment, how is the mental model of user?

To answer these questions, the EMBASSI project team of Humboldt University Berlin conducted a study, whereby the appropriateness of possible interface technologies for intelligent houses was analyzed. The interfaces tested were: conventional remote controls, graphical user interfaces (GUI on Touchscreen), artificial persons (Avatar), and an empty room scenario that could be operated by speech. To compare the interfaces, the wizard of Oz technique was used. The goal was to find the respective mental model of the user, i.e. his conception of the functionality of the intelligent living room. Fig. 2.3 shows a summary of the results of that survey [59].

The study clearly identifies the differences between the user interfaces. If the user is forced to use the interfaces of the individual devices, the relationship between them remains unknown, even if the devices are linked. Using a GUI requires explicit knowledge about the system functions (high affordance[16]) and due to the complexity the cognitive load is very high. When using an avatar, the user perceives this artificial assistant as the representative of the system that is responsible for the autonomous behavior and execution of the actions. For speech interaction the users need to have an abstract knowledge about the functionality of the environment, and if they do, the interaction becomes very goal-oriented. In the case of an empty room and speech interaction the affordance is minimal. But the users need to have an imagination of the "purpose" of this environment. Then the interaction can be maximum goal-oriented.

2.7 Chapter Summary

With the paradigm of goal-based interaction we now have an interaction principle of extensible and – at least conceptual – considerable efficiency, which relieves the user from as many details

---

[16]*Affordance* – in the context of HCI – refers to the possible functionalities of a device or a system which are readily perceivable by the user.

Goal-based Interaction

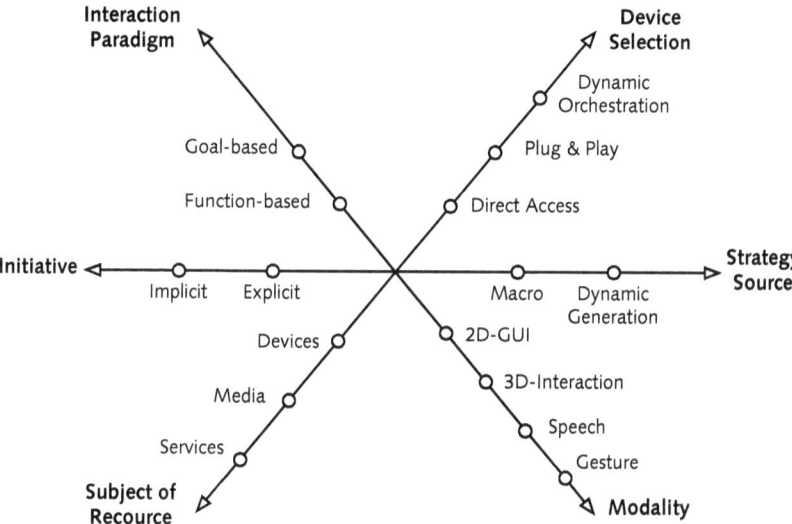

Figure 2.4: Multidimensional Classification of Human-Environment-Interaction, adapted from [60]

as possible and allows him to think in holistic goal patterns. Technological interaction barriers will disappear with the further development of new I/O-modules. The functionality will then be limited only by the imagination and the confidence in the underlying system. The task for assistance and usability research is now to show the potential of this interaction technology, and to make a new quality of usability for complex systems accessible to the user.

Fig. 2.4 displays a multidimensional classification model [60] of human-environment interaction and the underlying configuration methods of assistive environments. This sketch also serves as a bridge to the remaining chapters of this thesis. With goal-based-interaction as a foundation for the architectural concept of this thesis, all alternatives of all dimensions of the classification model of Fig. 2.4 can be implemented.

Initiative: Both explicit and implicit interaction is supported through the use of explicit declarative goals. Therefore we must use a Dialogue Management System (see e.g. [61]) or an Intention Analysis (see e.g. [62]) to promote this.

The Dialogue Management System (DM) must be able to process for example speech or GUI interactions to cover explicit interaction and offer the initiative of the interaction to the user. Such a component was part of the EMBASSI project and the provider of the

43

system goals. The Intention Analysis (IA) must be able to use sensor and context data to infer the goal of the user and translate that into a system goal, allowing for an implicit interaction and leaving the initiative of the interaction to the system.

Although DM and IA are not directly a part of this thesis, it fits well in the architectural concept and is necessary for a complete system.

Interaction Paradigm: Due to the fact that the whole concept of this thesis is based on the utilization of explicit goals, it allows goal-based interaction for the user. But equally the direct access to functions is of course still possible. The architecture would allow to implement direct access to functions, because to use a function could also be interpreted as a goal.

Device Selection: The developed middleware SODA-POP (see Section 4) is able to accomplish true self-organisation and dynamic orchestration of devices, which is the most desirable option of device selection.

Strategy Source: The semantic self-description of the device functionality (Section 5) and the definition of optimal goal functions (Section 6) are the key features that enable a dynamic generation of strategies. Although the architecture also allows macros to be used, strategy generation is essential, as clearly indicated in the system requirements.

Modality: The presented architecture and the paradigm of goal-based interaction are powerful enough to support all kinds of interaction modalities. It is only a question of the used I/O technology and the capability of the intention analysis to deliver a system goal from different interaction modalities.

Subject of Resource: For the integration of components into the device ensemble and for the self-description of functionalities, there is no difference, whether they are devices, media, or services. All the resources can be integrated in the system without difference.

Chapter 3

Related Work – Smart Environments

Relevant subject areas for this thesis are without limitations, Pervasive/Ubiquitous Computing, Context-aware Computing, Mobile Computing, Human-computer Interaction, Internet Services, Distributed Systems, Artificial Intelligence, and Ambient Intelligence. However, since the main topic is a distributed system architecture for Goal-based interaction with ad hoc Smart Environments, I have structured this state of the art chapter around Smart Environment projects.

A lot of research is going on in the field of smart environments, especially in the area of smart homes and smart meeting rooms. Some projects focus on relatively static, instrumented environments where the devices remain the same over a long period of time, some focus on ad-hoc ensembles where devices can be added or removed dynamically at run time.

This chapter will provide a survey of current smart environments projects, with a focus on how each project addresses the issue of architectonic integration and operational integration.

The research projects will be briefly described and their major benefits and shortcoming will be examined. The projects are grouped according to the device cooperation strategy they pursue, because strategy generation is the main component of this thesis. The used software infrastructure and frameworks (architecture) will be discussed also. Other relevant aspects and methods from the state of the art will be discussed when needed later in the document.

3.1 Device cooperation / user assistance in smart environments

3.1.1 Custom-tailored by the designer

The following smart environments projects focus on device cooperation in instrumented environments. Thus, the ensemble is static and strategies are defined at design time.

EasyLiving

The EasyLiving project [40] deals with the development of a middleware, geometric world modeling, perception and service description for instrumented smart environments. Key components of the EasyLiving system architecture are the geometric model (EZLGM) and the rule engine. The EZLGM provides a general geometric service for ubiquitous computing that represents the existence of an object in the physical world. Measurements are used to define geometric relationships between entities. In particular, a measurement describes the position and orientation of one entity's coordinate frame, expressed in another entity's coordinate frame. EZLGM provides a mechanism for both determining the devices that can be used for a user interaction and aiding in the selection of appropriate devices. The EasyLiving system has 'behavior rules' that cause things to happen automatically when certain relationships are satisfied in the world model.

The primary benefits of using geometric context are [63]: **Physical parameters for UIs**: Device selection and control is performed using physical context. **Simplified device control**: Device aggregation is performed without requiring explicit user action. **Shared metaphor**: User experience is simplified through a common understanding of the physical world shared by system and user. To make clear what geometric awareness can offer they used the simple task of turning on a light as example [63]:

1. Manual: Flip a wall switch.

2. Traditional GUI: Use a dialog box with a list of lights and buttons for on/off.

3. Physically-enhanced GUI: Select from a map of house/room with lamp indicators.

4. Direct Speech: Say "Turn on the living room lights".

5. Gesture: Make a funny gesture, observed by a camera, indicating a need for light.

6. Indirect Speech: Say "I could use more light".

7. Implicit Request: Sit down at comfy chair while holding a book.

If the system has an understanding of the physical world, a wider range of interaction becomes possible, *e.g.* items 3,5,6 and 7.

The system architecture of EasyLiving is rigorous centralistic. Flexibility in case of new components is not possible without adaptation of the world model and the rule engine. However, the primary goal of the EasyLiving project was not decentralization or ad hoc integration of new components. The goal of the project was more to expand the applications of a conventional computer desktop to the dimensions of a room. To realize that, the needed interaction devices (*e.g.* keyboards, fingerprint scanner) become accessible for all users in the entire room.

The major drawbacks of the EasyLiving system are a fully centralized architecture and a static rule engine. If the system should be extended by new devices or services, new rules have to be added manually by the developers. Also, the approach of EasyLiving works only in a fully instrumented environment.

Intelligent Room / Metaglue

The Intelligent Room project [64, 65] is a part of MIT's Oxygen project and focuses on device interaction in an instrumented room called Hal. Within the project, a middleware called *Metaglue* was developed that enables software agents to find one another through a catalogue. Furthermore, agents can subscribe to the events of other agents. An advantage of Oxygen over other approaches (e.g. EasyLiving) is that an agent is not linked to one particular device. Thus, if one device fails, it can be replaced by a functionally equivalent one. The agents are organized in a layered architecture with different levels of abstraction (inspired by Rodney Brooks' subsumption architecture [66]). The agents in the lowest layer (which is called the *Scatterbrain*) are called *SodaBot* agents. They control and interconnect the devices in the environment. Agents in higher layers can use a combination of agents in a lower layer in order to perform more sophisticated tasks. These combinations are hard-wired by the system designer. For example, the SodaBot Netscape agent communicates with the SodaBot Display agent to make sure that web pages are displayed in an area in the room that is visible for the users. These two agents are in the lowest layer. Any agents on subsequent layers that use the Netscape agent need not worry about information being visible to the users as the lower-level agents deal with this task autonomously. The agents on the highest level are invoked by the user, for example via speech. In that case the user addresses the system explicitly by uttering a command preceded by the word *computer*.

Agents can call methods of unknown agents, however these methods have to be known at the time of the development of the system. Before the development of a distributed system based on Metaglue, a specification of all functions and methods must be available. For that reason Metaglue can not be extended at runtime with components that would bring new functionalities.

IHome

Within IHome [67], another smart home project, every device has an associated agent and a plan specifying which actions it can perform and which subtasks are necessary for an action. This plan, called a TAEMS[1] task structure, must be hand-coded by the designer. Thus, it is only suitable for a certain application in a certain scenario. A TAEMS task structure is similar to a hierarchical task network[2], but it contains different alternatives to complete a plan. Which of these alternatives is executed depends on the context and is determined by a problem solver incorporated into the agent. To this end, the reasoner evaluates the quality, cost, and duration of each alternative and chooses the appropriate action sequence for the given situation. For example, if the agent has a fixed deadline, it may choose to produce a solution with a lower quality which it can guarantee to complete before the deadline expires. Furthermore, agents negotiate with other agents using the agent communication language KQML and a special protocol called *SHARP*. They negotiate over the use of shared resources, such as electricity and hot water, and over shared tasks. For example, the air conditioning agent and the heater agent both control the room temperature. Thus, they negotiate about which of them does which part of the task.

Defining the device cooperation strategy at design time has the advantage of using little computation time and power, but it is also the least flexible solution as it is only suited for the environment it was tailored to. Thus, it is not applicable for dynamic environments.

3.1.2 Device cooperation by Plan Recognition

This section deals with projects that pursue a plan recognition approach. The basic idea behind this is to have a large library of possible action sequences which are compared to sensor data at run time in order to determine which of the stored plans is being carried out by the user.

---

[1]TAEMS (Task Analysis, Environment Modeling, and Simulation) task structures are described in more detail in [68].
[2]An introduction to hierarchical task networks can be found in [69].

Related Work – Smart Environments

The Intelligent Classroom

The Intelligent Classroom project [70] at the Northwestern University aims at assisting a user in a smart classroom. It focuses on a well-defined set of tasks that can be carried out within this classroom, for example recording a video of the user's activities. To achieve the assistance, the Intelligent Classroom project pursues a plan recognition approach: Detailed plans of the tasks that might occur are available in a large plan library. A component called the *process manager* receives signals from sensors and tries to infer what the user is doing. Whenever there is a change in the user's activity, the process manager does the following: At first, it tries to explain the activity of the user as a new stage of an ongoing plan. Should this fail, it tries to figure out which of the plans in its library the activity might belong to. It does so by evaluating the temporal relations within the user's activities after receiving more sensor data. For each hypothesized plan, the process manager knows what should come when, that is, after which time interval certain stages of an action should be completed. Thus, the process manager can rule out plans that do not match to the sensor data. The process manager does not deal with sets of plans being pursued in parallel because it assumes that the activities in a classroom all have a linear nature. The plan recognition approach is feasible because of the constrained nature of the domain and the environment being static. That is, the Intelligent Classroom does not deal with devices being added or removed dynamically.

DOMUS

The DOMUS project [71] uses techniques similar to those of the Intelligent Classroom, but in the field of smart homes. The aim is to assist cognitively impaired persons, such as people suffering from Alzheimer's disease. The system developed in the project consists of a set of agents. A low-level agent receives sensor data and uses these to recognize a person's actions and classify them with respect to a stored taxonomy. The results of this process serve as input to higher-level agents which perform logical operations in order to find out which higher-level plan the input corresponds to.

The plan recognition approach is very inflexible as it assumes a static environment. It requires a library of predefined plans designed for all possible situations. As the programmer will not be able to foresee every situation that might occur in the real world, this approach clearly has its limitations.

3.1.3 Learning by observing the user

This section will introduce some systems that learn the control strategy by observing the users' activities and use this knowledge to automate routine tasks.

MavHome

The MavHome smart home project [72] ("Managing an Adaptive Versatile Home") is a multidisciplinary research project focused on the creation of an intelligent and versatile home environment. The goal was to create a home that acts as a rational agent, perceiving the state of the home through sensors and acting on the environment through effectors (device controllers). Several prediction algorithms are used to realize an adaptive and automated environment. The key component behind MavHome's decision layer is a hierarchical reinforcement learner.[3] In the MavHome framework, the agent explores the effects of its actions over time and uses this experience to form control policies which optimize the expected future reward.

The Adaptive House

The Adaptive House project [73] is a project in the field of smart homes. This Adaptive House stands in Boulder, Colorado and is controlled by a neural network which observes the users' activities and tries to learn patterns in order to optimize lighting conditions in the house. It has two conflicting objectives: The user should feel comfortable (thus, a room should not be dark when occupied) and energy consumption should be minimized. Hence, if a room is not occupied, the light should be switched off.

iDorm

The iDorm project [74] uses a laboratory equipped like a student dormitory as a testbed for their environment control system. This system consists of agents that control lamps, heating etc. and uses a genetic algorithm to learn the users' preferences. Agents use services provided by other agents, for example a service that provides information whether a chair is occupied or not. Which services an agent uses is learned by the genetic algorithm. To this end, a population of chromosomes is generated where each chromosome encodes the importances of the services

---

[3]Reinforcement learning is an effective method for training robots and artificial agents which permits the agent to acquire control policies autonomously from potentially delayed rewards without the need for constant teacher input.

for the corresponding agent. Thus, a gene corresponds to an importance value for a service. These chromosomes are optimized whenever the user is not satisfied with something in the environment, e.g. switches on a light because he thinks the room is too dark. The genes of the best[4] chromosome are then used to establish links between an agent and the services. That is, when the services and agent is linked to provide certain information, it performs an action such as switch on a light.

The main problem with systems that learn the control strategy from the user is that the user has to know the right strategy which would lead to the desired goal of the user. In today's modern technical infrastructures the users are often overwhelmed by the abundance of available functionality and are not able to provide the appropriate strategy.

Let's remember the visions of the invisible computer and disappearing computing and the questions they introduced: (I) How do you interact with smart things you are not aware of? (II) How do you control devices you do not perceive?

If a number of devices are *invisible* to the user, they can not become part of a control strategy the user might develop. Another problem is that such a system cannot easily be extended. Introducing a new device will lead to a new learning process so it will take a while before the device functions appropriately.

3.1.4 Device cooperation by Matchmaking

The projects described in the following draw a lot of inspiration from the field of web services, and some of them even use web services as a design principle. That is why the devices' actions and the users' tasks are called services. The matchmaking approach requires a library of abstract plans the designer has to specify. At run time, these are matched against the descriptions of services available in the environment.

Amigo

The approach of the Amigo project [75] is to automatically compose device services, so that users can benefit from higher level services. In the composition process, they also use context information such as users location, current needs and preferences. The architecture is centered around a Service Infrastructure which keeps track of available devices and manages the services

---

[4]According to a fitness function.

they offer. To fulfill a user's goal, they use a predefined abstract plan (task) description and use a task matching between the task description and the service description model (OWL-S). The context information is included through a composition algorithm based on a constraint problem solver.

Ozone

The Ozone project [76] developed a framework which is quite similar to the approach of the Amigo project. This framework is called WSAMI (Web Services for AMbient Intelligence) and comprises a declarative language for the description of web services and a middleware that enables service composition depending on the context. For this to work, the developer of a composite service must specify abstract interfaces of atomar services the composite service must call when executed. Through the WSAMI middleware these interfaces can then be matched against the interfaces of existing services at run time in order to instantiate the service. Interfaces match if the documents they relate to are syntactically equal. To keep processing costs low, the Ozone team even goes a step further: The documents actually even have to be identical, that is, have the same URI. This solution is, of course, not very flexible and not suitable for dynamic environments.

DIANE

In DIANE [77, 78], services are described in service description language *DSD* (Diane Service Description). They propose an approach that integrates automated service composition into service discovery and matchmaking. The goal was to build an automated matcher that is able to compose services, provides fine-grained and precise ranking among competing offers (also automatically composed offers) and is able to automatically invoke the best offer, incorporating the preferences of the requester. The requests are descriptions of goals, precisely the set of acceptable goal states and preferences. Service offer descriptions contain the set of achievable goal states.

The agents manage and distribute services to clients in the following way: A client can ask a request agent for a service, which in turn calls other agents to search for available services, choose a suitable service and invoke it. Services can be either atomic or composed of several atomic services.

In DIANE, there are three possibilities for linking devices to services: 1) The combination of services is already known at design time and services are thus statically linked. 2) Which kinds of services are needed is known at design time, but not which services will really perform the task. Thus, at run time services are dynamically linked using a matchmaking algorithm. 3) The decomposition of a higher-level service is not known at design time. Hence, it must be generated at run time.

The third case is the most sophisticated one and is dealt with through an approach that integrates service composition, discovery and matchmaking [77]. Service requests are described via the effects they should fulfill. Then a suitable composite service is built in three steps: 1) All available service offers that fulfill some of the effects are picked. Variables are not yet instantiated. 2) All possible compositions of these offers are computed. The ranges of the variables are lowered by computing the cuts on the parameters if services depend on one another. 3) The variables are filled in such a way that the service composition yields the best possible results.

This is only working if there is a match between the service request (*e.g.*, $A+B+C$) and service offers that provides subsets of the request.

Aura

In Aura [79], user tasks are described as compositions of abstract services. The actual services offered by devices are described in XML, so that they can be wrapped as abstract services by special components called *suppliers*. A component called a *task manager*, which is something like a user's personal assistant, knows about the user's tasks and their decompositions into abstract services. Every smart environment is assumed to be equipped with an *environment manager* which is a kind of an interface between the user and the smart environment. The environment manager knows about all of the users' task managers, as well as the available suppliers. When the user enters a smart environment, the user's task manager registers with the local environment manager. Whenever the user wants to perform a task, his task manager decomposes this task into a set of abstract services. For this to work, a huge set of decompositions must be available to the task manager. It then queries the environment manager to pick an appropriate combination of service suppliers available in the environment. Should there be several combinations, it picks the best one by evaluating each configuration.

The matchmaking approach is a bit more flexible than fixed strategies and learning from the user because it performs part of the strategy generation process, namely linking services to suitable devices in the environment, at run time. Another advantage is that this approach is tightly coupled to research in the field of web services and can thus benefit from advances in this area. Its main drawback is the requirement of a library of abstract plans designed for all possible situations. Creating and maintaining such a library will not be possible in real-life scenarios, where an unlimited number of situations may occur and where systems will have to be extended dynamically.

3.1.5 Device cooperation – Projects focusing on middleware

This section will introduce some projects where the focus lies not so much on combining devices' abilities into higher-level services, but more on the communication among devices and the communication between the system and the user. The applications developed in these projects do not include sophisticated strategies for device cooperation but provide the functionality of a middleware, yet specially designed for smart environments.

FLUIDUM

The FLUIDUM (FLexible User Interfaces for Distributed Ubiquitous Machinery) project [80, 81] aims at developing interaction strategies for instrumented environments. That is, it focuses on ensembles that have a static core, but devices can be plugged and unplugged dynamically. It focuses on the development of a standard for accessing devices and interacting with them. To this end, a software infrastructure called the *Fluid Manager* was developed within the project. This software infrastructure provides plug-and-play functionalities for the devices in a smart environment. The Fluid Manager knows about all the devices connected to the system. Devices are not viewed as a whole, but as a collection their capabilities like video capturing or text entering. The Fluid Manager provides a lookup service, which services can query in order to find appropriate devices. This approach does not address strategy generation.

Gaia

The developers of the Gaia middleware [82] call it a *metaoperating system*. It extends the functionality of traditional operating systems for the use in smart environments, which are called *Active Spaces* in the project's terminology. The Gaia kernel basically consists of five components. The *event manager* notifies all interested applications in the system of events, like new services or people entering the environment. The *context manager* makes it possible for applications to query for and subscribe to specific context information. The *presence service* constantly acquires information about the entities that are present in the environment. The *space repository* lets applications query for detailed information about the connected components. The *context file system* makes data available to applications depending on the context. Furthermore, Gaia includes a mechanism that maps the resources an application needs (specified by the application developer) to the resources that are available in the environment. For this purpose, it uses a scripting language called *LuaOrb*. The Gaia system is distributed among several computation nodes, though the information needed for this to work is hard-coded into a configuration file.

EasyMeeting

The EasyMeeting project [83] focuses on how to grant users access to certain services of the environment depending on the context, e.g. the identity of the user or the location. To manage context information, a central broker called *CoBrA* (Context Broker Architecture) is used. Devices in the environment communicate with this broker using an ontology. Depending on the context the user is granted access to certain services.

The above approaches do not comprise strategy generation. They might well provide the basis for a truly intelligent environment control system, but in order to achieve this must be augmented by a component that performs strategy generation.

3.1.6 Strategies for cooperation from other research areas

The approaches described above all have their benefits and shortcomings. Some are relatively straight-forward and work well for constrained scenarios, but lack the flexibility required for the use in dynamic ad-hoc environments. In a truly dynamic environment with heterogeneous devices that are brought into a room and are expected to exhibit coherent behavior right from the start, hand-coded rules are certainly not an option. Neither is learning from the user or plan recognition. Other, more flexible strategies for device cooperation are required for this kind of environment. This section discusses some approaches from other areas that might provide inspiration to smart environments research in order to address this challenge.

Joint intentions

The Joint intentions theory stems from the field of multiagent systems and was developed by Cohen and Levesque [84]. It explores how agents should coordinate their activities when working together and how agents can reason about the mental states of other agents. One core principle is that of commitments. When an agent has committed to a joint action and discovers that it is impossible to perform this action, it cannot break its commitment but must first inform the other agents. This way, the agents can rely on all the other agents still being committed to the action if no agent explicitly breaks this commitment. A more recent approach that draws on principles of Cohen and Levesque is that of Michael Brenner [85]. He focuses on the question how agents can synchronize for a joint action. Joint actions can only be performed if the agents acquire the mutual belief that they can perform the action and that the other agent is going to perform the action as well. This mutual belief can be generated either via direct communication or via copresence: If an agent senses the presence of another agent it can conclude that the other agent also knows about its presence, thus the joint action can be performed. This idea might be crucial if Levesque's approach is to be transformed into smart environments because it can reduce communication overload.

Swarm intelligence

The field of swarm intelligence draws a lot of inspiration from nature.[5] The key idea behind this field of research is that the principles that e.g. ant colonies or swarms of birds employ in order to form coherent behavior can be copied for computer science. These swarms of animals are truly self-organizing. None of the animals has global knowledge and each animal only interacts with its neighbors. Yet the system as a whole exhibits sensible behavior. Servat and Drogoul [87] discuss in detail what makes the principles of such systems desirable for smart environments. Some of their relevant properties are lightweight architectures and the ability to cope with dynamic environments and poor communication possibilities. Servat and Drogoul suggest combining this approach with amorphous computing. In amorphous computing, lots of unreliable, identically programmed computing units with small computing power and small memory collaborate.

Situated agents with goals

The approach of Pattie Maes [88] relies on the agent paradigm but also draws a lot of inspiration from artificial life research. Agents consist of sets of *competence modules*, which correspond to the actions the agent is capable of. These competence modules are described in terms of preconditions and effects, just as in traditional AI. The effects are viewed as an agents' goals. That is, a service has a kind of "motivation" to become active. Furthermore, each service

---

[5]A detailed account of swarm intelligence is given in [86].

has an activation level. If this activation level exceeds a certain threshold, the service becomes executable. Services are connected to other services through links. Through these links services can send activation energy to other services which can help them in fulfilling their goals. They can also take away activation energy from services that might hinder them. Energy is inserted into the network by the context in the first place. The activation then spreads throughout the network. Eventually enough energy will accumulate in some service and it will become active, provided that all its preconditions are fulfilled. Through its execution the service alters the state of the world by changing the truth values of conditions, thus providing new context information and new energy. Notice that no central controlling component is required, only local interactions take place and intelligent behavior emerges as a side-effect of the local interactions. These properties makes Maes' approach feasible for the use in dynamic environments. Projects that have implemented and refined Maes' ideas are [89, 90, 91, 92].

The approaches of this section are very well suited for dynamic environments. They also do not need a central controller. However, they are not able to generate solutions for complex goals. Furthermore, their parameterization is difficult. They do not deliver a constant high solution quality, which is needed for assistive systems, where the user expects that his goals will be fulfilled.

3.2 Software infrastructures for distributed systems

To create intelligent environments, we need to provide the communication of the distributed components. Hence, different software infrastructures, frameworks, and middleware technologies were build in the known projects. I already mentioned the important aspects of the analyzed projects in the last section. In this section I will introduce a few software infrastructure of other projects, that didn't fit into the classification of the last section. However, it is only possible to present some example approaches that I find particularly interesting or that had a huge impact. A survey of 29 software infrastructures and frameworks which support the construction of distributed interactive systems can be found in [80], but also this overview is only an extraction of the huge number of systems in this research area.

A common goal of this systems and their middleware[6] is the provision of basic functionalities

---

[6]A middleware shall manage the complexity and heterogeneity inherent in distributed systems. It is defined as a layer of software between the operating system and the application program. This software infrastructure enables the interaction between the different involved distributed software modules and is responsible for the basic communication mechanisms. It allows for the interaction of heterogeneous

for the composition of dynamic device ensembles: the mediation of messages between agents (*Routing*) and the identifying of agents with specific functionalities (*Yellow Pages*).

Open Agent Architecture: The Open Agent Architecture (OAA)[7] [93, 34] had the goal to shift the paradigm of static defined agent systems to more flexible systems. The objective was to avoid the shortcomings of known approaches, like *distributed objects*, *conversational agents*, and *blackboards*. Distributed objects have the disadvantage of fixed embedded interface definitions and explicit method calls, *c.f. e.g.* CORBA [94]. *Conversational Agents* based on an agent communication language like KQML [95] or FIPA [96], have often a fixed core set of atomic performatives and also a static agent addressing. *Blackboards* are based on the concept that all connected components process all messages and events, which leads to a difficult prediction of the behavior of the system.

The OAA uses *delegated service requests* for the communication, which allows to submit requests without direct addressing. Four different kind of components provide the communication within OAA: (I) **Requester:** specifies the goals for the facilitator, (II) **Provider:** service agents that can perform goals and subscribe these goals at the facilitator , (III) **Facilitator:** manages a list of available service agents and holds a set of domain-independent global strategies that can fulfill the goals, and (IV) **Meta-agents:** are equipped with domain- and goal-specific knowledge and reasoning methods. Meta-Agent are also used by the facilitator to resolve conflicts. Hence, the facilitator is responsible for the execution of requests, the coordination of provider agents and requester.

This delegation model aims to release the agents from the responsibility of task planning, task decomposition, and execution control. The Open Agent Architecture provides interesting approaches and is as a result an often cited reference. It was one of the first agent platforms that realized the communication of agents on the basis of events and not on agent names. The processing of the events is realized by the facilitator, based on the provided knowledge of the meta-agents. However, the OAA has several central components that complicates the dynamic extensibility: the facilitator and the meta-agents.

Galaxy communicator: The Galaxy Communicator Infrastructure [97, 98] defines an architecture that was developed specifically to integrate speech technology. Galaxy uses a client/server

---

device ensembles, *i.e.* devices with different operating systems and communication principles.
    [7]Although the first version of the architecture was developed in the middle of the last decade, it is still a widely used architecture. According to the projects website, more than 35 applications have been implemented using the Open Agent Architecture. [93]

approach where users can communicate with the system from light-weight clients. Specialized servers handle the computationally heavy tasks such as speech recognition, language understanding, database access and speech synthesis. Galaxy's key architectural component is a central programmable Hub which controls the flow of data between the various clients and servers and retains the state and history of the current conversation. At the first start of the Hub-component, it loads a dedicated file that contains informations about the connected clients, *e.g.* IP-address. Furthermore, the configuration file contains a number of rules that describe in what context what messages have to be send. With that Galaxy aims to support complex dialogue procedures that can initiated by the user with a GUI, speech input or special desktop agents. Due to the fact that all routing rules are static in the central Hub-component, the Galaxy architecture is not easy extensible.

INCA: The INCA [99] infrastructure is able to support specific goals (*e.g.*, the recording, saving, and rendering of multimedia data) for the automatic creation of applications from different components, that are registered at a central service. The foundation of that component cooperation is the automatic creation of a data flow from the data source over transducer to the data sink. Such a data flow based approach for the cooperation in a device ensemble will be illustrated in Chapter 4.

BEACH: The BEACH infrastructure [100] enables the flexible creation of intelligent environments from individual devices. However, the causal relation of the ensemble functions have to be predefined by global models (UI model, tool model) by the developer. The system does not support strategy generation, the user controls the applications via a GUI.

3.3 Summary

This chapter surveyed the current research in the field of smart environments with respect to sources of strategy for device cooperation (*operational integration*) and how their software infrastructures handle *architectonic integration*. The projects in Section 3.1 were grouped according to the strategy generation methods they use and their benefits and shortcomings were shown. Additional software infrastructures were introduced in Section 3.2.

Table 3.1: Smart Environment Projects

Project	Intention Analysis	Strategy Concept	Strategy Source
MavHome, UTA	Learning and Prediction, ALZ	Learned Procedures	Learned from User
The Adaptive House, Boulder	Learning and Prediction, NN	Learned Procedures	Learned from User
The Aware Home, GaTech	Context Widgets; MySQL	Rule Set (manually eng.)	System Designer
Easy Living, Microsoft	Geometry Model	Rule Set (manually eng.)	System Designer
AIRE, MIT Oxygen	Rule-based Programming	Rule Set (manually eng.)	System Designer
Intelligent Classroom, NWU	Plan Recognition	Rule Set (manually eng.)	System Designer

3.3.1 Verdict on operational integration

Table 3.1 summarizes the intention analysis and strategy generation mechanisms for a variety of well-known Smart Environments projects. As can be seen, there are two basic approaches to strategy generation: (a) learn from user – by observing the user's interaction with the infrastructure, as is done by MavHome (b) learn from system designer – by receiving a set of behavioral rules, as has been done for EasyLiving.

Unfortunately, both approaches are not viable any more, as soon as we look at dynamic ensembles. The consequense of disappearing computers and dynamic ensembles is that we need appliances that cooperate spontaneously and are able to generate strategies that accomplish the goal of the user.

In Section 3.1.6, it is given an account of approaches from other fields that might be of interest for future research. The ideas sketched in Section 3.1.6 are decentralized and rely on self-organization. They might thus be worth considering for future research, especially Maes' approach.

None of the presented approaches is able to dynamically create strategies for the kind of goals that I have identified in the Sections 2.4.3 and 2.4.4.

3.3.2 Verdict on architectonic integration

How applicable are the presented approaches for the coordination and communication of ad hoc ensembles? We can see that many current projects rely on a centralized architecture. A central component (router, hub, resource manager) is responsible for communication and coordination. These components provide often very complex functionalities, however that complicates the realization in distributed and dynamic varying ensembles. A great challenge is the fact that concepts like OAA or Metaglue are *universal* communication infrastructures. The individual components handle one or more functional roles (*e.g.*, input device, strategy source, execution control). Specific communication relations between these components defining the architecture or application topology. Universal communication mechanisms don't define the application topology[8] for a domain, such a topology would be inconsistent with the universality. In these approaches, the role of a component within the topology is part of the components logic. Hence, it is difficult to use them in different ensembles with varying strategies for the coordination of components.

---

[8]See Section 1.4.2 for an application topology example.

Chapter 4
Architecture Framework

Creating multimodal assistant systems supporting the intuitive interaction with technical infrastructures of the everyday life is one important goal of current HCI research and one of the goals of Ambient Intelligence.

I will look at some of the challenges of creating architectures for such systems and I will outline the developed solution approach. This approach aims to be a solution for the system requirement No. 1 that I identified in Section 1.3.2: "Smart Environments will have to be composed from individual components that have to assemble themselves into a coherently acting ensemble."

It also serves as an answer to the aspect of architectonic integration. Reminder: Architectonic Integration refers to the integration of the device into the communication patterns of the ensemble. The presented approaches in Chapter 5 and 6 for operational integration are implemented on the basis of the architecture of this chapter.

In this chapter, I will outline the architecture of a multi-agent system that supports multimodal interaction with technical infrastructures of the everyday life, based on the principles of goal based interaction. Furthermore, I will discuss the underlying middleware mechanisms, the SODA-POP model that provides the essential communication patterns of a data-flow based multi-component architecture.

4.1 Introduction

The presented architecture originated in the EMBASSI project, where I was part of the development team. To achieve the dynamic extensibility of the EMBASSI architecture, I developed the

SODA-POP middleware.

The EMBASSI-project [101, 44] was a joint project with 19 partners from industry and academia that aimed at establishing an interoperable system infrastructure for multimodal and multimedia assistance systems.

EMBASSI[1] was a focus project supported by the German Ministry of Education and Research (Bundesministerium für Bildung und Forschung, BMBF) within the strategic research area Man-Technology-Interaction. With 19 partners from industry and academia and a time scope of four years, EMBASSI intended to provide an integrated approach to the development of assistants for our everyday technologies.

The primary application area for EMBASSI were technical infrastructures of the non-professional everyday life – in particular, application scenarios were being developed in the home, automotive, and public terminals environments.

The EMBASSI architecture is conceptually based on two important paradigm shifts:

- Transition from essentially unimodal, menu-based dialogue structures (with a fixed interaction vocabulary provided by the system) to polymodal, conversational dialogue structures (with an unrestricted interaction vocabulary provided by the user).

- Transition from a function-oriented interaction with devices to a goal-oriented interaction with systems.

While these paradigm shifts are being discussed in the research community for some time now, it is a substantial challenge to make these results accessible to the user of, *e.g.*, home entertainment infrastructures or meeting rooms.

Building such systems is a substantial challenge – not only with respect to the individual concepts and algorithms that are required at the various levels of multimodal interaction processing, but also with respect to the overall system architecture. Especially, when we try to address systems that can be extended dynamically and that are not built by a single vendor.

Following I will look at the challenges of creating architectures for such systems and will outline the solution approach we used and developed within the EMBASSI project.

This chapter is further structured as follows: Section 4.2 gives an overview over the challenges of self-organizing multi-modal multi-agent systems. Section 4.3 outlines the architectural

---

[1] "EMBASSI" is a German acronym for "Multimodal Assistance for Infotainment & Service Infrastructures"

Architecture Framework

framework used in EMBASSI. Section 4.4 describes the underlying concepts of the middleware SODA-POP. I will relate this work to other approaches in Section 4.5 and look at future work in Section 4.6.

4.2 Middleware challenges

A central requirement for an Ambient Intelligence architecture is that it should support technical infrastructures that are built from individual components in an ad hoc fashion by the end user. This situation is for instance common in the area of home entertainment infrastructures, where users liberally mix components from different vendors. Furthermore, some infrastructures may change over time – due to hardware components entering or leaving the infrastructure or due to changes in the quality-of-service available for some infrastructure services, such as bandwidth in the case of wireless channels.

Also, it is not possible to rely on a central controller[2] – any component must be able to operate stand-alone. Using a central component where all devices would register and use it as a broker and communication server would have a number of disadvantages. Firstly to mention is of course the single point of failure or bottlenecks. May be with some redundancy and quality of service methods this problem could possibly be overcome. However, this would only function in instrumented environments. But imagine an empty room scenario where a video projector, a PDA, and a mobile phone come together. Who should serve as a server component in this scenario?

The functionality of devices should not generally be dependent on the availability of other components. The basic functionalities of devices in an ensemble should be available directly for the user. An existing device ensemble should be expandable in an ad hoc fashion by new components. Also the removing of a component should not hinder the functionality of the remaining ensemble. For that, new components have to be integrated in the communication flow of the existing ensemble. Additionally to the above arguments, the demand for dynamic extensibility excludes the option to depend on a central component. Dynamic extensibility includes the special case that an ensemble starts with zero devices (empty room scenario) and

---

[2]Besides my own arguments I would also like to reference the experience of Coen [65] that he made in the Intelligent Room project. He argues that a monolithic controller for the coordination of all components and functions has to be avoided. He calls the central controller of the Intelligent Room a "Big Messy C Program" and adds "... adding new functionality to the room required modifying the monolithic controller and manually determining the interactions and conflicts between old and new room functions."

forms up ad hoc by adding new components.

The demand for a distributed realization is the result of the avoidance of central components. If no central component coordinates the data flow and the cooperation of components, the software infrastructure has to be distributed. The distributed implementation is the precondition for the self organization of the ensemble.

Therefore, such an architecture should meet the following objectives:

- Ensure independence of components,
- Allow dynamic extensibility by new components,
- Avoid central components,
- Support a distributed implementation,
- Allow flexible re-use of components,
- Enable exchangeability of components,
- Provide transparent service arbitration.

When interacting with their personal environment, users may be driving car, enjoying a TV show at home, calling a colleague over the mobile phone, etc. These very different situations do not only influence the assistance strategies provided by the conceptual architecture's components – they also have a strong impact on the hardware infrastructure available for implementing the assistant system. It becomes clear that a broad range of different hardware infrastructures has to be considered as implementation platform – for example:

- mobile personal communicators with wireless access to stationary servers,
- wearable computers using augmented reality displays for interaction,
- a set of networked consumer electronic components, without a central controller,
- the local information network of modern cars,
- the user's PC at home, communicating with globally distributed information servers,
- public terminals, etc.

From these considerations, substantial challenges arise with respect to the software infrastructure that is required for implementing the conceptual architecture. It needs to support functions such as:

Distributed implementation of components. As soon as more than one host is available (or required) for implementing the architecture, a distribution scheme must be developed. The distribution scheme may either simply allocate different functional components on different hosts (relying on the assumption that inter-component communication is less frequent than intra-component communication) or it may distribute individual components across multiple hosts (making each component virtually available everywhere, but creating challenges with respect to managing a consistent internal state). Clearly, the right choice depends on the concrete infrastructure that is available.

Communication mechanisms. Once a distributed implementation is considered, the choice of communication concept is no longer a matter of taste. Distributed shared memories or distributed blackboards for example are a much more heavyweight communication scheme than message passing and bus architectures – but simplify communication design for knowledge based systems. Again, the right choice cannot be made without considering the concrete infrastructure, the specific communication needs of the components in question, and the distribution model.

Ad-hoc discovery of system components. In some infrastructures, new components may join an existing system in an ad-hoc fashion. Consider, *e.g.*, a personal communicator establishing contact to a point of sales terminal, where both components are equipped with their own version of the assistance system. Both systems must be able to integrate with each other and discover each other's components and functionalities, in order to provide an interoperable service (such as using the mobile communicator's input and output devices for the stationary terminal's analysers and dialogue management).

Ad-hoc (re-) distribution of software components. In case the infrastructure changes during system life, it may become necessary to adapt the distribution scheme towards the new resources. It may even be of interest to change the allocation of software components in an ad-hoc fashion – *e.g.*, by using mobile agents.

4.3 The EMBASSI architecture

The generic architecture that we have developed within EMBASSI (Fig. 4.1) is a pipeline approach to the problem of mapping user utterances to environment changes. Each "level" in the architecture represents one function within this pipeline, while the level interfaces have been introduced at "meaningful" places, separating different ontologies. These "ontologies" (the sets of objects that are discussed at a level) become visible at the level interfaces. The level interfaces make up the EMBASSI protocol suite.

Each level consists of a number of processes ("components") that co-operatively implement the level's function. Processes can be added or removed dynamically: suitable co-ordination mechanisms at each level are responsible for managing the interactions between the processes at this level. There is deliberately *no* central co-ordination component (see Section 4.4 for further details on component co-ordination).

The use of this rather fine-grained level-model in conjunction with the feature of dynamically adding or removing processes at each level allows us to create systems that can be incrementally built and extended in an *ad hoc* fashion, using modular components. Specifically, it allows us to build interoperable systems, where different components are provided by different vendors and where components are added and removed over time by the end-user.

Also, this allows us to collect components in a "technology toolkit", from which specific assistant systems can be built by simply "plugging" these components together.

4.3.1 The Multi-Modal-Interaction (MMI) levels

An EMBASSI system has to accept multimodal utterances which it needs to translate into goals before it can begin to think about changing the environment. According to the architecture in Fig. 4.1, this translation process can be broken down into three distinct steps[3]:

1. First we translate physical interactions into atomic interaction events (lexical level).

   The transformation of physical user interactions into unimodal atomic events is done by the *I* components (I = Input).

2. The stream of atomic interaction events is then sent via the *Event* interface to the *F*

---

[3] The reader should note that this three-level approach is a rather straightforward adoption of the LANGUAGE model described by Foley and Van Dam [102].

Architecture Framework

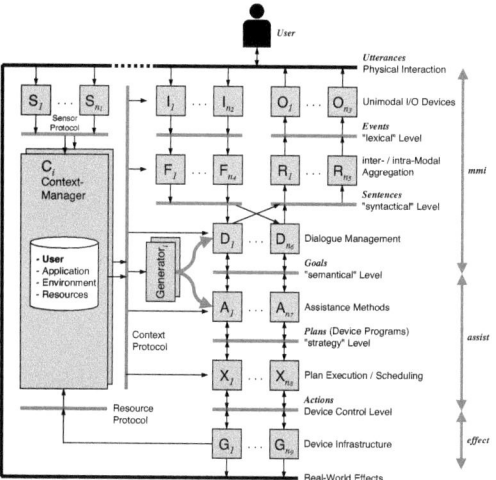

Figure 4.1: Generic EMBASSI architecture

components (F = Filter). These components are responsible for inter- and intra-modal aggregation of atomic events into amodal *sentences* (syntactical level).

3. The stream of sentences arrives at the D components (D = Dialogue manager). D components are responsible for translating sentences into goals denoted by these sentences (semantical level). Also, D is responsible for managing inter-sentence relations (dialogue memory) and dialogue dynamics (such as turn-taking).

The process is reversed when producing output: D sends amodal output "sentences" to the R components (R = Renderer) which in turn map these sentences to multiple atomic output events for the available output channels, the O components.

4.3.2 The assistance levels

The assistance levels operate on goals which are identified by the MMI levels. The process of mapping goals to changes of the environment consists of the following steps:

1. A components (A = Assistant) take goals (which specify state changes of the environment) and try to develop strategies for fulfilling these goals (strategy level). These strategies are called *plans*.

69

There is no predefined way to produce a plan. Some A components may use hardwired plans, others could use decision trees or even complete inference systems.

2. The plans are sent to the X components (X = eXecution control), which are responsible for the (distributed) scheduling and execution of the plans. (This means, the EMBASSI-architecture advocates a two step planning policy, as described *e.g.* in [103], where strategy planning (A-level) and execution scheduling (X-level) are distinct processes.)

   The scheduling-components ensure the correct sequential processing of the individual steps in a plan. Also, they are responsible for managing the parallel execution of multiple plans and for the management of execution resources needed by the plan.

3. Finally, individual action requests are sent to the (abstract) devices (device control level), the G components (G = Gerät – German for "device"). The G components execute the action request by employing the physical device they control, thus changing the state of the environment and causing an effect as intended by the user.

The **Context Manager** C is responsible for managing the system's view of the world – information about the user, resource profiles, the environment, and also the availability and state of the individual EMBASSI components. Attached to the context manager, we have sensors to obtain biometrics and environmental information – such as the current position of the user or the ambient light level. The context manager supports both pull interface (queries) and a push interface (notifications) to the information it stores.

Finally, based on a self-description deposited by a G-component in the context manager, a *Generator* may be able to automatically create simple A and D components for it. See [44] for further details on this concept.

4.3.3 Additional notes on the generic architecture

Before addressing the main point of this section – the middleware infrastructure that is required for building dynamically extensible interactive assistance systems based on the EMBASSI architecture – a few additional aspects of this architecture should be noted:

- The above generic architecture has been instantiated for the various application scenarios investigated in EMBASSI – home control, car infotainment, and point-of-sales / point-of-information terminals. The instance architecture for home control is shown as example in Fig. 4.2.

Architecture Framework

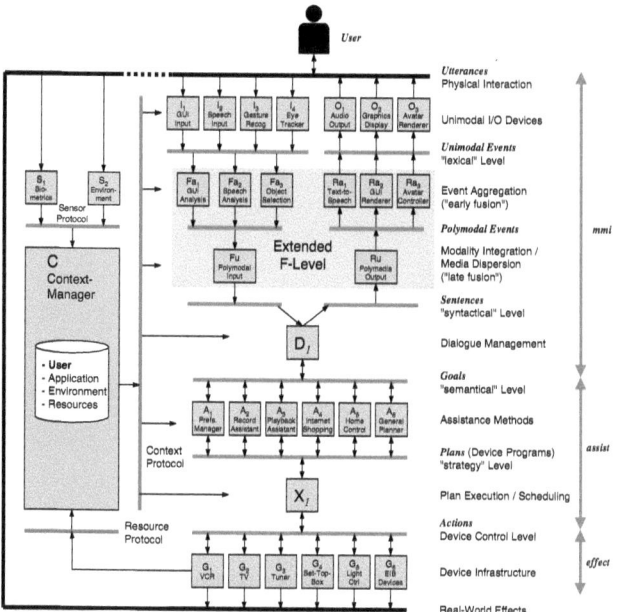

Figure 4.2: EMBASSI architecture – Home Control Instance

- Conventional widget-based user interfaces are quite easily mapped to the EMBASSI architecture: within the Home Control scenario, they correspond to the GUI Analysis / GUI Renderer components.

- The feedback loops *within* an EMBASSI level – *e.g.*, the connection between GUI Input and GUI Renderer are *not* explicitly shown in our architecture. Such feedback loops cleary do exist – but we have not yet ventured into designing a *generic ontology* for these them. Hence, they are not yet part of the EMBASSI protocol suite.

- It is of course possible to map the EMBASSI architecture to existing architecture models for man-machine interfaces such as the ARCH model [104, 105]. In ARCH, the levels that map user interaction to system actions are: Interaction Toolkit, Presentation Component, Dialogue Component, Domain Adaptor Component, and Domain-specific Component. Without going too much into the details, one possible mapping of EMBASSI to ARCH would be: I/O-Level = Interaction Toolkit, F/R-Level = Presentation Component, D-Level = Dialogue Component, A-Level = Domain Adaptor Component, X & G-Level = Domain-specific Components.

In this context, the reader should be aware of the fact that it was *not* the primary goal of EMBASSI to present yet another model for interactive architectures. Rather, we tried to build an infrastructure that allows the *dynamic composition* of interactive systems from components in an ad hoc fashion. It is the dynamic composition functionality that is the "interesting" aspect of this architecture – at least at the architectural level.

Next, I will look at the middleware model that we used for implementing the dynamically extensible architecture of EMBASSI.

4.4 The middleware model SODA-POP

The goal of our middleware-work is to develop a system model that provides the essential communication patterns of a data-flow based multi-component architecture such as EMBASSI. At the same time, we also want to have an experimental platform implementing this model (a reference implementation) that allows to quickly build and empirically verify experimental applications – specifically with respect to functions such as service arbitration.

Here, the focus of empirical studies is the way *systems* can be build dynamically from individual components and how the mechanisms provided by the model are used for building such systems – a software engineering focus.

The model should have the following properties:

- Support data-flow based event processing topologies.
- Support conventional remote procedure calls.
- Support self-organization of system components.
- Support decentralized problem decomposition and conflict resolution (service arbitration).
- Support dynamic extension by new components.
- Support unification / partitioning of complete system topologies.

The model we have developed so far is called SODA-POP (for: Self-Organizing Data-flow Architectures suPporting Ontology-based problem decomPosition.). Following, I give a brief overview over the salient features of this model.

4.4.1 Component types

The SODA-POP model [106] introduces two fundamental organization levels:

- Coarse-grained self-organization based on a data-flow partitioning (basic topology).

- Fine-grained self-organization for functionally *similar* components based on a kind of "Pattern Matching" approach.

Consequently, a SODA-POP system consists of two types of components:

Channels, which read a single message at time *point* and map them to multiple messages which are delivered to components (conceptually, *without delay*). Channels have no memory[4], may be distributed, and they have to accept *every* message.

Channels provide for *spatial distribution* of a single event to multiple transducers. The interface buses of the EMBASSI architecture are channels.

Transducers, which read one or more messages during a time *interval* and map them to one (or more) output messages. Transducers are *not* distributed, they may have a memory and they do not have to accept every message.

Transducers provide for *temporal aggregation* of multiple events to a single output. Note that a transducer may have *multiple* input and output channels ($m : n$, rather than just $1 : 1$). The I, F, ...components of EMBASSI are transducers.

The criterion for discriminating between transducers and channels is the amount of memory they may employ for processing a message – *i.e.*, the complexity they create when trying to implement them in a distributed fashion: Channels may use no memory. This requirement clearly makes sense when considering that we may want to use channels as "cutting points" for distributing a system: Implementing distributed shared memory is expensive. Communication primitives for potentially distributed systems therefore should not provide such a facility "for free". In addition, the "No Memory" Constraint provides a *hard* criterion for discriminating between the functions a channel is allowed to provide and functions that require a transducer.

Finally, it becomes obvious that persistence functionality (such as provided by blackboard-based communication infrastructures, *e.g.* LINDA [107] or FLiPSiDE [108]) shall not be part of a channel, as persistence clearly violates the concept of memory-free channels.

---

[4]Channels may have internal memory for their own use, but provide no memory like *Blackboard* architectures.

4.4.2 Channels & systems

Channels accept (and deliver) messages of a certain type t, Transducers map messages from a type t to a type t'. A system is defined by a set of channels and a set of transducers connecting these channels. So, a system is a graph where channels represent points (nodes) and transducers represent edges[5]. Channels and transducers are equally important in defining a system – a minimal complete EMBASSI system for example consists of 10 channels and 10 transducers (9 and 9 if sensors are omitted).

Channels are identified via *Channel Descriptors*. Conceptually, channel descriptors encode the channel's ontology (the meaning of the messages), so that transducers can be automatically connected to channels that speak the languages they understand.

Communication patterns The middleware for multimodal event processing and multi agent approaches should support at least the following two communication patterns:

- *Events* that travel in a data-flow fashion through the different transducers. When an event e is posted by a transducer t, it (t) does not expect a reply. Rather it expects that other system components (*i.e.*, the *called* transducer) know how to continue with processing the event.

- *RPCs* that resemble normal remote procedure calls. When a RPC is called by a transducer, it expects a result. Here, the *calling* transducer determines the further processing of the result.

Events and RPCs describe different routing semantics with respect to result processing. When considering the EMBASSI architecture, the flow from I to G is a typical event processing pipeline, where at each level we have a set of transducers that cooperate in order to translate an event received at the input (upper) level into an event posted at the output (lower) level.

Event- and RPC-like result routing semantics correspond to different types of channels, a transducer may subscribe to. Event- and RPC-Channels are the two basic channel types provided by SODA-POP.

With respect to events, there is one important additional requirement: In the normal course of action, events are delivered by a *push* mechanism, initiated by the producer. However, there are also situations when the consumers need to *pull* events – here, event delivery is initiated by

---
[5]Rather: a multigraph, because we may have several edges connecting the same two nodes.

Architecture Framework

the consumers. One specific instance of this pull situation arises when the transducers receiving an event need to *ask back* to the producing level for further information that may be needed to understand the event (*e.g.*: D may ask back to F for further multimodal event information it may need to disambiguate a given user utterance). So each event channel implicitly contains an inverse RPC channel on which an event-pull can be performed.

4.4.3 Subscriptions

Events and RPCs are (in general) posted *without* specific addressing information: in a dynamic system, a sender never can be sure, which receivers are currently able to process a message. It is up to the channel on which the message is posted to identify a suitable message decomposition and receiver set (service arbitration).

A channel basically consists of a pipe into which event generators push messages (events or RPCs) which are then transmitted to the consumers (transducers) subscribing to this channel. When subscribing to a channel, an event consumer declares:

- The set of messages it is able to process,
- how well it is suited for processing a certain message,
- whether it is able to run in parallel to other message consumers on the same message,
- whether it is able to cooperate with other consumers in processing the message.

These aspects are described by the subscribing consumer's *utility*. A *utility* is a function that maps a message to a *utility value*, which encodes the subscribers' handling capabilities for the specific message. A transducer's utility may depend on the transducer's state.

The definition for Utility values in SODA-POP is[6]:

```
type Quality = Int                    -- just as example
data UtVal = NotApplicable            -- Can't handle msg
         | Exclusive Quality          -- Expect to handle it exclusive
         | Nonexclusive Quality       -- Don't mind if others are involved
         | Cooperative [(Quality,Msg)] -- Can do some parts, but need help
```

And a simple transducer that is able to handle only a single kind of message m0 might provide a utility function such as

---

[6]The current version of SODA-POP is defined in Haskell [109], the current "standard" functional language

```
isForMe :: Msg -> UtVal
isForMe m | m == m0 = Nonexclusive 0.5   -- if m is m0
          | True    = NotApplicable      -- otherwise
```

The `Cooperative` value needs further explanation: with this utility value, a transducer may return a list of partial messages it is able to handle, together with a quality value for each sub-message. This gives the Channel the opportunity to select the best tradeoff for decomposing a message across multiple transducers[7].

4.4.4 Message handling

On a given SODA-POP channel, messages are delivered between communication partners based on a refined publish / subscribe concept. Every channel may be equipped with an individual strategy for resolving conflicts that may arise between subscribers competing for the same message (the same request).

Receiver selection & message decomposition. When a channel processes a message, it evaluates the subscribing consumers' handling capabilities and then decides which consumers will effectively receive the message (receiver set). Also, the channel may decide to *decompose* the message into multiple (presumably simpler) messages which can be handled better by the subscribing consumers. (Obviously, the consumers then solve the original message in cooperation.) The basic process of message handling is shown in Fig. 4.3.

How a channel determines the effective message decomposition and how it chooses the set of receiving consumers is defined by the channel's *decomposition strategy*.

Both the transducers' utility and the channel's strategy are eventually based on the channel's ontology – the semantics of the messages that are communicated across the channel.

For some channels, the concept of cooperative message processing may already be a part of the channel's ontology. This means that the channel's language contains a means for embedding synchronization statements into a (presumably compound) message – such as "wait for completion of sub-request i" and "announce completion of sub-request j". The channel's strategy then embeds suitable synchronization statements into the messages it creates for the receiver set. Corresponding announcements are to be exchanged over a synchronization channel that needs to be established between the receiver set. This mechanism is used in EMBASSI for distributing

---

[7]This is a rather experimental feature.

Architecture Framework

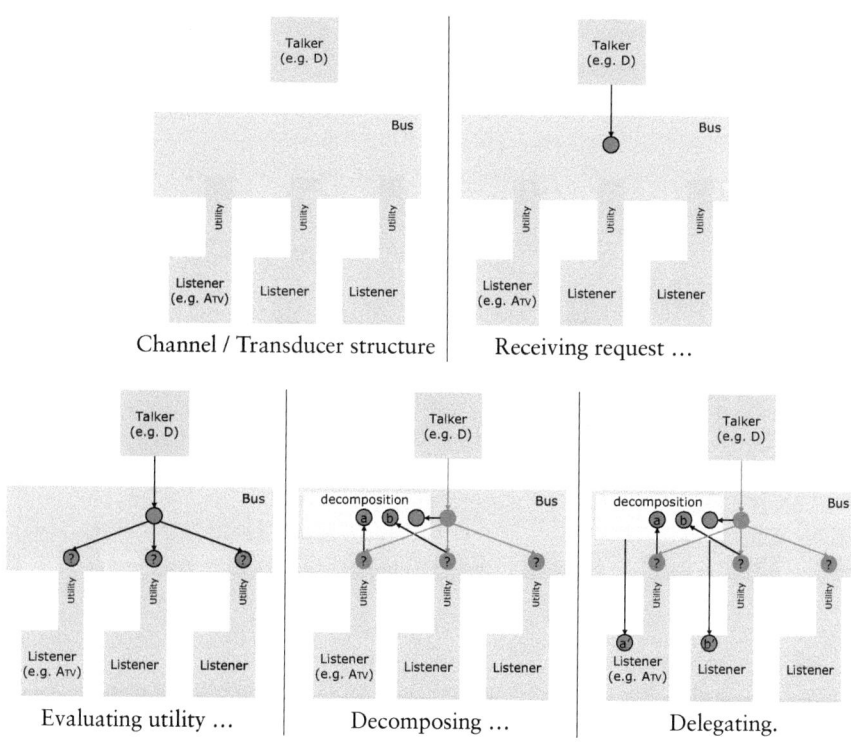

Figure 4.3: Basic message handling process in SODA-POP

the execution of strategies computed by the A level across multiple scheduling components at the X-level. (Note in this context that *temporal scheduling* is *not* a channel function as it clearly requires memory in the channel.)

Reply recombination. A channel's strategy may also describe the method for how to assemble the reply messages created by cooperating (or parallel) message consumers into a single aggregated reply. This strategy describes how to wait for the different transducers that have received (partial) messages and what algorithm to use for aggregating these replies. The most simple approach is to just return the first reply that is received. Another simple approach is to wait for all results, put them into a list, and return this list.

Unfortunately, it requires memory to perform this reply recombination: the component responsible for recombination has to remember from whom it can expect replies and which replies it already has received. Therefore, this component can not be handled by a channel. Instead, the channel creates an *implicit transducer* that performs the reply recombination strategy. By factoring reply recombination out of the channel, the design choice of *where* to do recombination in a distributed environment (at the receiver side? at the processing side?) becomes explicit, while at the same time keeping channel functionality lean: The channel may decice *where* to place the recombination transducer – but it does not have to implement its memory functionality.

Note that by putting decomposition and recombination into the channel rather than leaving this to the requesting component, we ensure that message decomposition and reply recombination is *transparent* to a component. This has two effects:

- Component designers are relieved from the task of doing receiver selection and reply recombination, this greatly simplifies implementation.

- The danger of misbehaved components that always select the same kind of receivers (*i.e.*, only receivers from the same vendor ...) is minimized.

4.5 Related work

SODA-POP is not the first concept for addressing the problem of dynamic, self organizing systems. Other approaches are for example HAVi [110] and Jini [111], the Galaxy Communicator Architecture [97, 98], and SRI's OAA (Open Agent Architecture) [93, 34], where specifically Galaxy and OAA intend to provide architectures for multi-agent systems supporting multimodal interaction.

Compared to the state of the art, the pattern-matching approach in SODA-POP itself is not new. Comparable concepts are provided by Galaxy, by SRI's OAA, as well as by earlier work on Prolog [112] and the Pattern-Matching Lambda Calculus [113]. Here, SODA-POP simply intends to provide a certain refinement at the conceptual level by replacing language-specific syntactic pattern-matching functionality (such as the Prolog-based pattern matching of OAA) by a language-independent facility based on utility value computation functions that are provided by transducers.

The *important* differences of SODA-POP to the above approaches are

- SODA-POP uses a *two-stage* approach to system decomposition and self organization.

Coarse-grained structuring is provided by defining channels, fine grained structure is supported by "pattern matching".

- SODA-POP supports data-flow architectures by providing event channels besides conventional RPC channels.

The *combination* of these two approaches is an important extension over the above systems.

HAVi, Jini, OAA, and Galaxy all provide a *single* mechanism for message routing. In HAVi and Jini, we have a simple event subscription mechanism on a global bus. Furthermore, Havi and Jini both do not provide transparent service arbitration. OAA basically provides a single SODA-POP RPC channel with a Prolog-based decomposition and recombination strategy. Galaxy provides a centralized hub-component, which uses routing rules for modeling how messages are transferred between different system components. Galaxy too can be modeled by a single SODA-POP RPC channel that uses a decomposition approach built on top of Galaxy's frame language.

On the other hand, both Galaxy and OAA could be used to model SODA-POP – simply by representing channles with *message tags*. (Galaxy and OAA both use heavyweight routing components that incorporate arbitrary memory and are therefore not suited for a distributed implementation – but this is a different issue.)

So the question is not so much which approach is more powerful, but rather: which approach provides those abstractions that best help to structure a system architecture. Specifically, SODA-POP aims at supporting systems that are created by multiple (*e.g.*, 19[8]) partners in parallel.

In our experience it is dangerous to provide only a single granularity for decomposing a complex system structure such as EMBASSI. The single granularity necessarily has to be fine in order to provide the required flexibility. When trying to fix the overall structure of the system, such a fine granularity provides too much detail and quickly leads to a proliferation of interfaces that are shared by only a few components. This danger specifically exists, when the interface discussion is carried out by several project partners in parallel[9]. However, the proliferation of interfaces is a Bad Thing, because it obstructs the interoperability of system components – a prime goal of EMBASSI.

The SODA-POP approach provides abstractions that allow a top-down structuring of the system (channels) *as well as* a bottom-up structuring (within-channel decomposition). In addition, it

---

[8]In EMBASSI the consortium had 19 partners.
[9]Systems with a similar scope as EMBASSI are known that implement well above 100 interfaces, based on a single structuring mechanism.

explicitly includes a data-flow based mechanism for constructing systems out of components, based on SODA-POP Event Channels. As a design paradigm, the SODA-POP approach has already been used successfully in implementing the EMBASSI demonstrator systems.

4.6 Summary and outlook

4.6.1 What has been achieved so far

This section outlined the architecture of a multi-agent system that supports multimodal interaction with technical infrastructures of the everyday life – the EMBASSI architecture. Furthermore, I have outlined the underlying middleware mechanisms, the SODA-POP model, that provides the essential communication patterns of a data-flow based multi-component architectures such as EMBASSI.

The SODA-POP model defined so far contains the following properties:

- Support data-flow based event processing topologies.
- Support conventional remote procedure calls.
- Support self-organization of system components.
- Support decentralized problem decomposition and conflict resolution (transparent service arbitration).
- Support dynamic extension by new components.

The aspect of dynamic unification / partitioning of complete system topologies has not yet been integrated, but should be comparatively straightforward based on the current definitions.

The SODA-POP infrastructure described here was implemented using the functional language Haskell [109]. This implementation[10] served as a proof of concept of SODA-POP, as well as a testbed for experimenting with different data-flow topologies and alternative channel ontologies (*e.g.*, decomposition and recombination strategies).

It should be mentioned that SODA-POP aims at providing a core facility for self-organization of appliance ensembles, not a comprehensive software infrastructure covering all aspects conceivably being required for ubiquitous computing systems. So, security, privacy, authentication,

---
[10]The source code of SODA-POP is included in [106].

context management, strategy planning, dialogue management, etc., are currently not part of SODA-POP, as these functionalities have to be provided by layers above (resp. below) SODA-POP.

4.6.2 Additional considerations

Temporal patterns. The definition of SODA-POP currently is more or less elaborate with respect to *decomposing* an event into a set of sub-events that is to be distributed to a set of receivers (spatial decomposition). However, there is currently no comparable mechanism for describing the *aggregation* of several events into one compound event – as is required for a simplified definition of transducers that are doing temporal aggregation. The concept of recombination strategies is just a first step in this direction[11]. Most notably, temporal aggregation could be described by such things as state machines, petri nets, or by parsers.

QoS guarantees. Currently, SODA-POP provides no mechanisms for specifying and verifying QoS properties such as:

Local QoS: *e.g.*, a reply with a certain minimum precision is guaranteed to arrive within a given time interval. Channels provide currently no mechanism for describing QoS guarrantees. The minimum would be that an answer – without a guarantee on its precision – is being made available after a given time. This could be achieved by incorporating strategies such as *successive refinement* into reply recombination.

Global QoS: *e.g.*, the current set of transducers and channels fulfills a certain data-flow topology (*i.e.*, for each required system function, at least one transducer is available).

There is currently no mechanism defined for making global statements about a set of channels and transducers. These statements could contain both constraints on the topology of the channel / transducer network as well as constraints on their temporal behavior. Although technologies for specifying *and verifying* such properties exist (*e.g.*, temporal logic, petri nets, process calculi, ...), it has not yet been investigated, which of these technologies suits best the needs of SODA-POP and how they can be integrated into an essentially *decentralized* system concept.

---

[11] A recombination strategy exactly produces such a temporal aggregation.

4.6.3 Enhancement of SODA-POP with an agent selection algorithm

The definition of concrete channel ontologies for the Ambient Intelligence infrastructure was an important item for the next steps – after all, the need for transparent and self-organizing service arbitration in EMBASSI has been one of the main motivations for developing SODA-POP. The focus is the $D - A$ channel (goal-channel): how do we automatically select between different A components that all claim to be able to solve a specific user goal detected by a D component?

This question was answered to some extend in the EMBASSI succession project DYNAMITE [28, 29, 32]. In this project, SODA-POP's subscription (see Section 4.4.3) and message handling mechanisms (see Section 4.4.4) were extended by an *opinion based agent selection algorithm* inspired by [114].

When a component of the intention analysis emits a goal into the goal-channel, the most appropriate assistant has to be found. But how should the channel provide this functionality in a distributed and dynamically changing ensemble? The chosen approach uses the assistants' opinions (the assistants are the only available domain experts) in a suitable way. The objective ability of each assistant is calculated by using the assistants' subjective opinions. Thus every assistant that takes part in a request to tender for accomplishing a goal, provides the channel with several aspects it considers as relevant to solve it. For each aspect, every assistant provides the channel with the following values [29]:

- the relative importance of each aspect

- a confidence value for each aspect describing the confidence of the component that the aspect indeed has the assigned importance

- a fidelity value that describes, how well the component thinks it can consider this aspect or adjust it to the ideal value

These values are used to calculate effective objective importances of each raised aspect. Multiplied with the individual fidelity values the objective performance can be estimated (The mathematical algorithms behind this are described in [114, 32]).

Example: Imagine the user wishes to hear relaxing music and the dialogue manager sends a goal that incorporates *render music* and *low ambient brightness*. The pictured system has two assistant components raising their aspects they could take into account to develop an effective strategy to reach this goal. The first assistant belongs to a sound system and would raise the aspects *render music* with a high importance and fidelity value and *low ambient brightness*, with a low importance and low fidelity value. The second assistant is capable of device comprehensive strategy generation and would raise the aspect *render music* with almost the same value of importance and fidelity than the first one, but additionally the aspect *low ambient brightness* with high values of importance and fidelity. According to the agent selection algorithm - and according to rationality - the second assistant would be selected to fulfill the goal.

To summarize, self-organization is achieved by two means in SODA-POP:

1. Identifying the set of channels that completely cover the essential message processing behavior for any appliance in the prospective application domain.

2. Developing suitable channel strategies that effectively provide a distributed coordination mechanism tailored to the functionality, which is anticipated for the listening components.

Then, based on the standard channel set, *e.g.*, as outlined in Fig. 4.2, any device is able to integrate itself autonomously into an ensemble, and any set of devices can spontaneously form an ensemble.

4.7 Ensemble Communication Framework – ECo

The ECo middleware (Ensemble Communication Framework) is a subset of SODA-POP and is used as the underlying software infrastructure of the MMIS[12] Smart Appliance Lab (see Picture 1.3). Fig. 4.4 has a schematic view of the room. This environment is heavily instrumented with sensors and actuators, but also ready for ad hoc added appliances. For that, the room features WiFi-connectivity, a number of LAN-connections, Bluetooth, and several connections for video and audio signals. The primary goal of this Lab is to create ad hoc device ensembles that are able to react to users' behavior and provide intrinsic computational assistance to users in a workspace, which – in the current scenario – is a smart meeting room. The key goal of the current research is to create a system infrastructure that provides a continuous concept of adjusting the environment in which users are working. The configuration of the Smart Appliance Lab includes among other things a steerable projector, 4 static ceiling mounted projectors, a mobile projector, 8 motor-screens, different network connected sensors and actuators, like dimmable lamps, air-condition, temperature and light-sensors, cameras and a sound system.

---

[12]MMIS – Mobile Multimedia Information Systems, Computer Science Department of the University of Rostock

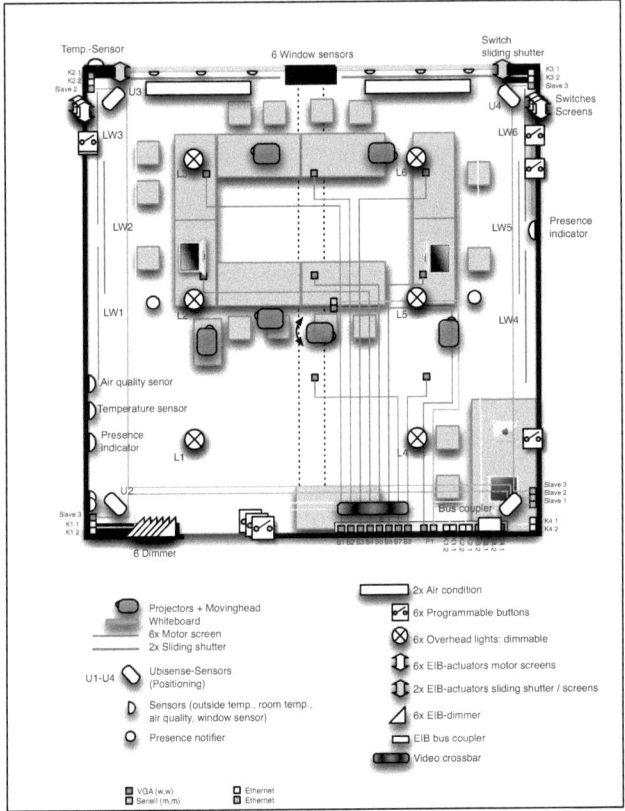

Figure 4.4: MMIS Smart Appliance Lab, schematic view

For the localization of the users in the room we use a Ubisense real-time location system, that utilizes ultra-wideband technology to locate assets and people.

Fig. 4.5 shows some of the ECo components of the Smart Appliance Lab. ECo provides the middleware mechanics for the components of our Smart Environment in a distributed manner where no central component is required. For the underlying communication, ECo uses *Zeroconf* channels [115] that enables auto configuration for IP networks. Zeroconf communication channels enable seamless subscription of appliances and take care that sent message get through to their addressees. ECo provides two channels, a ContextChannel and an ActionChannel. According to their role or purpose, the appliances or devices of the environment subscribe to these communication channels.

Architecture Framework

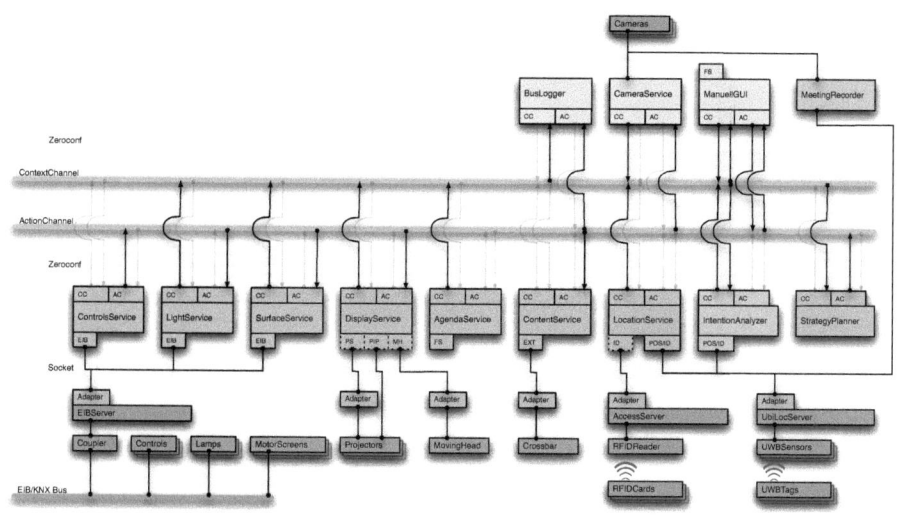

Figure 4.5: ECo Architecture of MMIS Smart Appliance Lab

Several appliances act as perceptual components, *e.g.*, LightService, SurfaceService, DisplayService, AgendaService, LocationService and provide context, status or sensor information to the ContextChannel (CC). The IntentionAnalyzer is the reasoning component that reads data from CC, interprets it, and writes its interpretations or predictions back to CC. Note that ECo don't uses a central context manager anymore. Every component that needs context information is subscribed to the ContextChannel and handles the context information that it is tailored to use.

StrategyPlanner is a decision making component that reads appliance states and goals (intention interpretations) to decide for a set of appropriate assisting actions. The resulting actions are requested via the ActionChannel (AC). The components with execution functions (actuators), *e.g.*, LightService, SurfaceService, DisplayService, ContentService are subscribed to the ActionChannel and perform the requested actions.

From a physical point of view, every component could run on its own computer, or even better, the computer itself could be integrated into the smart appliance. With the usage of ECo, these appliances can form and configure[13] a smart environment in an ad-hoc fashion, by sharing their functionality and negotiating about user needs.

---

[13] Of course, ECo is only able to provide the architectonic integration, not the operational integration.

Chapter 5

AI Planning as Source of the Assistance Strategy

The requirements for Ambient Intelligence include without limitation the need for dynamic strategy generation of the device ensembles. In this chapter I will show that Artificial Intelligence planning technologies are able to accomplish this requirement.

5.1 Introduction

In the previous chapters I already exemplified that creating multimodal assistant systems supporting the intuitive interaction with technical infrastructures is a substantial challenge - both with respect to the individual concepts and algorithms that are required and with respect to the overall systems architechture. While some systems attempt to build solutions with a fixed set of allowable functions and environment variables, like Jini [111], I focus on a system which is dynamically expandable by new components with completely new functions. This chapter presents a planner-based approach, first-time proposed in [23], to helping the user to interact with complex technical infrastructures of the everyday life.

Planners are software components that allow the automatic creation of strategies for reaching a given goal based on a given set of possible actions. Providing such a system component with planning capability – this is, relieving the user of coming up with a control strategy by himself (which would require him to know all possible operations of his infrastructure) – might allow to make more of the available functionality *accessible* for the user. The goal of our research is the creation of an interactive environment based on multimodal interfaces and is conceptually based on this important paradigm shift: the transition from a function-oriented interaction with devices to a goal-oriented interaction with systems. Such a system will be able to interact with its users through speech (or gesture), will be context sensitive through perception of the environment, and will therefore provide a kind of situation aware assistance. The presented concept supports not only syntactical interfaces, but also semantical interfaces, which means that the components provide a description of the meaning and the effect of their functions. Thus, a planning assistant is able to develop system comprehensive strategies, even with new devices.

The remainder of this Chapter is structured as follows: Section 5.2 gives an overview about the embedding of planning and scheduling into the architectural framework. Section 5.3 starts with the resulting requirements for a planning component and outlines the planning approach. Section 5.4 gives arguments why planning is a suitable inference method and Section 5.5 elucidates the reasons that led to the usage of PDDL as planning representation language. Section 5.6 describes the downstream scheduling algorithm and Section 5.7 deals with the necessary ontology. In Section 5.8 we will have a closer look at the actual implementation and the functionality and Section 5.9 discusses the limits of AI planning. Finally, Section 5.11 gives a summary and an outlook.

5.2 Architecture overview

The idea of using AI planning for creating system comprehensive strategies is embedded in the architectural concept that I have explained in Chapter 4. As described, this generic architecture (Fig. 4.1) is a pipeline approach to the problem of mapping user goals to environment changes. Each "level" in the architecture represents one function within this pipeline, while the level interfaces separating different ontologies. Components can be added or removed dynamically: suitable co-ordination mechanisms at each level are responsible for managing the interactions between the components at this level. There is deliberately *no* central co-ordination component. In Chapter 4 I have outlined the underlying middleware mechanics, the SODA-POP model, that provides the essential communication patterns of a data-flow based multi-component architecture such as EMBASSI. In Section 4.6.3 you can find the description of an agent selection algorithm, which is able to choose the best suited agent to perform a given task in a dynamic environment.

This architechture allows us to build interoperable systems, where different components are provided by different vendors and where components are added and removed over time by the

AI Planning as Source of the Assistance Strategy

end-user.

An important aspect of the generic architecture is the context manager component. It is responsible for managing the system's view of the world – information about the user, resource profiles, the environment, and also the availability and state of the individual components. Attached to the context manager, we have sensors to obtain biometrics and environmental information.

The planning assistant – which is the main topic of this chapter – is part of the assistance level:

The assistance levels

The assistance levels operate on goals which are identified by the MMI levels. The process of mapping goals to changes of the environment consists of the following steps:

1. A components (A = Assistant) take goals - which specify state changes of the environment - and try to develop strategies for fulfilling these goals.
2. The plans are sent to the X components, which are responsible for the (distributed) scheduling and execution of the plans.
3. Finally, individual action requests are sent to the devices that execute the action request.

Lower level communication

The components in an EMBASSI system communicate with each other using the Knowledge Query and Manipulation Language (KQML) as agent communication language, which runs on top of TCP/IP. KQML distinguishes within one act of communication between "performatives" and "parameters". Performatives destine what impact a message should have. The essential content of a message resides in the parameter "content". For this content we decided within the project to use the standard of XML. Especially during the development and debugging phase, where we had to make sure that the components provided by 19 different partners all use the same syntax, it has been very helpful to be able to verify that the message sent by a component indeed did correspond to the syntax it claimed to have. The comunication between all components is controlled by a KQML-Router which is positioned underneath the presented architecture.

Media streams

Media data, *e.g.* images, video or mp3-files are composed of two components, the data itself and the meta data which are describing these data. For example for the description of media data the XML structure *AVProgram* was specified, which allows the meta data specification of audio-files, videos, images and documents. We have consciously avoided the predefinition of a certain transmission protocol for media streams, to be open for both existing and prospectively protocols. But to build a completely dynamic system, in which all component co-operatively work together, controlled by an assistant like described in the next sections, we need at least a declaration of the procedure for the transmission of media data and their associated meta data. Therefore I have defined our *Mediastream Protocol*. With this we have predefined the way how the transmission of mediastreams has to proceed and how the components has to describe their provided busses. Thus, the generic addressing of different bus types, *e.g.* IEEE1394 or TCP/IP is possible.

5.3 Planning as assistance

Once an explicit declarative representation of the user goal is available, it becomes possible to exploit partial-order planning mechanisms. This requires to describe the operations provided by the available devices as *precondition / effect rules*, where the preconditions and effects are based on the environment state model. These rules then can be used by a planning system for deriving strategies for reaching user goals, which consider the capabilities of all currently available devices. The planning system receives the goal identified by the Intention Analysis. It must then find a strategy that changes the environment from its current state to the goal state. This can be understood as a classical planning problem:

- The goal is given as a set of positive and negative literals in the propositional calculus.

- The initial state of the world (resp. the state of the system and the environment-condition which is known to the system) is also expressed as a set of literals.

- The actions provided by the available devices ("operators") have to be characterized using a suitable definition language. It describes the action's relation to the environment: it contains a set of preconditions that must be true before the action can be executed and a set of changes, or effects that the action will have on the world. Both the preconditions and effects can be positive or negative literals.

The critical aspect here is the expressive power of the model used for describing device operators, which needs to be strong enough to capture at least the operational semantics of today's consumer appliances.

5.3.1 Concrete example

As example, consider the situation outlined in Figure 5.1, left, where a user would like to increase the brightness of his TV set. Assuming the TV is already set to maximum brightness, the sensible reaction of the ensemble would be the one given at right: reduce ambient light. In order for an ad hoc ensemble to arrive at this conclusion, TV set, lamp, and shutter must provide a description of their capabilities, similar to the one given below[1]:

THE LAMP'S IMPACT ON THE ENVIRONMENTSTATE:

Action: *dim-down*(?x)
  Precond: *luminosity*(?x) = **high**
  Effect: *luminosity*(?x) = **low**

THE SHUTTER'S IMPACT ON THE ENVIRONMENTSTATE:

Action: *closeShutter*(?x)
  Precond: *open*(?x)
  Effect: ¬*open*(?x) ∧ *luminosity*(?x) = **low**

THE TV'S DEPENDANCE OF THE ENVIRONMENTSTATE:

Axiom: *ambBrightness-low*
  Context: ∀?x ∈ dom *luminosity* : *luminosity*(?x) = **low**
  Implies: *ambientBrightness* = **low**

Axiom: *increaseTVBrightness*(?x)
  Context: *brightness*(?x) = **max** ∧ *ambientBrightness* = **low**
  Implies: *brighter*(?x)

Then, based on a specific situation given by
Inits: (*brightness*(**TV**) = **max** ∧ *luminosity*(**Lamp**)= **high** ∧ *dimmable*(**Lamp**) ∧ *open*(**Shutter**))
a suitable plan for the Goal: *brighter*(**TV**) could then be computed as Plan: [*dim-down*(**Lamp**), *closeShutter*(**Shutter**)].

---

[1]For sake of brevity, this capability definition has been very much simplified.

Chapter 5

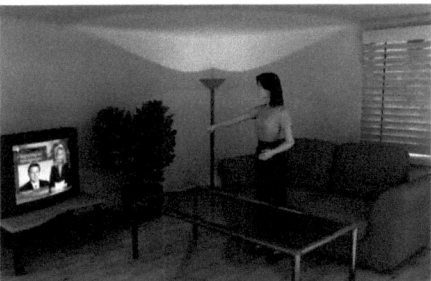

Figure 5.1: Goal-based ensemble control: Example

5.4 Why Planning as Inference?

5.4.1 Reasoning Methods in AI

With the previous shown examples it is already clear that the assistive system must do more than simply reacting to the environment. The users have goals they want to be achieved. In order to do so, the system has to look ahead. The Smart Environment must plan its course of action. Planning is the process of generating representations of future behavior prior to the use of such plans to constrain or control that behavior. The objective is a set of actions, with temporal and other constraints on them, for execution by the device ensemble.

To generate such a plan, we cannot use *e.g.* problem solving by search, where we describe a problem by a state space and then implement a program to search through this space. We need to specify the problem declaratively (using logic) and then solve it by a general planning algorithm. Also the following approaches from the area of artificial intelligence[2] cannot be used, like expert systems, finite automata, artificial neural networks or genetic algorithms for either one of this reasons: (I) A powerful representation language is missing. (II) The inference system is not able to generate new strategies, only to select pre-existing strategies. (III) Learning is required to acquire the strategies. (IV) They need a complete representation of the state space. (V) Parameterization is difficult, that means that it is difficult to find parameters that deliver constant (sub)-optimal solutions.

As determined acting is one of the most remarkable abilities of humans, planning has been studied since the beginning of research in artificial intelligence and cognitive science. Planning

---

[2]This is not a complete list of possible options, but the reasons why they are not considered are the same.

AI Planning as Source of the Assistance Strategy

research has led to many useful tools for real-world applications, and has provided significant insights into the organization of behavior and the nature of reasoning about actions. AI planning – also called action planning – introduces two general questions:

- How can we represent the knowledge about complex dynamic systems and the statement that has to be solved?

- How can we generate instructions (plans) to achieve a goal, based on a suitable represented problem description?

5.4.2 Planning vs. Service Matching

Another good reason to use planning is the option to use an environment ontology as the basis for the representation of the problems. If we would use service descriptions as the basis of the assistive system, the number of different services could become really huge and we were not able to consider new services in an dynamic environment. That means that the number of environment states variables are limited, whereby the number of possible services will not be limited. Therefore, it will be easier to define an ontology of environment states instead of an ontology that contains all possible services.

Remember the examples of Fig. 1.6 or Section 2.3. In that examples we identified that we need a mechanism for discovering and combining services, a mechanism that is based on the *semantics* of services rather than on their names. The advantage of using an environment ontology is that it will consist of a rather finite number of entities. Such an environment ontology maintains all environment states and their relations and these states are finite, in contrast to the possible number of syntactical service descriptions (names). In the example of Section 2.3 we had a service called `moveFromAtoB`. If we now use a location model embedded in the environment ontology, we can describe that we want to have something `(at B)` with the initial state of having something `(at A)`, and with an action that is able to `(moveFomTo ?x ?y)` we don't need a new name for a new service that can move something.

5.5 The planning domain model

A representation language is necessary to specify planning problems in a way that can be solved by a computer. More expressive representation languages allow one to model a greater variety of planning problems but are also more complicated, which makes it harder to encode planning problems and understand planning problems that have been encoded by others.

Providing a suitably expressive operator definition language is not a completely trivial requirement when looking at the host of features included in modern infotainment systems. But with expressiveness comes computational intractability – the more expressive a language is, the more computation is required to reason about sentences in that language. On the other hand, the solution capability of the planning system determines the space of the possible functionality of the device components. For example, the choice of discrete operators obviously excludes devices that provide continuous functions. So finding the right balance between expressiveness and computational tractability is very important for our application domain. Furthermore operator sets for devices must be compact in order to keep the number of operators that have to be managed by the system small and in order to simplify the creation of (compatible) operator sets by device vendors.

In the next section I will show what led to the decision to use PDDL as representation language for the planning problems in smart environments.

5.5.1 Representing Plans

In AI planning the task is to find a sequence of operator instances that transforms an initial state into a state in which the goal is satisfied. To do that we need a representation for states, actions, goals, and plans.

Classical planning is mostly represented in terms of deterministic state models characterized by the following elements (see *e.g.* [116]):

- A discrete state space S;

- The initial situation given by the state $I = s_0 \in S$;

- A goal situation given by a non empty set $G = S_G \subseteq S$;

- Actions $A(s) \subseteq A$ applicable in each state $s \in S$;

- A deterministic state transition function $f(a, s)$ for $a \in A(s)$;

- Positive action cost $c(a, s)$ for applying action a in s.

A solution for a planning problem of this type is a sequence of actions $(a_0, a_1, ..., a_k)$ that is corresponding to a sequence of state transitions $(s_0, s_1, ..., s_k)$ such that each action a_i is applicable in s_i, i.e. $s_1 \in f(s_0, a_1), s_2 \in f(s_1, a_2), ..., s_k \in f(s_{k-1}, a_k)$, where s_k is a goal state, i.e. $s_k \in S_G$ and $a_i \in A(s_i)$. An optimal solution is found, when the total costs are minimal: $\sum_{i=0}^{n} c(a_i, s_i)$. In classical planning it is assumed that all costs are equal and thus that the optimal plans are the ones with minimal length.

Classical planning has been dominated by research on domain-independent planning. Because of the difficulty of developing a domain-independent planner that would work well in all planning domains, most research has focused on domains that satisfy the following set of restrictive assumptions (*e.g.* [117]):

Finite system: The system has a finite number of states: $|S| < \infty$

Full observability: The system is fully observable, that is, one has complete knowledge about the state of the system. Associated with this assumption is the "closed world assumption", which states that any fact not known to the system can be taken to be false.

Deterministic transitions: The system is deterministic, that is, for every state s and action a: $\forall (s, a) | f(s, a) | \leq 1$. If an action is applicable to a state, its application brings a deterministic system to a single other state.

Static model: The system is static, that is, the set of events E is empty ($E = \emptyset$). The system has no internal dynamics; it stays in the same state until the controller applies some action.

Offline planning: The planner is not concerned with any change that may occur while it is planning; it plans for the given initial and goal states regardless of the current dynamics, if any. In other words, planning and execution are independent.

Reachability goals: The only kind of goal is a reachable goal that is specified as an explicit goal state or a set of goal states S_G. The objective is to find any sequence of state transitions that ends at one of the goal states. This assumption excludes, for example, states to be avoided, constraints on state trajectories, and utility functions.

Sequential plans: A solution plan to a planning problem is a linearly ordered finite sequence of actions.

Implicit time: Actions and events have no duration, they are instantaneous state transitions. This assumption is embedded in the state-transition model, which does not represent time explicitly.

Some of this restrictive assumptions make it difficult to use classical planning in real word applications. That is why we have to look which of these assumptions can be relaxed to use planning in smart environment applications.

5.5.2 Choosing a planning language

Why is it useful to use a standard planning language? With a standard language it is possible to use the same planner for many classes of problems, but more importantly it allows us to compare different planning algorithms and to solve a problem with the planner of choice. It was not the intention of this thesis to develop a new planning language or a new planning algorithm. The objective was to show that AI planning – which is a wide and active research area with many different approaches – is a reasonable method to implement goal based interaction for smart environments. Hence, I will now look at the state of the art and substantiate my selection of the planning language and algorithms.

If we look at possible options to represent planning domains it is clear that it is impossible to list all possible states S explicitly. Even for very simple domains, the number of states in a system could be very large and it would not be possible to represent all states in a graph and use a standard search algorithm. Therefore, we need implicit representations that can describe useful subsets of S in a way that both is compact and can easily be searched.

In the literature we find three different ways to represent classical planning problems. All three have about the same expressive power. Any problem that can be represented in one representation can also be represented in the other two.

Set-theoretic representation: uses propositional logic, each state of the world is a set of propositions and each action is a syntactic expression specifying which propositions belong to the state in order for the action to be applicable and which propositions the action will add or remove to change the state of the world.

Classical representation: uses predicate logic, the states and the actions are like the ones described for set theoric representation except that first order literals and logical connectives are used instead propositions.

State variable representation: represents states in terms of variables used, each state is represented by a tuple of value n state variables $(x_1, ..., x_n)$ and each action is represented by a partial function that maps this tuple into some other tuple of values of the n states.

AI Planning as Source of the Assistance Strategy

For more information about these three representations see *e.g.* [118]. Mostly used today is the classical representation, with STRIPS [119] as the first widely accepted language. STRIPS originated from a planning system called the Stanford Research Institute Problem Solver in 1972 to control the Shakey robot. Further developments of STRIPS are ADL (Action Description Language) [120] and the UCPOP formalism (Universal Complete Partial Order Planner) [121]. Other important formalisms in the history of planning are *e.g.* PRODIGY [122] or UMCP (Universal Method-Composition Planner) [123].

But what representation language should be used for the application area of smart environments? The experience from the modelling of our domain has shown that we need a planning environment that supports conditional effects[3] and disjunction in the preconditions – this allows a compact representation of device operator sets. Furthermore it is mandatory to have universal quantification in the preconditions and the effects. This for instance allows to define operators that apply to an arbitrary number of objects – which is extremely important in an environment that is dynamically extensible.

Also, it is an advantage, if the planning system supports domain axioms, because they provide a convenient way to decouple operators from the environment: Instead of describing the environmental preconditions and effects of an operator in the operator's definition itself, we only describe the operator in terms of the device's internal state. Environmental aspects are attached by providing suitable domain axioms. This approach simplifies an incremental definition and extension of the environment state – which relieves us from the complex task of coming up with a complete environment model before defining the first operator. This advantage has to be contrasted with the fact that some of the fastest planning systems available today – *e.g.* Metric-FF [124] – unfortunately do not support domain axioms.

Finally, the planning system should generate partially ordered plans (rather than totally ordered plans), so that independent actions can be executed in parallel. Moreover, it is thus possible that the scheduler can apply refined strategies – such as least cost scheduling – for determining the concrete execution sequence. Some current planning systems don't support partially ordered plans. A solution for that is to use a filter between the planner and the scheduler which attempts to modify the plan order to put the scheduler in a better position [125]. Such filters could remove certain over-commitments in the ordering, which is called deordering.

For our first running prototype we used the UCPOP planner. But the experiences have shown that the expressiveness of this system's operator definition language was not well suited for

---

[3]The language features mentioned in this paragraph will be explained in more detail in the PDDL-section.

modeling various problems of our application domain. Especially the feasibility to modeling temporal and continuous processes was missing, that is necessary to provide a reasonable time and resource management. Important is also to be able to represent mixed discrete/continuous domains. Amongst other approaches from different researchers the newer versions of the PDDL language are going in this direction.

In the last years PDDL (Planning Domain Definition Language) has become the quasi standard for the modeling of planning domains. PDDL is also the given language for the "International Planning Competition" (IPC). This competition is a biennial challenge for the planning community, inviting planning systems to participate in a large scale evaluation. Consequently there are now quite a lot planning systems which can process domains modelled in PDDL. Moreover it gives an overview about the performance of the available systems. PDDL is also an atempt to standardize planning domains and problem description languages.

There are currently four versions: PDDL1.2 (IPC 1998 and 2000) [126], PDDL2.1 (IPC 2002) [127], PDDL2.2 (IPC 2004)[128] and PDDL3.0 (IPC 2006) [129]. Each version introduced new features, but not all have survived. In the next section I will give an overview about the main features of PDDL. For a detailed treatment, please have a look at the respective documentations (cited above).

5.5.3 PDDL

PDDL was introduced as the input language for the first International Planning Competition by the AIPS-98 Planning Competition Committee [126]. The basic paradigm of PDDL is to express the "physics" of a domain, i.e. what predicates exists, what actions are possible, what is the structure of compound actions and what are the effects of actions. PDDL has a Lisp based syntax, follows the formalism of UCPOP and has STRIPS-style description of the possible actions. Other description formalisms that influenced PDDL are ADL, Prodigy, and SIPE-2 [130].

PDDL uses different files for the definition of domains and problems. This separates the descriptions of parameterised actions that characterise domain behaviors from the description of specific objects, initial conditions and goals that characterize a problem instance. Therefore, a planning problem is created by the combination of a domain description with a problem description. Each domain defines the "requirements" a planner should comply with to run it. In Fig. 5.2 we have the structure of a domain file that specifies the necessary definitions and in Fig. 5.3 we have an example domain file.

Structure of a domain:

```
(define(domain<name>)
    (:requirements <:req 1> ... <:req n>)
    (:types <type 1> ... <type n>)
    (:constants <cons 1> ... <cons n>)
    (:predicates <p 1> ... <p n>)
    (:action 1)
    ...
    (:action n)
)
```

Figure 5.2: PDDL domain structure

The *:requirements* field is used to declare what kind of problems are stated in the domain file. The *:types* field structures the types of the objects in a domain, typing the parameters that appear in actions and constraining the types of arguments to predicates. The *:predicates* field is used to declare predicates and the arguments of each one. An action (operator) consists of parameters, preconditions, and effects. The *:parameters* is a list of variables that are used by the action. The *:precondition* is a goal description (GD) that must be true before an action can be executed. The *:effect* describes the effect that an action has. They list the changes that the action imposes on the current state of the world. For an example see the action EIB-ShutterUp of Fig. 5.3. This action uses a parameter of the type device and has the preconditions that the device ?d must be (not open) and be a shutter. If the action is executed the device ?d will be open and the luminosity for ?d will have the value of outsideBrightness. Also the environment variable ambientBrightness will be increased by the value of outsideBrightness. This action will also add to the overall cost by 1. With this PDDL operator we can see the dependance and the impact of actions on environment variables.

List of operators which can appear at an action preconditions or effects:

- Preconditions:
    - and / or / not
    - imply
    - exists <variable> <literal>
    - forall <variables> <literal>

- Effects:
    - and / not
    - forall <variables> <effect>
    - when <expression> <effect>

Example of a domain file:

```
(define (domain embassi-domain)
  (:requirements :strips :equality :fluents :typing :adl :universal-preconditions)
  (:types integer float - number device)
  (:predicates (lamp ?x)
    (shutter ?x)
    (eib-dimmer ?x)
    (on ?x)
    (brighter)
    (darker)
  )
  (:functions (ambient_brightness)
    (costs)
    (old-ambient_brightness)
    (luminosity ?x - device)
    (outsideBrightness)
  )
  (:action LAMP-SwitchOff
     :parameters (?lamp)
     :precondition (and (on ?lamp) (lamp ?lamp))
     :effect (and (not (on ?lamp)) (decrease (ambientBrightness) 20)
             (decrease (costs) 20)))
  (:action LAMP-SwitchOn
     :parameters (?lamp)
     :precondition (and (not (on ?lamp)) (lamp ?lamp))
     :effect (and (on ?lamp) (increase (ambientBrightness) 20) (increase (costs) 20)))
  (:action LAMP-DimmUp
     :parameters (?d)
     :precondition (and (eib-dimmer ?d) (< (luminosity ?d) 50))
     :effect (and (increase (ambientBrightness) 10) (increase (luminosity ?d) 10)
             (increase (costs) 10)))
  (:action LAMP-DimmDown
     :parameters (?d)
     :precondition (and (eib-dimmer ?d) (> (luminosity ?d) 0))
     :effect (and (decrease (ambient_brightness) 10) (decrease (luminosity ?d) 10)
             (decrease (costs) 10)))
  (:action EIB-ShutterUp
     :parameters (?d - device)
     :precondition (and (not (open ?d))(shutter ?d))
     :effect (and (open ?d) (increase (costs) 1)
             (assign (luminosity ?d) (outsideBrightness))
             (increase (ambientBrightness) (outsideBrightness))))
)
```

Figure 5.3: PDDL domain file

Fig. 5.4 shows an example problem file. This problem defines the initial state of the world, the goal description, and the metric.

The definition of PDDL is domain independent and gives deliberately no "advice" to planners, *i.e.*, annotations about which actions to use in reaching which goals, or selecting which actions under which circumstances. However, due to the fact that few planners will handle the entire PDDL language, PDDL is factored into subsets of features, called *requirements*. A domain's set of requirements allows to quickly tell if a planner is likely to be able to handle a domain, and to choose an appropriate one. For PDDL1 the following requirements are defined.

PDDL 1 requirements:

Example of a problem file:

```
(define (problem t1)
(:domain embassi-domain)
  (:objects EIB01 - device
      EIB-Shutter - device
      EIB-Dimmer - device
      TV - device
      SON-MP3 - device
      stringAVProg - string
      )
  (:init (lamp EIB01)
      (on EIB01)
      (eib-dimmer EIB-Dimmer)
      (= (luminosity EIB-Dimmer) 0)
      (shutter EIB-Shutter)
      (open EIB-Shutter)
      (= (ambientBrightness) 0)
      (= old-ambientBrightness 0)
      (= outsideBrightness 30)
      (= costs 0)
      )
  (:goal and (= (ambientBrightness) 20) (RenderAudio))
  (:metric minimize (costs))
)
```

Figure 5.4: PDDL problem file

:strips Basic STRIPS-style adds and deletes.

:typing Allow type names in declarations of variables.

:negative-preconditions Allow `not` in goal descriptions.

:disjunctive-preconditions Allow `or` in goal descriptions.

:equality Support = as built-in predicate.

:existential-preconditions Allow `exists` in goal descriptions.

:universal-preconditions Allow `forall` in goal descriptions.

:conditional-effects Allow `when` in action effects.

PDDL2.1

PDDL2.1 was created in 2002 by Fox and Long for IPC3 [127]. The main new features are *fluents* (numbers), plan quality measures: *metrics*, that is an objective functions for measuring the quality of plans, and *durative actions*, which take time (explicit representation of time and duration) and may have continuous effects.

The most important innovation in PDDL2.1 is the introduction of objective functions for plans, thus making plan quality as important as plan existence. The use of numbers in a domain allows for measuring consumption of critical resources and other parameters. A metric that can be modeled is for example that energy consumption must be minimized. This is very important for many goals in our domain in which plan quality might be dependent on a number of interacting factors.

Fluents: Allow handling of numeric values in PDDL. New requirements flag [:fluents]. Functions (fluents) can be used in actions preconditions, together with relational operators (=, >, <, <=, >=), or effects (as they were predicates). Values are modified using: `increase, decrease, assign, scale-up, scale-down`.

Metric: The use of functions allows also to define plan quality measures beyond the use of plan length. Requirements flag [:metric]. Options for plan optimization are `maximize` or `minimize`. Example:
`(:metric minimize (+ (* 2 (costs power)) (costs bandwith)))`

Durative Actions: Actions can now have a duration. Requirements flag [:duration]. A duration can be given a numeric value, calculated using fluents, can be given as an interval, or can be empty, the actions lasts until a precondition becomes false. Both preconditions and effects must be temporarily annotated, using: `at start, at end, over all`. Example:

```
(:durative-action pan_to
   :parameters (?x - projector ?y - coordinate ?z - coordinate)
   :duration (= ?duration 5)
   :condition (and (over all (movable ?x))
             (at start (available ?x)) (at start (at ?x ?y))))
   :effect(at end (at ?x ?z))
)
```

PDDL2.2

PDDL2.2 was created in 2004 by Edelkamp and Hoffmann for IPC4 [128]. The main new features are *derived predicates* and *timed initial literals*.

Derived predicates: Labeled as "axioms", derived predicates were already a part of the first version of PDDL, but they have never been used in a competition benchmark and for that reason only view planners could handle these. They are predicates that are not affected by any of the actions available to the planner. Instead, it allows predicates whose true value is defined by a set of rules of the form (if formula(x) then predicate(x)).

Timed initial literals Allows the initial state to specify literals that will become true at a specified time point. Example:
(at 7 (daylight)) (at 20 (not (daylight))))

PDDL3

PDDL3 was developed by Gerevini and Long for IPC5 [129]. The main new features are *goal preferences* and *state trajectory constraints*. With PDDL3, the focus of the language has shifted more to quality instead of planning time or plan length. Goal preferences also allows for the definition of intermediate goals, *i.e.* goals that have to be met not at the end but at certain moments of the plan.

State Trajectory Constraints: With this constraints we can define goals to be met not at the end but at certain moments of the plan. The constraints are expressed through temporal modal operators over first order formulae involving state predicates. Requirements flag [:constraints]. They are defined in the :constraints section of an operator, they are not allowed in the preconditions. Allowed constraints definition operators are: always, sometime, at-most-once, at end, within, sometime-before, sometime-after, always-within, hold-during, hold-after. Example: within t <GD> – Fact must be true during t time
(:constraints (within 10 (at projector2 screen3)))

Goal and state preferences: Until now, both goals and constraints had to be accomplished for the plan being valid. That means that the planning system would not deliver a plan if it is not possible to deliver exactly the goal state and to observe the constraints. In real domains that can often be a problem. Sometimes there are goals we would like to be accomplished but don't want the plan to be invalid if it is not exactly possible. To deal with this, PDDL3 introduces preferences that are applicable to goals and constraints. Requirements flag [:preferences]. These preferences can appear in the constraints field, the operator preconditions, and in the goal description. Example:
(:constraints (forall (?x - user)
  (preference PrefName1 (sometime (haveSeen ?x Document)))))
Whether a plan accomplishes preferences or not, it would still be valid. Of course it is the objective to prefer plans that pay attention to the preferences. For that reason,

preferences can be given a weight (in the metric part of a problem) to establish which is more important. Example:

```
(:metric minimize
   (+ (* (is-violated PrefName1) 4.1)
      (* (is-violated PrefName2) 6.4)))
```

PDDL Conclusion

In its initial purpose, PDDL has been as a communication language – so that (I) planners could be compared in competitions and (II) problem sets could be shared and planning algorithms independently validated. It's purpose now is also to be a practical language, to help an engineer accurately and efficiently encode an application domain into a planning domain model.

With PDDL we have a series of languages that suit planners with different capabilities. The basic requirement in PDDL is [:strips] which indicates the underlying semantics of the language are considered as sets of situations (states), where each state is specified by stating a list of all predicates that are true. The syntax is clear and precisely defined within the manuals, and parsing tools, solution checkers and domain analysis tools are available publicly.

That PDDL is a very expressive language for a variety of planning applications has been shown by the range of problem domains used in competitions and in benchmark sets.

In the beginning of this section, I listed a number of restrictive assumptions that were the basis of classical planning domains. With the development of the modern versions of PDDL and the consideration of the requirements of our application domain, we can resolve the most restrictive assumptions.

Evaluation of classical planning assumptions:

Evaluation of finite system: A possibly infinite set of states may be needed, for example to handle numerical state variables. But, functions in PDDL are restricted to be of the type $Object^n \rightarrow \mathbb{R}$, for the finite collection of objects in a planning instance, Object and finite function with n arguments [127]. The decision not to allow numbers to be used as arguments to actions rules out some actions that might seem reasonable. However, this constraint has the benefit of keeping the logical state space finite which is needed for most of the current planning approaches to handle issues about decidability and termination. Still, this can make the modeling of some actions a little difficult.

Evaluation of full observability: We can assume that we can observe the effects of actions we apply. Therefore, this assumption is still true but is not a problematic restriction.

Evaluation of deterministic transitions: Within our application domain we can expect that the system is deterministic. However, there may be situations in which an action can lead to different states. With the option of *conditional effects* in PDDL we can now deal with such situations. For the case of unpredictable effects we need to introduce special preparation operators that can be executed during the generation of a plan. These operators are described in Section 5.8.1.

Evaluation of static model and offline planning: During the planning, the planner is not concerned with any change that may occur. As the average planning time for a problem in our domain is less than one second, the probability of an external event during that time is rather low. If an external event should happen that would lead to a plan failure during the execution, the system will have to replan with the result of the event incorporated in the initial state.

Evaluation of reachability goals: Reachability or achievement goals are still the main kind of goals. However, with *goal preferences* and *state trajectory constraints* it is now possible to model goals where states have to be avoided or constraints on state trajectories have to be observed. With *fluents*, *preferences* and the option to define a *metric* we are now also able to use utility functions.

Evaluation of sequential plans and implicit time: When time is introduced into the modelling of a domain it is possible for concurrent activity to occur in a plan. Actions and events can now have a duration, a start and an end time.

To sum it all up it is to say that PDDL is by now an applicable description language for the modeling of planning problems in Smart Environments.

5.5.4 Choosing a Planning System

As mentioned before, one advantage of PDDL is the fact that it is used for the International Planning Competition. That gives us the opportunity to compare different planning systems and to choose appropriate ones. In these competitions many different planning problems are used, for a number of different planning domains[4]. The most important performance measures

---

[4]A domain is mainly a set of planning operators. For each domain it is possible to generate an unlimited number of random problems by specifying different initial and goal states.

to choose a planning system are success rate and speed, i.e., the fraction of problems solved and the CPU time needed to solve them. From these measures, we can get a good idea of what kind of problems the planners can solve in a reasonable amount of time. There are basically two type of planning systems in these competitions, (I) "fully automated" planners [127] where the problem input consists only of the information described above: initial state, goals, and operators, and (II) "domain configurable" planners, where the input includes detailed information about how to solve problems in the relevant problem domain.

The domain configurable planners require a significant amount of up-front work to formulate the domain specific knowledge, and this work must be redone each time one switches to a new domain. This is of course out of the question for our dynamic scenarios. In the domain of Smart Environments, we need fully automated planners, as the planning domain will be created dynamically from the available devices.

To choose appropriate planning systems I used the results of the 2002 International Planning Competition[131]. The competition was run with a series of domains, e.g. transportation related domains and space-applications. The domains were represented by several variants, including STRIPS, numeric, simple-timed, timed and, in some cases, more complex problems, usually combining time and numbers.

Table 5.1: Extract from the IPC 2002 Planning Competition results [131]
S - Strips, N - Numeric, HN - Hard Numeric, ST - Simple Time, T - Time, C - Complex

Planner	Problems solved	Problems attempted	Success ratio	Capabilities
FF	237	284	83%	S, N, HN
LPG	372	428	87%	S, N, HN, ST, T
MIPS	331	508	65%	S, N, HN, ST, T, C

A qualitative judgement of the planners can be based on the coverage (what kind of problems can be handled), the ratio of successful plans to approached problems, and the quality of the solutions generated. The speed of the planners is also of interest, but not that important. Most essential is a high coverage and high ratio of success in combination. A detailed look at the results shows that certain planners achieved outstanding performance in particular tracks even though they did not display broad coverage of the entire data set. For example, FF outperformed its competitors in many of the Numeric and Strips problems, but it didn't compete in the temporal domains, giving it lower overall coverage.

In Table 5.1 we have an extraction of the results of the mentioned competition. In that competition no planner was able to solve all the problems. Also the different planner had varying key skills. Planners that have demonstrated distinguished performance in the competition are

AI Planning as Source of the Assistance Strategy

Metric-FF [124], LPG [132] and MIPS [133]. Therefore these planners were chosen for the implementation of our planning assistant.

When in our scenarios a domain is dynamically created with the operator files of the available devices, the domain file is containing the requirement flags that describe the necessary functionalities for the planning system. Based on these requirement flags, we can choose a capable planner. Should it find no solution for the given problem, automatically one of the other systems gets the task to find a solution.

5.5.5 What about HTN planning?

The attentive reader might wonder why I have not considered to use HTN[5] planning (*e.g.* [134]). HTN planning reasons at the degree of high-level tasks instead of lower-level actions. In HTN planning, high-level tasks are repeatedly decomposed into simpler ones until all tasks have been reduced to primitive actions (tasks). High-level tasks are called methods and encode how to achieve a compound task. Methods consists of three elements: (I) the task being achieved (method head), (II) the set of preconditions, and (III) the subtasks needed to achieve the head. The low-level tasks are the operators. Like STRIPS operators, an HTN operator consists of the primitive task it achieves and its effects, indicating how the world changes when it is applied. However, HTN operators have no preconditions because applicability conditions are determined in the methods.

The problem with HTN is that a lot of knowledge has to be coded into the high-level task descriptions. For some domains this may be no problem, even an advantage, as it is often easier to define complex knowledge in HTNs. But for our domain, where we want to combine many different devices that offer many different low-level actions, HTN planner are not so suitable. That is also reflected by the fact that HTN planner have their good results at the planning competitions only at the hand coded tracks (domain configurable).

Possible shortcomings of the usage of HTN planning can be seen *e.g.* in [135] where the SHOP2 [136] planner is used to automatically compose Web services. There, the system depends on the task lists that are given and it does not attempt to generate new solutions on its own. For example, query actions are not called because the system identifies the need for information; instead the query action is explicitly predefined in the task list. For the domain of Smart Environments we need more flexibility, for instance to deal with situations where no predefined strategies exist yet.

---

[5]HTN – Hierarchical Task Networks

5.6 The Scheduling Coordination Algorithm

Please recollect the data flow in our system architecture. The dialog manager (D) sends interpretations of the user's desire as a goal to the assistants. These will be processed by the assistants and transfered to the scheduler (X) for execution and execution monitoring. There may be one or more schedulers, which will be coordinated by the algorithm described below. A scheduler transfers the operations to the devices over the uniformed device drivers (Xd).

A plan tells which actions to do and in which order to do them, while a schedule assigns exact release times to these actions. Planning and scheduling follow in a sequence such that scheduling can be viewed as a post-processing step to planning, where planning is concerned with causal relations and qualitative temporal relations between actions, while in scheduling systems, activities are organised along the time line having in mind the resources available. Scheduler can handle temporal reasoning and resource consumption, together with a quality criteria (*e.g.* resource consumption) but they cannot produce the needed activities and their precedence relations because they lack an expressive language to represent the actions.

Given: Plan with actions to perform; Set of resources to use; Time constraints;

Objective: Allocate times and resources to the actions;

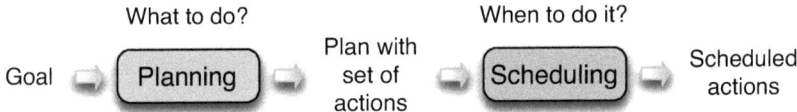

Figure 5.5: Planning and Scheduling Procedure

The scheduler is controlling all single operations on the devices, respective the device drivers in front of the devices. It controls the operation processing and notifies other schedulers in a distributed scheduler application about the state of the sequencing progress. At the end of the execution program plan there are two cases: (I) All operations are finished without an error. Then an okay-message will be sent back to the ordering assistant. (II) In at least one operation an error occurred. Then an failure-message will be sent back to the ordering assistant. The message about success or failure of the execution program plan goes back to the assistant. This one decides about the following steps, e.g. an alternative plan.

In an execution program plan $x - prog$ it is possible to address many different X-components (schedulers), which are responsible for certain operations in $x - prog$. Therefore a mechanism

AI Planning as Source of the Assistance Strategy

is necessary, which coordinates the distributed execution of $x - prog$ by a free number of schedulers parallely. The applied algorithm works as follows:

1. The planning-component sends the program $x - prog$ to all X-components which are responsible for at least one operation of $x - prog$.

2. Each X-component finds all operation in $x - prog$ within its own responsibility $O_x := \{op \in x - prog \mid xmoduleID(op) = x\}$ and initializes the quantity of success-messages E with an empty quantity $E := \emptyset$.

3. A X-component has to send a termination message in the case of the responsibility for a finished operation with no successor. The initial quantity of termination-message responsible X- components is $X_t = \{x \mid \exists op \in O_x : post(op) = \emptyset\}$.

4. The X-component decides the quantitiy of executable operations O_a by the election of operations, which have success-messages for its predecessor.
   $O_a = \{op \in O_x \mid pre(x) \subseteq E\}$.
   In the case of this quantity is not empty, it follows:

   (a) The X-component executes the operations in O_a in any sequence.

   (b) As soon as the X-component has executed an operation op successfully, this will be deleted in O_x and a success-message is send to all X-components, which are responsible for any operation $post(op)$.

5. In the case of receiving success-messages e at the X-component, the quantity E is extended accordingly.

6. In the case of quantity O_x is not empty, proceed with step 4.

7. Default: if the X-Component is member of the quantity X_t it has to send a termination message to the ordering A-component.

8. If an A-component receives a termination message from a X-component, it will be removed from X_t.

9. As soon as the ordering A-component gets a termination message from all responsible X-components (X_t is empty), it can notify the successful processing of the user's goal to the dialog manager.

5.7 The joint ontology

The description of the component functions and capabilities as operators for the planning domain is essential. (See Section 5.5.3 for an example of a domain file.) In order to support the interoperability of devices provided by different vendors, we need a shared understanding of the common environment domain they operate upon – a uniform ontology[6]. Standardized environment ontology concepts such as *ambientBrightness*, *luminosity*, ... make it possible to develop the components' operator definitions independently from each other. Different vendors have to adhere to these ontology concepts as an explicit specification of the environment aspects for their specific planning subdomains. If different components use common concepts for the same features, *e.g. ambientBrightness* for the capability of a lamp and of a venetian blind (by daylight), a cooperation is feasible. The vendor of a component characterizes its products in accordance with the specification of the ontology and the potentialities of the chosen problem-specification language. The planning operators will reasonably abstract from the device's concrete internal state and use a simplified state model that is tailored towards attaching the operators' environmental effects.

To make sure that operators of different origin are compatible, they must comply to a common ontology. A widely excepted ontology for the definition of environment states / variables has not yet emerged. Within the scope of this thesis an ontology was developed that was used as basis for the modelling of the devices' PDDL operators. However, this ontology is only a first concept for the implementation of prototypes. New impulses for the development of an excepted environment ontology may arise from the currently very popular research area of Semantic Web (see *e.g.*, [138]).

5.8 Prototype

The sections above presented the overall architecture and the theoretical foundations to use a planning algorithm as inference system to allow goal oriented assistance for extended multimedia systems and other dynamic technical infrastructures. I will now outline the details of the

---

[6] "An ontology defines the terms used to describe and represent an area of knowledge. Ontologies are used by people, databases, and applications that need to share domain information (a domain is just a specific subject area or area of knowledge, ...). Ontologies include computer-usable definitions of basic concepts in the domain and the relationships among them ... They encode knowledge in a domain and also knowledge that spans domains. In this way, they make that knowledge reusable. The word ontology has been used to describe artifacts with different degrees of structure. These range from simple taxonomies, to ... ontologies with a significant degree of structure." [137]

current implementation which was an integral part of various demonstrators for the EMBASSI project.

5.8.1 System extension

To enable the system for dynamic extension special requirements are needed. In this section I will present the mechanisms for the self description of the appliances / devices which makes it possible to create a dynamic extensible assistant system. Every appliance at the G-level has to provide three concept-components: an operator file, an action class and a goal class. If a new appliance connects to the system, it has to upload these three components to the context manager. The planning assistant is subscribed to this concepts at the context manager and get immediately messages which contains the new device concepts.

The Operator file

The operator file has to be compatible to our ontology specification which is defined in DAML+OIL Language (see Section A.2). This ontology specification is an attempt to define and describe all environment variables which are necessary for our current application domain, which is multimedia entertainment and room control. According to this ontology the operators have to be defined in PDDL syntax. If the planning assistant gets the new operator file from the context manager, it performs a PDDL syntax check on that operator file and if the syntax check was successful it subjoints this appliance subdomain to the overall planning domain and creates a global operator file. This operator file will then be validated with the tool VAL[7][139]. This PDDL validating is very important, because an invalid operator file would damage the whole planning domain.

Preparation Operators

As described before, the generation of the plan and the execution of the plan are two separated steps in the current approach. This separation can sometimes lead to problems, because it is based on the assumption that the planner has perfect knowledge. Examples for insufficient knowledge are that the state of the environment is not fully known or that actions may have unpredictable effects.[8] In those cases, the planner may need to execute some of the steps of the generated plan to observe more of the state of the environment or the effects of some actions. An example for insufficient information could be that the planner need to know if and where a

---

[7] VAL, The Automatic Validation Tool For PDDL
[8] This does not contradict the full observability assumption. It means that the planner needs to apply some actions to get some information or that the planner needs to observe the effect of some action to know the outcome.

document or other type of media is available, what would lead to a different plan, depending on the result of the query. An example for an unpredictable effect is the situation were the planner decides to open the shutter to use the daylight to increase the ambient brightness. If the planner has no knowledge about the outside brightness, the effect of that action is unpredictable (depending on the weather) and the planner has to observe the effect and potentially to re-plan.

To allow the execution of actions during the planning I have defined *preparation operators*: (:action IGD-MEDIALIB-FindMusic-PREP ...). These operators differ from ordinary operators only by the added ending "-PREP". With this policy for the naming of preparation operators it is possible to query information or observe effects of actions that are in the middle of a plan.

In the case of a preparation action in a plan, the plan will be processed until the first preparation action is executed. The result of this action will lead to a new initial state and that will be used for a re-planning. This time the planner should have sufficient knowledge to create a correct plan.

The Action class

The action class defines the interface between the PDDL operators in the operatorfile and the syntax understood by the corresponding appliances at the *G*-level. The reason for this is that the described planning component had to work in the EMBASSI demonstrators. Within these demonstrators we used XML[9] for the communication of the components in the architecture. For the planning component, it would be easier to address the devices directly via their PDDL operators. From a scientific point of view, this interface between PDDL and XML is not interesting. I only mention it, because this engineering aspect was part of the implementation and necessary that the planner could be used in EMBASSI.

For every PDDL action provided by a component a corresponding function has to be defined, which implements the interface to this component. The planning assistant of EMBASSI is implemented in Java and so the action class is defined to be a java-subclass of a default superclass. That allows the planning assistant to use the dynamic class loading of java and to add new action classes dynamically, even without to restart it. Because the action class has additional tasks, we could not use just a simple configurationfile for the conversion of PDDL to XML. One example is dynamic information gaining. During the planning process it is sometimes necessary to gain special sensor data or to find out which appliance has the seeked media data (*c.f.* preparation operators). Only the device which provided the PDDL operator which leads

---

[9]XML being the standard for inter-component communication in EMBASSI, the ontology is exchanged in form of an XML DTD specifying concepts and their roles as nested elements.

AI Planning as Source of the Assistance Strategy

to a request, knows how to handle the answer and how to expand the init state (fact file) to proceed with the planning. The actionclass is responsible for providing all the functions that are necessary to parse such an anwser and to add the new facts in the predetermined syntax to the active context.

The Goal class

The goal class is responsible for providing the concepts for the interpretation of user utterances and user goals. In this class has to be defined which user behavior (speech, gestures, interaction) are associated with what goal states of the environment. These states have to be modelled as PDDL goals. These goals don't have to be limited to environment states that can be changed by the added device. I can also contain global (system-wide) goals. As the intention analysis is responsible for translating user goals into system goals, the planning assistant transferes this new concepts to the intention analysis components and subscribes itself for this new goal.

Additionally to goals that are added by new devices, the planning assistant holds a database of goals that are predefined. These goals were identified by usability experts and describe the desired environment state for various user goals.

After having the semantic selfdesription of this new component, the planning assistant is now able to integrate this appliance into the system comprehensive strategy planning, creating environment changes based on the users goals, including the features of the new component. The Figures A.1 - A.4 illustrate the joining of a new device to an ensemble. Fig. 5.6 contains an example of the planning procedure.

5.8.2 Operating sequence example

Imagine the example the user says "I want to see 'Terminator' now!". The multimodal dialogue management recognizes the goal: $\text{Goal} \equiv render(\textbf{Terminator}) = \textbf{Terminator} \in renderedMedia \land \textbf{Terminator} \in perceivableMedia \land ambientBrightness = \textbf{low}$ and sends it to the planning assistant. The assistant gets the current context from the context manager and creates the init state, which - together with the goal - results in a problem file. With the problem file and the operator file a planning system gets started, *e.g.* Metric-FF. First, the planning systems finds out that it has to gain the information which appliance has the media file containing the movie 'Terminator'. The system is at this programmed to create plans which causes the least costs. It finds out that there is a Media Library which is able to provide 'Terminator' as *renderedMedia*. Then the system reasons that it needs devices that provide functions to have the *audio* and *video* part of the media data as *perceivableMedia*. Then it recognizes that there

Chapter 5

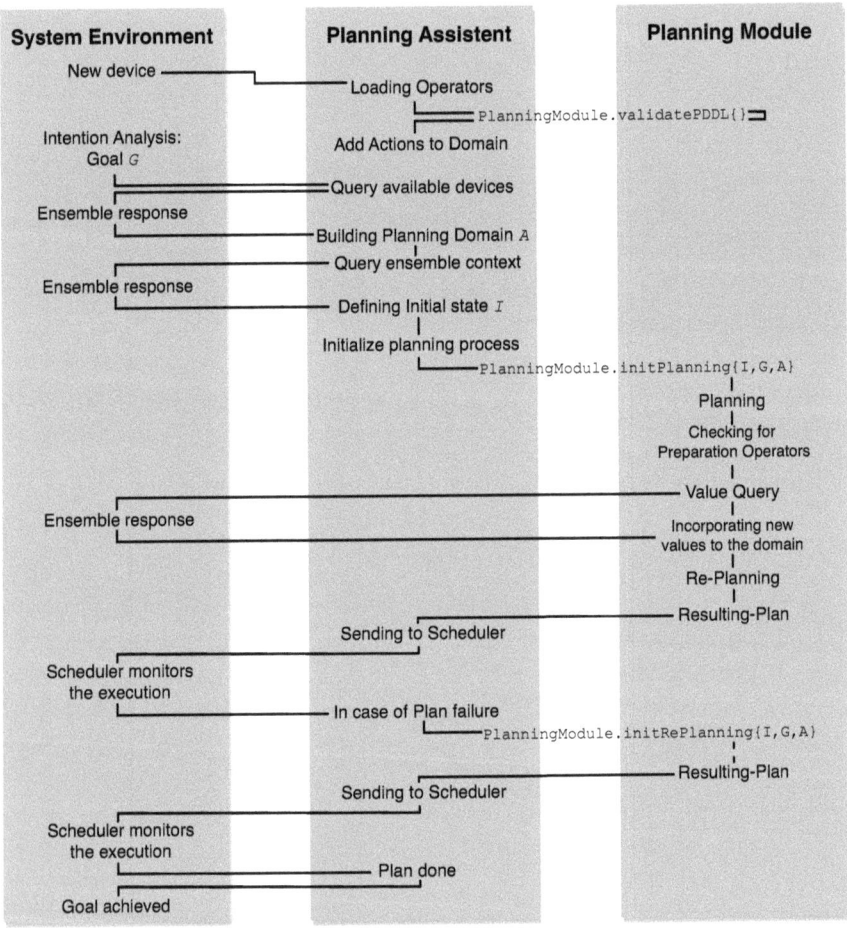

Figure 5.6: Planning Procedure

is a *dts*-amplifier and a videobeamer which provides the best quality for the seeked effects. Finally the system will choose actions which results in a low ambient brightness. After creating the appropriate partial ordered plan, the plan is sent to the scheduler (X component), which is responsible for the correct sequential processing of the plan and for the execution monitoring. Should something went wrong during the execution of a plan, the system would try to create an alternative plan.

5.9 Limits of the AI planning approach as assistance method

In Section 5.5.3 we have seen that the latest versions of PDDL are powerful enough to model the problems we encounter in the domain of Smart Environments. That does not answer the question whether current planning systems are really able to solve the modeled problems. But as before, we can look at the International Planning Competition for a guideline. It has become a common standard that a paper discussing new techniques for classical planning (as part of a new planning system) also presents performance results for some of the competition domains. This can be used to get an idea of what the planning systems can handle.

In [140] Helmert analyzed the complexity of the planning domain of the IPC3 and IPC4 domains, for the decision problems related to finding some plan, finding an optimal sequential plan, and finding an optimal parallel plan in these planning domains. He focused on propositional (i. e., non-numerical, non-temporal) domains. His results were that the analyzed domains belong already to the complexity classes P, NP, NP-hard, PSPACE, and PSPACE-hard. We can conclude that the domains with numerical or temporal problems will not be less complex.

As many of the planner were able to find solutions for this problems, the results of Helmert should be good news. However, one problem is that many of the planner are tailored for the domains of the planning competition and so the results are of limited value for other domains.

To find out if a planning system can handle certain kinds of problems, we have to test that system with this domain. In my own tests I learned that the tested planner were able to solve problems related to achievement goals (see Section 2.4.3) in our Smart Environment domain, also with plan quality metrics that are linear. However, optimization goals[10] (see Section 2.4.4) that have a non-linear optimization function, could not be solved by one of the planning systems I tested.

To overcome this limitation of the current planning approach, a second reasoning system had to be added to the architecture framework, which will be illustrated in Chapter 6.

5.10 Distributed vs. Centralized Strategy Generation

The described architecture is inherently decentralized, but the realization of dedicated assistance functionality is not necessarily decentralized. If we look again at the nature of Smart

---

[10]In Section 6.6.3 you will find an analysis of the complexity of the given optimization problem.

Environments that are build from dynamic ensembles, it is clear that the number and types of the distributed devices that are connected to an ensemble are not known in advance and continuously change during the operations of the system. We have a naturally distributed problem. This argument would call for a *distributed* planning approach. However, we must also consider that a number of these devices have limited computational and communicational power. Not all of the ensemble devices will be able to perform complex computations, in particular those required by planning tasks. This argues more for a *centralized* approach. We have to find a balance between these both approaches. These techniques have the following general characteristics:

- Centralized Coordination Mechanisms
    - Single point of data / knowledge and decision-making / authority
    - **Benefits:** Easier to show optimality, implement, ignore concurrency issues, communicate only twice (gather problem info, issue results)
    - **Shortcomings:** Central point of failure, difficulties in dynamic environments, privacy
- Decentralized Coordination Mechanisms
    - Decentralized knowledge / data and decision-making
    - **Benefits:** Parallel computation, communication constraints (e.g. privacy), robustness, organizational fit, realistic
    - **Shortcomings:** Rarely optimal compared to centralization, concurrency complexity, communication complexity, synchronization, not all ensemble-member are able to perform complex computation
- Reality: Hybrids (e.g. centralized control of individual resources in a decentralized environment / context)

In AI planning we can have different degrees of distribution:

1. Classical centralized planning
2. Centralized planning for decentralized plans
3. Decentralized planning for centralized plans
4. Decentralized planning for decentralized plans

For a number of reasons, I chose the second approach.[11] That we need distributed plans is obvious. The reasons for centralized planning are mainly the limited computational power of some of the ensemble devices and the lack of appropriate planning systems for distributed planning. In the current state of the art we don't have a system that is able to deliver decentralized planning for problems that can be modeled using the complexity of the latest versions of PDDL.

However, through the utilization of the agent selection algorithm of SODA-POP (see Section 4.6.3) it is no longer a big drawback that the planner is centralistic. Every component (device, appliance) is able to provide its features without the planner. The channel decides to use the planner if it offers more competence than the single components.

5.11 Chapter summary

This section describes a system infrastructure supporting goal oriented assistance with dynamic environments. It presents how we can create distributed technical infrastructures - even feature loaded multimedia systems - which are efficiently usable by the average person. It is displayed the architectural concept, which makes it possible to integrate classical Artificial Intelligence technology - such as planning and scheduling - into the domain of networked consumer appliances, like multimedia systems and room control. The different individual components provide a semantic self-description, and thus the technical infustructure is - with the help of a planning assistant - able to act like a united system, even with ad hoc integrated new devices.

Future work on the planning assistant should focus on the following aspects: So far we have not integrated all devices and appliances which are imaginable for our application domain. We will need to find out how the system reacts if it has a huge planning domain.
Further the experiences has shown that it is not always easy for the engineers of the device vendors to create planning operators for their appliances. Thus tools are needed which should helping the vendor engineers to create planning subdomains based on the specification of our environment ontology.

In standardizing a form of PDDL for practical domain model building, more structure, guidelines and tool support is required. To help engineers apply the technology, language conventions have to be achieved [141]. The requirements of future Smart Environments in particular will demand a common model for planning knowledge.

---

[11]This is the correct choice at the current state of the art. Future systems should try to avoid central components.

Planning component conclusion:

Benefits: Ad-hoc expandable, enables strategy generation, system comprehensive, weighted strategies;

Shortcomings: Centralistic, needs semantic self-description of all components to control, no support of goals with hard optimization;

Similar approaches and feedback: A similar approach to the one described in the last chapter were used in the work of Amigoni et al. [142], Saif et al. [143] and Lieberman [144].

In their book "Smart Environments" Das and Cook [13] states that this planning approach I described here seems to be very promising and should be considered in future smart environment developments.

To avoid the drawback of a central planning component, my colleague Reisse [145] is developing a decentralized version of Maes' [88] action selection algorithm. The approach is presented in the state of the art chapter, Section 3.1.6.

As outlined above, recent AI planning technologies have limitations. To overcome these, an additional approach is used which will be described in the next section.

Chapter 6

Optimization as Source of the Assistance Strategy

> *A key element of ubiquitous computing applications is knowing the precise spatial-temporal relationships between people and objects.*
> Roy Want et al., Disappearing Hardware, 2002 [146]

6.1 Introduction

This chapter serves several purposes. The first is to show that everyday functionality demands for modern technical infrastructures can be fulfilled by explicit goal descriptions that fit in the architectonic concept I proposed. The second is to show that the example problem I will introduce is a real life situation and that the solution I propose will be useful and appropriate.

In the last chapter we proceeded on the assumption that we can define a user goal as the desired state of the environment. But sometimes this is just not possible. Especially when there is more than one user, the exact setting needed to satisfy all users may be unclear. This is particularly the case when users with divergent interests and limited resources come together. We then need a collective agreement on the situation on how to proceed. This important application area is the definition of an optimal ensemble behavior regarding the mapping of (sub)-tasks to available resources. Here, a metric has to be defined that describes how "good" a certain mapping of tasks to the available resources is and which allows to compare different mappings with respect to their optimality. So, these types of goals provide an explicit statement of a system designer's idea of optimal ensemble behavior[1]. This can be regarded as a theory of optimal ensemble behavior. The ensembles responsibility w.r.t. unsupervised spontaneous cooperation is then to jointly approximate this global optimum as good as possible. These implicit goals will be triggered by the situation through the intention analysis and must then be achieved by the appliance ensemble.

This chapter illustrates the unsupervised solution of the Display Mapping problem for dynamic multiple display environments as an example for this special type of goals[2]. The contributions of this chapter are:

1. The proposal of a goal function q that provides a precise definition of a *globally optimal* display mapping in a multiple display environment.

2. The proposal of a distributed optimization algorithm that requires only *local knowledge* at each participating device. (This algorithm is applicable to arbitrary objective functions q.)

3. At the meta level, the observation that some aspects of a globally coherent behavior of a dynamic ensemble of ubicomp devices can be treated as optimization problems.

4. The evaluation of the proposed approach and proof that it is efficient and useful.

6.2 Smart Meeting Rooms

Modern conference or meeting rooms provide interesting functionality, but are very difficult to simply walk in and use. Most of these rooms must have resident experts who have to keep the room's systems functioning. To overcome this, many research teams are working on smart meeting rooms as an instance of smart environments (see *e.g.* SMaRT [147], EasyMeeting [83], or [148]). Smart meeting rooms foster creative team work by the automatization of the underlying mechanisms and processes, *e.g.* for the access, presentation, and analysis of information.

Examples are

- Tools that allow users to find the information they need quickly from a number of sources, like segments of recorded meetings, documents, or other media of interest;

---

[1] Interestingly, in contrast to the user goals discussed in the previous chapter, mapping objectives tend to be *predefined*, implicit goals.
[2] Goals as definition of optimal ensemble behavior.

Optimization as Source of the Assistance Strategy

Figure 6.1: Examples of multiple display environments. (I, left) Stanford's iRoom; (II, right) the "Management Cockpit" at Iglo-Ola, Unilever Belgium

- Automatic rendering of relevant information (*e.g.* agenda, protocol, topical presentation) on the available displays;

- Management of the meeting process (*e.g.* change to the next agenda item, proposing a break if the meeting participants begin to become unconcentrated);

- Automatic arrangement of appropriate room conditions (*e.g.* temperature, air quality, ambient light level and adequate spot light).

Other research goals are the same as for general smart environments, *e.g.* they provide meeting support that does not require explicit human-computer interaction. By monitoring the activities of the users using both video and audio analysis, the meeting room may be able to react appropriately to the users' needs allowing them to focus on their own goals.

6.3 Managing Multi-Display Environments

(...) for each person in an office, there should be hundreds of tabs, tens of pads, and one or two boards.
Mark Weiser, 1993 [149]

Since Weiser's vision, displays have begun to proliferate. For people coming together in a well equipped meeting room, the above numbers of devices are not quite achieved yet – but we seem to be getting close.

While this increased availability of displays opens up many new opportunities, the management of information across them is not trivial, especially when multiple users with diverging interests have to be considered. This particularly applies for *dynamic* ensembles of displays.

So called Multi-Display Environments[3] (MDEs) support collaborative problem solving and teamwork by providing multiple display surfaces for presenting information. Typical examples for such environments are meeting rooms, conference rooms, and "mission control centers", as shown in Fig. 6.1 and 6.2.

One difficult task here is the *Display Mapping problem* – that is, deciding which information to present on what display in order to optimally satisfy the users' needs for information. While this task is more or less trivial in single-user, single-display situations, it becomes challenging in multi-user, multi-display settings: Users and displays are spatially dispersed so that the visibility of (semi-) public and private displays varies across users. Also, information needs may vary across users, so that finding the "best" assignment of information to displays becomes a typical optimization problem[4].

Optimization problems are solved by defining an objective function $q(x)$, the "quality" to maximize, and then applying a suitable optimization algorithm to compute $x_{max} = \arg\max_{x \in X} q(x)$.

In this setting the Display Mapping problem gives rise to two subproblems:

- What is a suitable definition for $q(x)$? I. e., what is the objective function to be maximized in order to achieve an optimal (or at least: satisfactory) solution for the Display Mapping problem?

- How should the computation of x_{max} be distributed across the members of an ensemble of displays? – This is especially interesting when dynamic ensembles have to be considered (e.g., portable projectors carried into a meeting room, etc.).

The further structure of this Chapter is as follows: in Section 6.4, I motivate why an automated display mapping might be useful. Section 6.5 provides an in-depth discussion of the display mapping problem and the proposal of a global quality function q for this problem. How the quality function q can be computated by the ensemble is shown in Section 6.6. The experimental design and the results of an evaluation of an automated display mapping in comparison to a manual assignment is described in Section 6.9. A discussion of the results and further work is given in Section 6.9.5.

---

[3]See e. g. the UbiComp 2004 workshop on Ubiquitous Display Environments [150] or the Ubicomp 2006 workshop on next generation conference rooms [151].
[4]This kind of optimization problems is currently not solvable with the planning approach that I illustrated in Chapter 5. Hence we have to use an additional reasoning approach for this kind of problems.

Figure 6.2: Multiple display environment: Smart Appliance Lab at Rostock University

6.4 The Need for Automatic Display Mapping

Why do we need automated display mapping? – Could not the users just do the assignment manually, using a suitable interactive interface, resolving conflicts by social protocols (negotiations)? One example for such a manual display assignment is the ModSlideShow system [152], which is designed to manage presentation slides on multiple displays. Displays can be linked and grouped into flexible configurations depending on their physical layout in the environment and on the scenarios of use. For assignment of content to displays, meeting participants drag-and-drop presentations from their notebooks to any of the available displays. Another example providing a similar interaction mechanism is the PointRight software developed for Stanford's Meyer Teamspace [153].

However, manual display assignment has to cope with the following conflicts:

1. **Interest conflicts** between users might be solved faster by computer supported negotiation mechanism: Morris et al. [154] have already observed that social protocols do not always suffice for coordinating the use of shared resources, such as display surfaces, in teams – even in relatively simple situations. They suspect that the need for coordination may increase as the number of users, the number of documents, or the number or size of the surfaces increases. Indeed, they advocate the development of specific strategies for automating the negotiation process.

2. The need for **dynamic realignment** of Display Mapping is caused by topic changes in the user population – in this situation, the user's focus of attention will be on the changing

topic rather than on convincing the display infrastructure to change the topic.[5].

3. In a dynamic multiple display environment, the **user might not be able to know** the displays currently available to him. With dozens to hundreds of possible display configurations, the user might want to rely on the infrastructure to select the best choice for him.

Therefore, an automatic display assignment might be helpful in multi-display environments, specifically in multi-user settings. However, to my knowledge, it is not known if suitable automatic assignment heuristics do exist. Although there is substantial research in multi-display environments, the development of an automatic display assignment has not been addressed.

The question is now how to proceed. To answer this let us again have a look at the main challenge:

The Challenge: How to automatically allocate documents to displays in order to optimally satisfy users' information needs?

Methodological Problem: We do not have a really good idea, how users would like to interact with such environments. There is no empirical base of use cases. We do not know which kinds of conflicts would arise in such environments with what frequency.

Solution Alternatives: Wait for organizational psychologists and usability experts to investigate this setting or exploit own experience and „common sense" for scenario design.

Because MDEs are new, we have no experience on how they are used and which problems users have using them. So, in order to take a first step, we simply have to guess what the problems might be.

6.4.1 User Requirements

The obvious conjecture is that MDEs are not just about one presenter using multiple displays for delivering carefully authored content to an audience. It is more reasonable that MDEs should support teams of users for jointly exploring knowledge, comparing options, and trying to settle controversies. MDEs should be environments that help teams to assess the state of a system or decide upon a course of action by combining knowledge from many sources, *e.g.*:

---

[5] The classical counter-example: The next speaker mounts the stage, and instead of delivering a speech, he starts fidgeting with his notebook in order to get his presentation onto the screen ...

- System architects discussing alternatives for a system architecture
- Researchers trying to agree upon the interpretation of controversial data
- Management trying to get a coherent view on the state of a large enterprise (and deciding where to put investments)

As resulting requirements, MDEs should support teams where:

- Members have overlapping, but not identical „regions of interest" → resource conflicts
- Regions of interest are not known in advance
- Regions of interest change in the course of action

6.5 Defining Optimal Display Mapping

As discussed earlier, the mapping of tasks to the available resources can be seen as a typical optimization problem. To do so we need to define an adequate optimization function. In this section, I will discuss the basic properties of a quality measure – $q(x)$ – that can be used for solving the display mapping problem.

Note that I do *not* claim that the definition I provide for q is a *generally* applicable heuristics. This definition shall show the *existence* of situations (and quality heuristics) for which an automatic mapping can be as good as (or even superior to) a manual mapping.

The Basic Concept

Consider the simple Display Mapping problem outlined in Fig. 6.3, left. There are two users u_1, u_2 sitting at a table and three displays y_1, y_2, y_3 (for instance, backprojection displays or simply screens with an associated projector). User u_1 is interested in documents d_1 and d_2, user u_2 is interested in d_1 and d_3. Also, u_1 has very high interest in d_1 (maybe it is the presentation currently delivered by u_2). In this situation, considering the positions of users and displays, the resulting display visibility, and the user's information needs, an optimal mapping of documents to the available display surfaces is given by the mapping outlined in Fig. 6.3 on the right: u_1 gets optimal visibility of his most important document on y_3 and acceptable visibility of d_2 by looking sideways on y_1. Similarly u_2 gets acceptable visibility of d_1 and d_3.

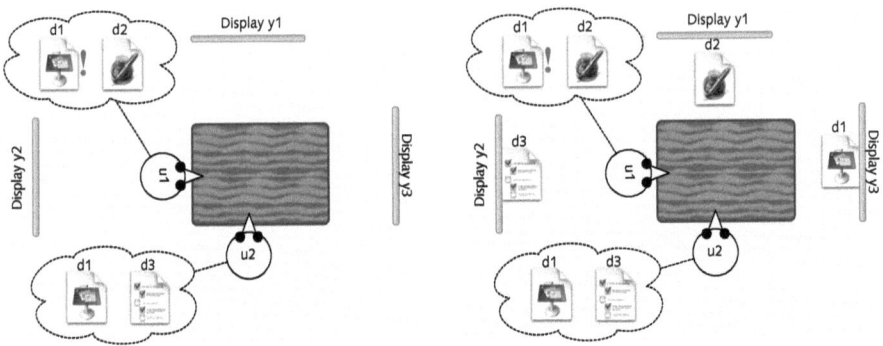

Figure 6.3: Mapping documents to displays. Initial situation (left) and optimal mapping

In order to enable an *automatic* assignment of documents to displays for a team of users, we need an explicit notion of the "quality" of a given display mapping. In the current proposal for such a quality measure, the following heuristics are considered:

Spatial Layout: For documents of high importance to a user, displays should be preferred that provide a good visibility for the user.

Temporal Continuity: When considering a display for a document, the system should prefer already existing assignments.

Semantic Proximity: Related documents should be presented close to each other to support the user in analyzing the semantic correlation between the documents. (Semantic proximity is not yet part of our implementation.)

Let D, U, Y be the sets of documents, users, and displays, respectively. Then, a *display mapping* is a function $m : D \to 2^Y$ which assigns documents to sets of displays. For a given document $d \in D$, $m(d) \in 2^Y$ gives the set of displays document d is assigned to. $m(d)$ is a set of displays, as it sometimes clearly makes sense to assign a document to more than one display. For the example given in Fig. 6.3, we have $m = \{d_1 \mapsto \{y_3\}, d_2 \mapsto \{y_1\}, d_3 \mapsto \{y_2\}\}$, so that $m(d_2) = \{y_1\}$.

The *overall quality* of a display mapping m, given a previous mapping m_0, is then given by a function $q(m, m_0)$, which consists of three components: $q_s(m)$, measuring the spatial quality, $q_t(m, m_0)$, measuring the temporal continuity (with respect to a previous mapping m_0), and $q_p(m)$, measuring the semantic proximity. In general, $q(m, m_0)$ may be an arbitrary complex

Optimization as Source of the Assistance Strategy

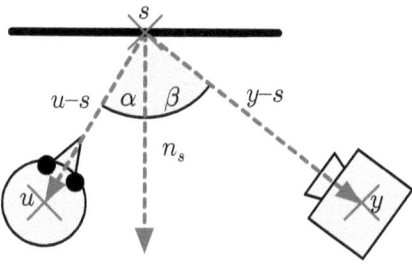

Figure 6.4: Visibility & Projectability

function of q_s, q_t, q_p. However, currently only a linear combination is considered, so that

$$q(m, m_0) = \alpha q_s(m) + \beta q_t(m, m_0) + \gamma q_p(m). \tag{6.1}$$

The relative weights $\alpha, \beta, \gamma \in [0 .. 1]$ balance the influence of the three components. (Currently used weights are the empirical determined choices $\alpha = 1$ and $\beta = 0.1$. These choices worked for the experiments, but definitely this should be based on additional research.)

I will now look at the component functions.

6.5.1 q_s – Spatial Quality

Let $impt(d, u) \in [0 .. 1]$ denote the importance of the document d to a user u and let $vis(y, u) \in [0 .. 1]$ denote the *visibility* of display y by user u. Then the spatial quality achieved by a mapping m can be defined as

$$q_s(m) = \sum_{\substack{u \in U \\ d \in D}} impt(d, u) * \max_{y \in m(d)} vis(y, u) \tag{6.2}$$

This definition represents the above spatial heuristic: in a good mapping, documents with high importance (for specific users) should be assigned to displays with high visibility (for this user). In addition, if a document is assigned to multiple displays, only the best one for a given user is considered when computing the quality for this user (this is the "max vis" term).

As a first approximation to computing vis we have chosen Lambert's law of reflection, which gives the visibility as cosine of the angle between the display's surface normal n_d and the user's forward vector. A similar approach has been taken by the EasyLiving Geometry model [63].

Note that deriving a reliable estimation of *impt* in general may be a substantial challenge – however, there may be additional information available that can be used as a surrogate (such as an agenda item listing a responsible person with a number of associated documents, etc.). For some scenarios in our Lab we used an intention analysis component [55] that provided the document importance based on an agenda. In the experiments described later, we have used a manual importance assigment. But there is also other research that seems promising to deliver the document importance. Badi et al. [155] developed an 'Interest Profile Manager' for collecting and analyzing user interest and document value, or Claypool et al. [156] describe a method that implicitly determines the interest of a user by observing his interaction.

There are possible extensions to q_s. Some are already considered in the current implementation: *steerable projectors*, *user roles*, and *accessibility*.

Steerable Projectors – Different Types of Displays

Steerable projectors are displays that are able to choose between different display surfaces. For some time, steerable projectors such as the Everywhere Display [157] have been investigated for a flexible information display by several research groups (see [158] for a short overview). Our lab infrastructure also provides such a device (cf. Fig. 6.5). The introduction of steerable projectors introduces another degree of freedom in the display mapping process, as a steerable projector may be able to choose between different projection screens. We therefore need to distinguish between *Displays* (devices which can present a document) and *Surfaces* (regions in space on which a display renders a document). For some devices, the mapping from display to surface is fixed (i.e., a notebook display will always render on the notebook's screen surface; a fixed projector will always render on the screen it is looking at), while for other devices it is variable (i.e., a steerable projector that can pick different screens to project on).

Let Y denote the set of displays and S the set of available (display) surfaces. Furthermore, let $rend(y, s) \in [0..1]$ be the rendering quality achievable by display $y \in Y$ on surface $s \in S$ (for devices with fixed display surface, $rend$ will be 1 for this surface and 0 everywhere else). We now have to replace m by *two* mappings: $dm \in D \to 2^Y$, mapping documents to sets of display devices, and $ym \in Y \to S$, mapping displays to surfaces. And our definition of q is changed to

$$q_s(dm, ym) = \sum_{\substack{u \in U \\ d \in D}} impt(d, u) * \max_{y \in dm(d)} (vis(ym(y), u) * rend(y, ym(y))) \qquad (6.3)$$

so that we now have to look for $(dm_{max}, ym_{max}) = \arg\max_{\substack{dm \in D \to 2^Y \\ ym \in Y \to S}} q_s(dm, ym)$.

Optimization as Source of the Assistance Strategy

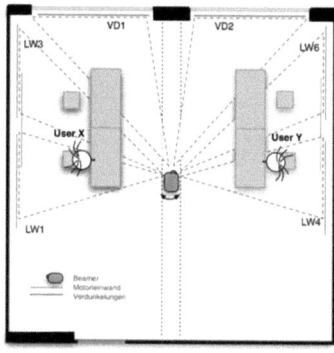 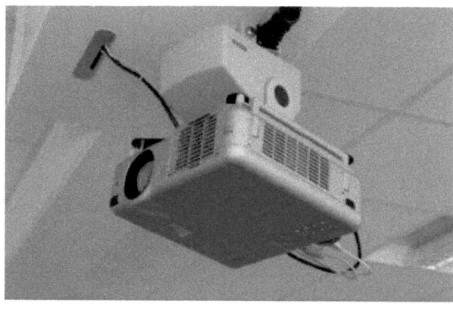

Figure 6.5: MMIS-Lab Steerable Projector

To compute $rend$, Lambert's law of reflection is used again, which gives the rendering quality as cosine of the angle between the rendering surfaces' surface normal n_s and the vector connecting the surface and the projector – see Fig. 6.4.

User Roles

For the different roles that a document may have for a user, the visibility vis may have quite different meanings. For instance, for a speaker, vis relates to the physical distance between himself and the presentation slides, rather than to the visual perceivability of the slides. So, in general $vis(y, u)$ should be written as $vis_{role(u,d)}(y, u)$: Depending on $role(u, d)$, different interpretations for vis can be selected.

Accessibility

The accessibility list contains information about the right of a user to see a document. If a user has no access right for a document, the respective mappings where she could see the document will be non valid solutions.

6.5.2 q_t – Temporal Continuity

Documents should not unnecessarily change their place between two display mappings. Therefore, we penalize display changes for documents. In a display mapping m, a user's *primary*

129

display for a document d is $\pi(m, u, d) = \max_{y \in m(d)} vis(y, u)$. It is that display showing d which is best visible for the user u. A relevant display change occurs between two mappings m and m_0 if a user's primary display changes:

$$shift(m, m_0, u, d) = \begin{cases} 0, & \text{if } \pi(m, u, d) = \pi(m_0, u, d) \\ 1, & \text{otherwise} \end{cases}$$

Then, q_t tries to minimize these shifts relative to the document's importance:

$$q_t(m, m_0) = -\sum_{\substack{u \in U \\ d \in D}} shift(m, m_0, u, d) * impt(d, u) \qquad (6.4)$$

Here, m_0 is the previous mapping and m is the mapping to be optimized. (Note the negation in front of the sum: the sum term denotes a penalty, hence we have to take the negative value if we use it in a maximization task).

6.5.3 q_p – Semantic Proximity

Semantic proximity is based on two functions: $\rho(d, d')$, measuring the semantic proximity of two documents and $\delta(y, y')$, measuring the physical distance between two displays (e.g., Euclidian distance). Based on this, the semantic proximity heuristic q_p can be defined as

$$q_p(m) = -\sum_{\substack{u \in U \\ d, d' \in D}} \rho(d, d') * \delta(\pi(m, u, d), \pi(m, u, d')) * impt(d, u) * impt(d', u) \qquad (6.5)$$

(Again, the sum denotes a penalty, therefore we negate it.)

Deriving a reliable estimation of ρ in general will be a substantial challenge. However, as in the case of *impt*, there may be additional information available (such as an agenda listing a set of documents for a given agenda item) that may be used as a surrogate for semantic distance.

Note that semantic proximity as defined here is an instance of the quadratic assignment problem (a combinatorial optimization problem that is NP-hard).

6.5.4 Discussion of q

I do not claim that this definition of q is a final and optimal one. It is based on common sense and own empirical investigation. There may be situations where this definition will not provide good results for all users. One example could be that it would be better to avoid very bad mappings for a single user (maybe depending on the user role) while neglecting the optimum for the other users. A mapping where one user would see nothing while all other users have a good view would be very unsatisfying for the first user. Another problem could be this one: imagine a user brings a mobile projector and places it in a non-optimal way in front of a screen. According to the function q a projector already present (static or steerable) provides a better projectability for the same screen and the system decides not to choose the mobile projector. Even if this would probably be a better solution, the user will be very annoyed that his effort was useless and he will dislike the system. With the evaluation of Section 6.9 I will try to answer how useful the current definition is.

6.5.5 Using q

q has been defined completely independent from a concrete ensemble of users, displays, documents, and surfaces. It describes the globally optimal behavior for any possible ensemble. Once machinery is available for computing the optimum for q, any ensemble will be able to behave optimally – as far as q is a correct definition of an ensemble's global optimum from the user's point of view.

Rephrasing the two subproblems identified in the introduction, two questions have to be answered now:

- Is q a useful representation of the user's needs? – This is the focus of section 6.9.

- Can q be realistically computed in a Multiple-Display environment (or even: in a general ubiquitous computing setting)? – This is the focus of section 6.6.

To briefly look again at the second question: Optimizing q is a difficult task in general (definitely NP hard, if we include semantic proximity)[6]. Therefore, heuristics have to be used for optimization. For my own work, I have chosen the Greedy Randomized Adaptive Search Procedure (GRASP heuristic) [159]. This heuristic is able to effectively compute solutions that are reasonably close to the true optimum. Of course, in a ubiquitous computing setting, where we might need to compute a display mapping for an ad-hoc ensemble of displays, the availability of a suitable decentralized optimization strategy becomes an important topic. In the next section I will show that a distributed version of GRASP can be developed which is able to

---

[6]See Section 6.6.3 for some further details.

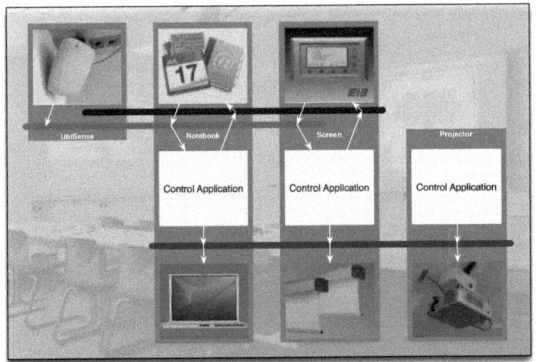

Figure 6.6: Ensemble creation

successfully solve problems such as display mapping. This algorithm has the further advantage that it requires only *local knowledge* at each participating device.

6.6 Distributed Optimization in ad-hoc Ensembles

In this section I will explain what reasons led to the development of the distributed optimization algorithm DGRASP for q. The mapping problem of our smart meeting room example is a problem where the solution is encoded with discrete variables and therefore belongs to the class of combinatorial optimization problems. Other examples for combinatorial optimization problems are the Traveling Salesman problem, the Quadratic Assignment problem or scheduling problems. In this kind of problems we have a fast growing search space if the problem size gets bigger, like in our case, if we add more components like displays and surfaces or documents. We also have a time limit to find an optimal mapping, so it is not possible to iterate over the whole search space.

For this kind of problems, many different metaheuristics[7] are proposed [160].

Fundamental properties to select an appropriate metaheuristic are completeness and efficiency. The goal is to find a method that efficiently explores the search space in order to find (near-) optimal solutions in the shortest possible time.

But in the scenario of document display mapping there are special requirements to the search process. We have different autonomous components: projectors, surfaces, documents, users:

---

[7]Metaheuristics are strategies that guide the search process.

we have a naturally distributed problem (see Fig. 6.6)[8]. Distributed optimization problems are problems where each variable and constraint is owned by an agent. Traditionally, such problems were gathered into a single place and a centralized algorithm was applied in order to find a solution. However, distributed optimization has a number of practical advantages over its centralized counterpart.

Centralized optimization is in our case infeasible due to privacy and data integration problems. As little information as possible should be exchanged between components and / or stored stored centrally. There may be components that do not wish to reveal specific information about themselves. Furthermore, it may be difficult for a (central) component to compute internal properties of other components. Take for example the calculation of the visibility by *vis*. Only the surface component may have the algorithm needed to calculate its visibility faithfully. If, for instance, two screens have a different gain-factor, then the visibility is different, even if the viewing angle and distance from the user to the screens is the same. In a fully distributed, local-knowledge approach, each surface is free to use its own tailored version of *vis*. In a centralized approach, these individual computations need to be shipped to (and evaluated by) the central component. The same drawback applies to classical distributed optimization approaches that just distribute the iterations of the optimization procedure or different slices of the search space (*e.g.*, [161]) across the available computing nodes: here too all nodes need global knowledge to assess the contribution of all available components to solutions in their iteration or of the search space slice.

The dynamic of the system is another reason. New components added in an ad hoc fashion, like notebooks oder mobile projectors, must be included in the search space. That means, by the time we would have centralized the problem, it may already have changed. Furthermore, the computing power of the different components is limited. We could not guarantee that there is a component in a dynamically created ensemble which would have the resources to compute the optimization problem alone.

Why distribution is necessary in this scenario:

- Autonomy of the components

- Privacy / Security

- Local knowledge

---

[8]The autonomous components are using the ECo middleware to create an ad hoc ensemble (see Section 4.7).

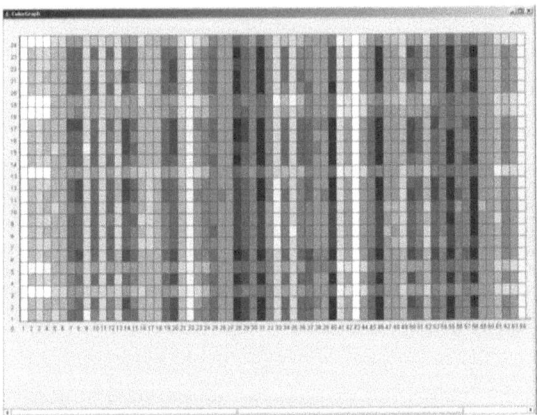

Figure 6.7: Visualization of the search space

- Robustness (single point of failure)
- Effective use of the resources

6.6.1 Related Work

If we look at the state of the art, there are a number of approaches that deal with the distributed solving of different problems in the context of ubiquitous computing or ambient intelligence. To name are without limitations distributed artificial intelligence [162], distributed problem solving [163], multi agent systems [164], and distributed constraint satisfaction problems [165]. But to my knowledge none of these approaches were engaged with the distributed optimization of a quadratic assignment problem (c.f. next section), a class of problems the display mapping belongs to.

6.6.2 The Search Space

If we look again at the goal function (Eqs. 6.1 and 6.3), we see that it is searching for the maximum of two assignments $(dm_{max}, ym_{max}) = \arg \max_{\substack{dm \in D \to 2^Y \\ ym \in Y \to S}} q(dm, ym)$. The first mapping is the assignment of documents to displays, e.g., projectors (dm), whereas the other mapping is the assignment of projectors to surfaces (ym). The search space consists of all possible assignments

Optimization as Source of the Assistance Strategy

of both maps (DM, YM). The number of the possible assignments is given by the number of projectors, surfaces and documents. The cardinalities of the maps are as follows:

- Document-Display-Map: $\#D^{\#Y}$

- Display-Surface-Map: $\binom{v}{v-w}$,
  where $v = \max(\#Y, \#S), w = \min(\#Y, \#S)$

As we can see, if we have a larger number of components, the search space will grow rapidly. To visualize the search space in Fig. 6.7 the mapping of documents to displays is presented by the x-axis and the mapping of display to surfaces by the y-axis. Here the brightness of the grey boxes corresponds to the value of the goal function q, where every box is a possible solution. The darker the grey of the boxes, the higher is the value of the goal function, where the red box represents the global optimum. This illustration clarifies the discrete character of the search space.

The Visibility value results from the angle between the view direction of the user and the respective surface:
Visibility $vis : Surface \times User \rightarrow [0; 1]$, e.g. simplified as:

$$v(s, u) = \max\left\{0, \frac{\langle \vec{n}_s, \vec{u} - \vec{s}\rangle}{\|\vec{u} - \vec{s}\|}\right\}$$

The rendering quality value results from the angle between the projection direction and the respective (electric) screens:
Rendering Quality $rend : Display \times Surface \rightarrow [0; 1]$

The visibility and the rendering quality will be calculated by the scalar product between the normal vector of the projector screen and the vector between projector (or user respectively) and the projector screen. Additional weighting factors can be the size of the surface, the gain factor in case of a canvas screen, or the visible viewing angle in case of a LCD or Plasma screen and also display size and resolution.

If in a mapping a document is displayed by multiple displays, only the maximum product of visibility and projectability for a given user will be incorporated to calculate q_{max}.

The Importance value depends on the agenda of the meeting and the role of the user in the different situations or the value will be specified by the user via a GUI:
Importance $i : Document \times User \rightarrow [0; 1]$

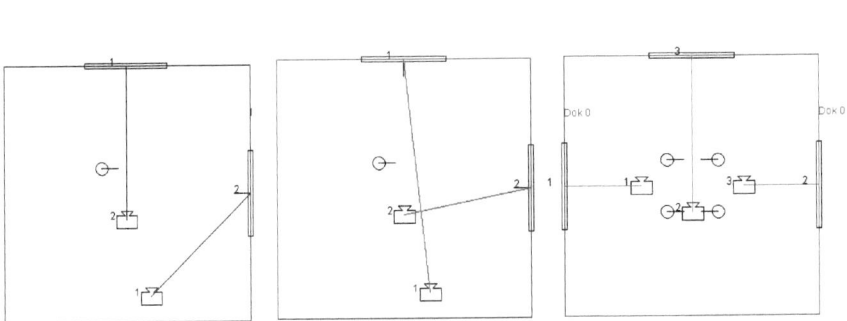

Figure 6.8: Simple examples for discussion of the search space

The Accessibility value provides the information about the authorization of a user for the respective document.

Accessibility $a : Document \times User \rightarrow \{0, 1\}$

The goal is the optimization of the function $q_{\max}$ in Eq. 6.1 which results in a Display Map, which associates each display (*e.g.* a steerable projector) with a display surface (*e.g.* a projector screen) and a Document Map, which associates each document with a display:

Display Maps: $YM = Display \rightarrow Surface$
Document Maps: $DM = Document \rightarrow \mathbb{P}Display$

Before describing the developed optimization algorithm, I will discuss some considerations which have influenced the algorithmic approach.

The first point is that, although we are looking for two separate maps (Display $\rightarrow$ Surface; Document $\rightarrow$ Display), we can not calculate these maps independently. Consider for instance the left sketch of Fig. 6.8. Assume there would only be the projector p_2. If the Display-Surface map was computed independently, then p_2 would always inevitably choose surface s_1, because this gives the best value for *rend*. With this choice, it is then impossible to arrive at the true maximum for q, as the user is looking at surface s_2.

Another problem are local maxima. A trivial example is displayed in the left and middle picture of Fig. 6.8. Although projector p_2 has a maximum projectability onto surface s_1, the overall maximum projectability is achieved when projector p_2 is directed to surface s_2. A somewhat more complex scenario is given in the right[9] picture of Fig. 6.8. Assume that the importance of document d_0 is for all users somewhat higher than the importance of document d_1, e.g. $\forall u \in U : imp(d_0, u) = 0.8 \wedge imp(d_1, u) = 0.6$. In this constellation it is then better to display the more important document d_0 on the surfaces s_1 and s_2, and the less important document d_1 on surface s_3, because the users are looking directly at s_1 and s_2 respectively. If an algorithm would choose to display d_0 on surface s_3, which would be the initial choice in a greedy approach, it could not reach the global optimum anymore. Greedy best-first algorithms tend to become stuck in the region around a local optimum. This example was used to choose an appropriate algorithm and also for testing the performance.

6.6.3 The Display Mapping Problem as a Special Case of the Quadratic Assignment Problem

In this section I will discuss the computational complexity of the display mapping problem and show that it belongs to the class of Quadratic Assignment Problems. The Quadratic Assignment Problem (QAP) is a well known NP-hard combinatorial optimization problem, first introduced by Koopmans and Beckman [166] to solve a facilities location problem. In the classical version, the problem consists of assigning n facilities to n locations with the objective of minimizing the transportation costs associated with the weight of materials between facilities and the distances between locations. The QAP can be formulated as a permutation problem as follows: Let F denote a matrix of facilities and L a matrix of locations, together with a weight function $w : F \times F \to \mathbb{R}$ and a distance function $d : L \times L \to \mathbb{R}$. Find – over all permutations p – the assignment $p : F \to L$ such that the following cost function is minimized:

$$c(p) = \sum_{\substack{a \in F \\ b \in L}} w(a,b) * d(p(a), p(b)) \qquad (6.6)$$

where $w(a, b)$ represents the flow of materials from facility a to facility b and $d(p(a), p(b))$ represents the distance from location $p(a)$ to location $p(b)$. The objective is to find an assignment vector which minimizes the total transportation costs given by the sum of the product of the flow and distance between all pairs in p. This problem statement is related to the linear assign-

---
[9]The right drawing of Fig. 6.8 shows test room 6. See the tables in the result section.

ment problem (LAP), only the cost function is expressed in terms of quadratic inequalities, for that reason it is called "quadratic" assignment problem.

If we now look at the definition of q (Eq.6.1) it is easy to see that the problem is similar to the one described above. When using only the q_s part (Eq. 6.2) of q, we have a LAP, where n documents would have to be assigned to n displays. In this case each set of assignments is a permutation of a set of n integers. There are $n!$ distinct ways in which n documents can be assigned to n displays. It is obvious that – even with a LAP – for large values of n, a brute force approach of examining all possible permutations is not feasible. For example, if one were to attempt to assign $n = 10$ documents to 10 displays, they would have to examine $10!$, or approximately 3.63 million different permutations.

If we now add the steerable projectors to the problem (Eq. 6.3), we have two assignment maps that are not independent of each other as described above. By adding the semantic proximity to q (Eq. 6.5) we have a QAP. As with the LAP, there are a number of permutations from which to choose the optimal assignment of both maps. However, there is a key difference between these two problems which makes the QAP considerably more difficult to solve. Unlike the LAP in which the assignment of a document to a display was made independently of the assignments of the other documents, with the QAP the assignments are not independent. That is, when considering an assignment of document a to a display b, one must consider the assignments of all other documents who have some semantic proximity defined for document a.

Let us now look at some issues pertaining to the computational complexity of the QAP. As seen above, enumeration of all $n!$ feasible solutions leads to an overwhelming number of permutations one would have to search to find the optimal solution, suggesting that the QAP is indeed a tough problem. In fact, the QAP belongs to the class of computationally hard problems, know as NP hard. The proof that the QAP is indeed NP hard was first shown by Sahni and Gonzalez [167] in 1976. As the Display Mapping problem belongs to this class of problems it is unlikely that an algorithm exists which solves the problem to optimality in polynomial time. Furthermore, the problem of finding an ε-approximate solution is also NP-hard. Especially problems of size n > 15 are hard to solve [168].

6.6.4 Distributed Optimization – The Approach

As described in the last section, it is useful to apply heuristics to estimate the solutions for instances of the QAP. These procedures do not provide the global optimal solution, but can produce good answers within reasonable time constraints. There are five basic categories of heuristics to approximate QAPs [169]:

- Construction methods
- Limited enumeration methods
- Improvement methods
- Simulated annealing techniques
- Genetic algorithms.

I decided to use GRASP (Greedy Randomized Adaptive Search Procedures) as a starting point for the distribution algorithm, because it seemed reasonably straightforward to transform GRASP into a fully distributed *local-knowledge* optimization procedure. GRASP is a combination of a construction method and an improvement method. For comparison, we used an auction based approach.

6.6.5 GRASP

Greedy Randomized Adaptive Search Procedures are metaheuristic methods for combinatorial problems (*e.g.* [159]). GRASP combines the advantages of a greedy proceeding for a search of good solutions with the positive features of randomizing to cover a wide area of the search space. GRASP is mostly implemented as a multi-start or iterative process, in which each iteration consists basically of two phases: a construction phase and a local search phase (*e.g.*, hill climbing). The construction phase incrementally builds a feasible initial solution, whose neighborhood is investigated until a local optimum is found during the local search phase.

At each iteration of the construction phase, the set of candidate elements will be formed by all elements that can be incorporated into the partial solution under construction without destroying feasibility. The selection of the next element for incorporation is determined by the evaluation of all candidate elements according to a greedy evaluation function. The evaluation of the elements by this function leads to the creation of a restricted candidate list (RCL), formed by the k best elements[10]. The element to be incorporated into the partial solution is randomly selected from those in the RCL. This random selection ensures sufficient variability in the construction phase, providing wide area coverage of the search space.

---

[10]For conciseness, I outline only the cardinality-based RCL construction. See [170] for a more thorough treatment.

To generate the RCL, different procedures are proposed in the literature [170]. In the *cardinality based* scheme, an integer k is fixed and the k top ranked candidates are placed in the RCL. In the *value based* scheme, the candidate elements depend on the value of the greedy function. In this scheme it is possible to define a minimum quality criteria for the partial solution.

The advantage of a constructed starting solution compared to a random starting solution is the possibility to influence it. Through proper choice and adaptation of the *greedy randomized function* it is possible to create solutions that are located in a promising area of the search space. This increases the chance to find a good local optimum or even the global optimum.

The solutions generated by the greedy randomized construction are in most cases not optimal. Hence a local search phase follows, which usually improves the constructed solution. A local search algorithm works in an iterative fashion by successively replacing the current solution with a better solution in the neighborhood of the current solution. It terminates when no better solution is found in the neighborhood. One iteration of the GRASP algorithm is now finished. In the case of the multi-start variant, the whole procedure will be iterated until a given criteria is reached, which can be the maximum number of iterations, a timeout or a minimum quality. The best overall solution is kept as the result.

---
procedure GreedyRandomized
$s := \{\}$;
Evaluate the value of each element $e \in E$;
while *s is not a complete solution* do
   | Build the restricted candidate list RCL;
   | Update the value of each element $e \in E \setminus s$;
end
return s

Algorithm 1: Procedure GreedyRandomized

Alg. 1 and 2 illustrates the main blocks of a GRASP procedure for the optimization of a combinatorial optimization problem, in this case the maximization of a function q. The used notations are: Let $q(s)$ denote the function to optimize and s the specific solution. $s \in X$ is defined by a set of elements that are part of a solution $E = \{e_1, ..., e_n\}$, a set of feasible solutions $X \subseteq 2^E$, and the objective function $f : 2^E \to \mathbb{R}$. The set of elements E, the set of feasible solutions X, and the objective function are of course specific to the problem. GRASP tries to find an optimal solution $s^* \in X$ where $f(s^*) \geq f(s), \forall s \in X$.

An advantage of GRASP is the fact that it is easy to implement. Only few parameters are needed to set and the algorithm is very robust. Despite its simplicity it is a very effective metaheuristic and produces the best known solutions for many problems (see e.g. [171] for examples).

Optimization as Source of the Assistance Strategy

```
procedure GRASP(MaxIterations)
q* := 0;
for k = 1,..., MaxIterations do
    s := GreedyRandomized;
    s := LocalSearch(S);
    if q(s) > q* then
        s* := s;
        q* := q(s);
    end
end
return s*
```

Algorithm 2: GRASP heuristic for maximization

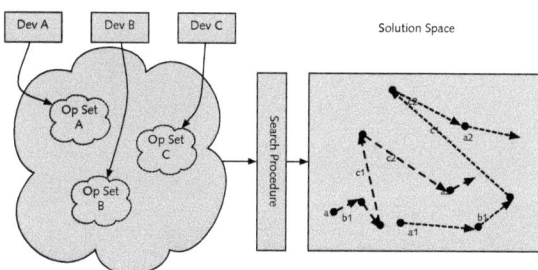

Figure 6.9: Finding solutions for multiple devices: Try multiple starting points and climb hills

6.6.6 Distributing GRASP (DGRASP)

The GRASP algorithm illustrated above operates in the multi-start variant as sketched in Fig. 6.9. Applied to our scenario of ubiquitous computing this means that all involved devices (*e.g.* screens, displays) provide their operator set into a global "knowledge cloud" and the search procedure operates on a global search space. But, as mentioned earlier, we need a fully distributed *local knowledge* version of the optimization algorithm.

Traditional distributed optimization approaches that are using multiple machines (devices) to apply the search procedure are using mainly two variants [172]. They either search in parallel over the whole search space (*c.f.* Fig. 6.10) or they split the search space (*c.f.* Fig. 6.11). Both methods still require to understand the global operator set in each search procedure instance. But the motivation for a distributed optimization of the ubiquitous computing setting of this thesis is not only to spread the search procedure over the available devices. The main goal is to apply an algorithm where the participating devices only need to share their part of the solution, not their complete operator set. The algorithm shall operate only with local knowledge of the involved devices.

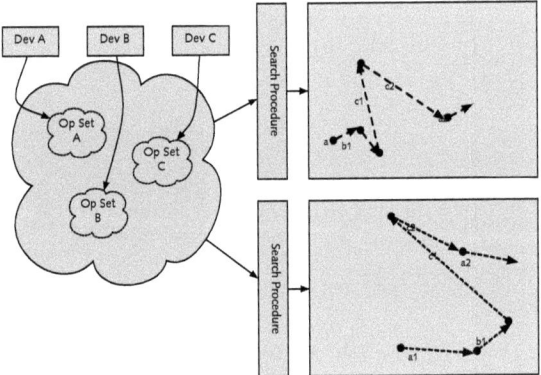

Figure 6.10: Multiple machines: search in parallel

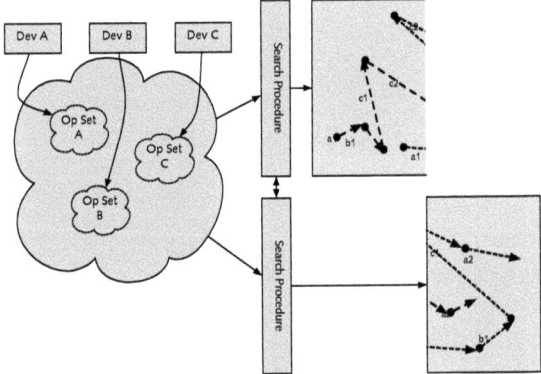

Figure 6.11: Multiple machines: Split search space

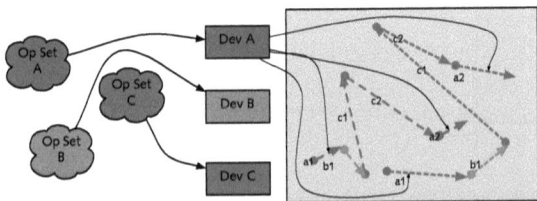

Figure 6.12: Distributed optimization with multiple devices: Approach

Optimization as Source of the Assistance Strategy

Fig. 6.12 illustrates the objective. Every device contributes its parts of a possible solution that adds up to an overall solution of the distributed optimization algorithm.

The developed approach, the distributed GRASP algorithm (DGRASP), operates in three main phases outlined below.

Initialization Phase. Every component of this scenario is considered (displays, surfaces, documents, users) as an individual agent. Every component of the room that joins the appliance ensemble broadcasts the information needed by the other components (*e.g.*, type, position, normal vector, ability to rotate (steerable projector), document importance etc.). In the current implementation, the surface agents are the main components in DGRASP. Surfaces will collect the relevant information about users, documents, and displays and they will note the presence of other surfaces. Surfaces themselves do not exchange any information about their capabilities, so that surfaces act purely locally with respect to other surfaces[11].

Construction Phase. DGRASP itself starts with the distributed generation of a feasible initial solution. The construction algorithm (Alg. 3) consists of the following steps:

1 - **MakeLocalRCL.** Starting from the current partial solution s^* (which is empty at the begining), every surface agent a generates several extended partial solutions by choosing a display $y \in Y$ and a document $d \in D$ and adding the the mapping $y \mapsto a$ and $d \mapsto \{y\}$ to the current display-surface resp. the current document-display maps of s^*.

Solution $s :: ([(Display \mapsto Surface, [(User, Value)]), Document \mapsto Display], QualValue)$
Solution $s = ([[(y \mapsto a, [(u,v)]), d \mapsto y], qv)$

Proposal $p :: ((Display \mapsto Surface, [(User, Value)]), Document \mapsto Display)$
Proposal $p = ((y \mapsto a, [(u, v(y, a, u))] | u \leftarrow User, d \leftarrow Display]), d \mapsto y)$

Candidate $c = s + p$

Using the definition of q (see Equation 6.1), the quality of these extended partial solutions will be calculated. Accordingly to the quality value, the k best solutions are put into the Restricted Candidate List.

RCL $= s \sim [c_i]_{i=1}^n$

---

[11] The fact that surfaces need to know about the capabilities of displays is a violation of the locality principle tried to achieve. Later in this section I will try to analyze if a further distribution is possible.

```
Executed by Every Agent i:
s* := {};
while Broadcast ≠ NIL received do
    s_i := s*;
    RCL := MakeLocalRCL(s_i);
    if RCL ≠ {} then
        s_i' := s_i + SelectRandom(RCL);
        Broadcast(s_i')
    else
        Broadcast(NIL)
    end
    Receive(s_j) from other Agents a_j;
    s* := max(s_j);
end
```
Algorithm 3: DGRASP Construction Phase

```
Executed by Every Agent:
v := value(s*);
repeat
    v* := v;
    s_i := s*;
    s_i' := LocalSelectBest(Steps(s_i));
    Broadcast(<s_i', value(s_i')>);
    Receive(<s_j, value(s_j)>) from other Agents a_j;
    v := max(value(s_j));
    s* := s_j where value(s_j) = v
until v* = v;
```
Algorithm 4: DGRASP Local Search Phase

2 – SelectRandom. Every agent choses randomly one solution from its local RCL.
SelectRandom = $s \sim [c_i]_{i=1}^n$

3 – Broadcast. This extended partial solution is broadcast to all other surface agents in the ensemble. Note that only solutions will be broadcasted, not local or private information. Partial quality values will be added to the solution if this information is necessary to compute the overall quality of the solution.

4 – SelectMax. All agents now have a synchronized list of all extended partial solutions. Each agent selects the best from this list as new current solution s^*.

Steps 1–4 are repeated until all surfaces resp. displays are assigned. Then the construction phase ends and the local search phase begins.

Optimization as Source of the Assistance Strategy

Local Search Phase. Local search (Alg. 4) operates on a complete solution and tries to improve it using the following steps:

1 – LocalSelectBest. Every surface agent changes the document assigned to its surface and calculates the new resulting quality value of that solution. It does this with all documents and consequently selects the best new solution. If there is no quality gain, the old solution is retained.

2 – Broadcast. Broadcast of the created solution to all other surface agents in the ensemble.

3 – SelectMax. All agents have now a synchronized list of all proposals for improved solutions. They then locally select the best proposal based on the quality value.

Steps 1 – 3 are repeated until no better solution is broadcasted by any agent. This process implements *hill climbing* as local search, i.e., the algorithm moves deterministically in the local neighborhood of the current solution towards the local maximum.

One iteration of the GRASP algorithm is now finished. Since GRASP is a multi-start approach, the whole procedure will be repeated n times (*e.g.*, $n = 5$). After finishing the last iteration, the solution with the best quality value of all iterations is the final result.

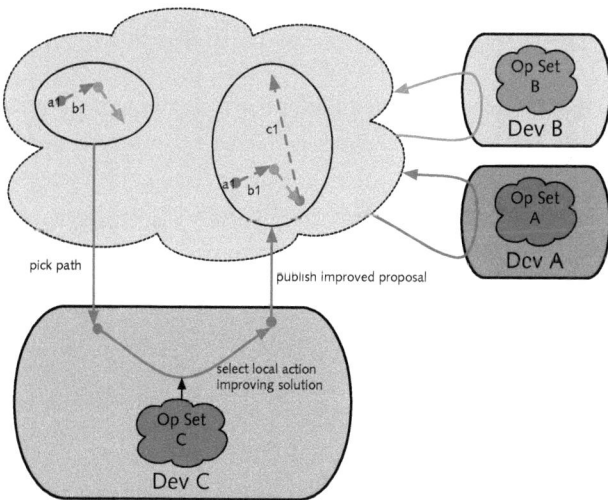

Figure 6.13: Implementation Approach

6.6.7 Running DGRASP

A rough sketch of the messages communicated between the components during a run of DGRASP is given in Table 6.1. This "trace" is based on a subset of the problem shown in Fig. 6.3. The message structure is defined below. First the messages for exchange of context information are shown.

$User_{context} = (uid, [imap = (uid, \{did \mapsto ivalue\})], [amap = (uid, \{did \mapsto avalue\})])$

$Document_{context} = \{(did, name)\}$

$displaY_{context} = (yid, pos = (x, y, z), normal = (x, y, z), res = (x, y))$

$Surface_{context} = (sid, pos = (x, y, z), normal = (x, y, z), size = (width, height))$

uid, did, yid, and sid are unique numbers identifying the individual components. $imap$ is the importance-map, a list of key-value-pairs where the keys are document-identiers, and the values range between 0 and 1. The access-map $amap$ connects the same key-values to access-rights. The other variables $pos, normal, res$, and $size$ are straightforward.

In the next section, I will look at the performance achievable with DGRASP with respect to the solution quality achieved and the number of messages required.

6.7 Evaluation of DGRASP

To benchmark DGRASP, we created 10 different test rooms on which DGRASP has been run using a simulation system. The rooms differ with respect to number and positions of the relevant components. We have tried to create a large diversity in the room design, so that the spectrum varies from awkward constellations to optimal constellations. Examples of these rooms are shown in Fig. 6.14 and in the right sketch of Fig. 6.8 and an overview of all test rooms is given in Appendix B.

In our tests, the algorithms were executed 100 times per room. In every run, the constellation of the respective room, including the positions of the users, were constant, but new documents with new importance values were created. This experimental setting should guarantee a realistic validation of the algorithms.

Table 6.2 gives the mean μ and the standard deviation σ of the solution quality achieved in the test runs. The solution quality is given relative to the true optimum (= 100), computed by an exhaustive search of the solution space. The mean is a direct indicator for the average

Optimization as Source of the Assistance Strategy

Table 6.1: Messages sent by the individual appliance components to acchieve the goal of an optimized document-display-mapping with distributed GRASP

Initialization: Components broadcast context information on context channel		
Users	U_1	$(u1, imap = (u1, \{d1 \mapsto 0.8, d2 \mapsto 0.6\}), amap = (u1, \{d1 \mapsto 777, d2 \mapsto 777\}))$
	U_2	$(u2, imap = (u2, \{d1 \mapsto 0.6, d2 \mapsto 0.8\}), amap = (u2, \{d1 \mapsto 777, d2 \mapsto 777\}))$
Projectors	Y_1	$(y1, pos = (0.0, 0.5, 0.6), normal = (1.0, 0.0, 0.0), res = (1280, 854))$
	Y_2	$(y2, pos = (0.75, 0.0, 0.6), normal = (0.0, 1.0, 0.0), res = (1280, 854))$
Screens	S_1	$(s1, pos = (1, 0.5, 0.6), normal = (-1.0, 0.0, 0.0), size = (80, 60))$
	S_3	$(s3, pos = (0.75, 1.0, 0.6), normal = (0.0, -1.0, 0.0), size = (80, 60))$
Construction phase: incremental creation of a initial solution		
construct...	S_1	$(s1, solution = (\{y1 \mapsto s1\}, \{d1 \mapsto \{y1\}\}, 1.0, C))$
	S_3	$(s3, solution = (\{y1 \mapsto s3\}, \{d2 \mapsto \{y1\}\}, 0.8, C))$
after receiving the initial solutions, $S_{1,3}$ improve solutions		
construct...	S_1	$(s1, solution = (\{y1 \mapsto s1\}, \{d1 \mapsto \{y1\}\}, 1.0, C))$
	S_3	$(s3, solution = (\{y1 \mapsto s1, y2 \mapsto s3\}, \{d1 \mapsto \{y1\}, d1 \mapsto \{y2\}\}, 1.8, C))$
Local search: improving current solution by searching the neighborhood		
local search...	S_1	$(s1, solution = (\{y1 \mapsto s1, y2 \mapsto s3\}, \{d2 \mapsto \{y1\}, d1 \mapsto \{y2\}\}, 2.1, L))$
	S_3	$(s3, solution = (\{y1 \mapsto s1, y2 \mapsto s3\}, \{d1 \mapsto \{y1\}, d2 \mapsto \{y2\}\}, 1.8, L))$
choose best solution for improvement of local search		
local search...	S_1	$(s1, solution = (\{y1 \mapsto s1, y2 \mapsto s3\}, \{d2 \mapsto \{y1\}, d1 \mapsto \{y2\}\}, 2.1, L))$
	S_3	$(s3, solution = (\{y1 \mapsto s1, y2 \mapsto s3\}, \{d2 \mapsto \{y1\}, d1 \mapsto \{y2\}\}, 2.1, L))$
local search is finished, no further refinement possible		
Multi-start: begin with new construction phase until max. iterations reached		
DGRASP solution: $(\{y1 \mapsto s1, y2 \mapsto s3\}, \{d2 \mapsto \{y1\}, d1 \mapsto \{y2\}\})$		

quality of the algorithms, while the standard deviation is a measurement for the robustness of the algorithm: the smaller the standard deviation, the more stable is the quality of the result.

We have tested DGRASP with two different parameter settings. DGRASP1_1 is run with $n = 1$ and $k = 1$, i.e., a single iteration with a restricted candidate list of length 1. DGRASP5_2 has been run with $n = 5$ restarts and a candidate list length of $k = 2$. The parameters n and k were determined empirically.

To get a feeling for the general performance of our DGRASP algorithm, we have compared DGRASP to a simple auction based [173, 174] display assignment algorithm.

Auction based procedure An auction is a market based procedure that joins requesting and offers with the help of special rules. Bidding mechanisms are suitable for our scenario because they don't need a central controller and the involved components can be autonomous. The basic idea of the auction based procedure[12] in our display mapping scenario is to create the mappings (document-display map and display-surface map) with auctions between the participating components. The quality measures for the respective maps are the basis for the bidding. The procedure contains three auctions that are sequentially ordered. We have a sale auction, where the displays are bidding for the offered surfaces. This leads to the display-surface map. In another auction the user agents bid with their visibility on the offered surfaces. After this auction every surface knows how good it is visible for all users. The last auction is responsible for the creation of the document-display map. For this purpose, the surfaces are bidding with their cumulated visibility for the offered documents.

The auction based procedure has several problems. One problem is that the order of the auctions is an issue. We altered the auctions sequences, but had no significant results. Another problem related to the first one is that the maps are created independent from each other. As we have seen in the discussion of Section 6.6.3, the maps are not independent and this leads to poor results sometimes. The algorithm also has the problem of local maxima, which we tried to avoid with Vickrey's sealed bidding (second price auctions) [176]. All tested variants had different problems and none produced constant good results.

Our naive auction mechanism is rather inferior to DGRASP with respect to quality[13], but this method seems to be quite effective considering the communication overhead: Table 6.4 displays the number of messages that were needed to execute the algorithms. This is a good indicator for the performance of the procedures in real world wireless infrastructures.

Table 6.3 compares the average execution times for DGRASP1_1, DGRASP5_2, and AUCTION. Because this timing data heavily depends on the performance of the used infrastructure, this measurement only allows a comparative statement about the algorithms.

The experiments show that the DGRASP1_1 parametrization already provides passably good results. But the missing randomization (RCL length $k = 1$) results in a high standard deviation and sometimes poor quality (see, *e.g.*, test room 7). DGRASP1_1 apparently sometimes gets stuck in regions around local maxima. The DGRASP5_2 parametrization, true multi-start in conjunction with the randomization of the RCL during the construction phase, delivers the re-

---
[12] A complete description would not fit into the scope of this section. See [175] for details.
[13] How good a solution really needs to be must be analyzed with dedicated usability studies. However, not only the average solution quality is important, also the reliability is very important. In contrast to the auction mechanism, DGRASP delivers consistent good solutions.

Optimization as Source of the Assistance Strategy

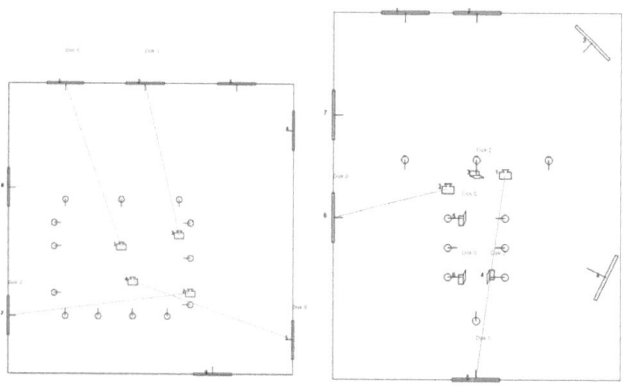

Figure 6.14: Test rooms number 4 and 5

Table 6.2: Average relative quality (mean, μ) and standard deviation (σ) of the solutions in relation to the global optimum in %

# test room	DGRASP1_1		DGRASP5_2		AUCTION	
	μ	σ	μ	σ	μ	σ
1	98.32	1.19	97.78	1.25	94.16	2.53
2	98.47	1.27	98.22	1.41	84.53	7.56
3	98.49	1.51	98.57	1.57	91.12	5.48
4	98.70	1.47	98.01	1.49	92.69	5.55
5	97.14	2.16	98.54	1.61	71.38	18.32
6	96.61	2.82	99.36	1.88	86.79	9.83
7	89.93	8.05	99.06	1.90	77.20	13.18
8	98.06	4.15	97.53	2.09	91.95	11.61
9	98.19	4.06	99.59	2.16	82.60	10.46
10	99.19	4.22	99.55	2.07	85.73	9.51

quired variability to browse the search space. The constant good quality and the small standard deviation allows the conclusion that DGRASP with 5 restarts and a RCL with 2 candidates will be appropriate for the multi-display constellations we can find in meeting rooms.

The disadvantages of the present implementation of the DGRASP algorithm is the low distribution of the procedure. Only the surfaces are actively involved in the search procedure and split the calculations among each other. The other components serve only as information providers. The question is now if it would be possible to implement a modified version that will also make the display agents active components (thereby avoiding the violation of the locality principle by the fact that surfaces currently need to understand the capabilities of displays). And the answer is probably no. The algorithm operates in the way that the agents broadcast

Table 6.3: Average computing time in ms

# test room	DGRASP1_1	DGRASP5_2	AUCTION
1	14	53	13
2	14	53	10
3	25	294	73
4	13	93	15
5	15	94	12
6	0	5	0
7	13	193	54
8	16	37	4
9	13	47	8
10	16	70	14

Table 6.4: Average number of communications during the whole search procedure

# test room	DGRASP1_1	DGRASP5_2	AUCTION
1	642	3315	225
2	645	3343	225
3	1216	6341	391
4	1233	6215	422
5	1540	7973	568
6	105	552	75
7	728	3721	195
8	394	2040	172
9	886	4720	329
10	2364	11882	306

their partial solution which leads to a (sub-)optimal solution in the end. To do so the agents have to provide the quality of their partial solution. That means it is only possible to distribute the algorithm to the degree that we can divide the quality function q. If we look for example at function part $((vis(ym(y), u) * rend(y, ym(y))))$ of Eq. 6.3, we see that it is needed to have the necessary information to determine vis and $rend$ and to assess the quality of that part of a possible solution. So the degree to that it is possible to distribute the algorithm is predefined by the used quality function.

The experiments with the auction based method produced no satisfactory results with respect to quality. It would be necessary to look deeper into useful auction mechanisms in order to give this approach a fair chance against DGRASP. What is interesting with the auction procedure is the significantly lower amount of messages that was needed in comparison to DGRASP. This justifies a further investigation of the market based approach.

Optimization as Source of the Assistance Strategy

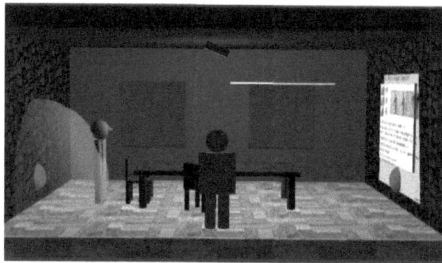 

Figure 6.15: Environment Simulation System

6.7.1 Environment Simulator

For a first informal evaluation of the applicability of this approach from the user's point of view, we have built a simple environment simulator. This is a visual simulation tool for smart / instrumented environments that provides a simple rendering & physics simulation server, to which all components of our system (mostly Java agents) can connect via sockets. The environment simulator is able to visualize the devices in the room and to display their behavior (*e.g.*, to project a document onto a wall). Furthermore, the simulator can be programmed to provide a test room with an environment geometry, sensor data, simulated users with a dedicated behavior, and interior. So it is possible to use this simulator to visually inspect the behavior of a typical ensemble controlled by q.

In the two pictures of Fig. 6.15, we have illustrated such an example. In the left image we have a scene with one steerable projector, one screen, and two users, where the user to the right gives a presentation. After adding a second projector and two notebooks, the ensemble calculates a remapping of the document display assignment (based on the maximum quality function of Eq. 6.1), resulting in the display mapping shown in Fig. 6.15 on the right. Initial results using the environment simulator system hint that q and its DGRASP approximation provide plausible behavior – this is no replacement for a user study, but was an encouragement that pursuing my approach is worthwhile.

6.7.2 Section Summary

To summarize, I make the following claims:

- The coherence of the behavior of an ensemble of devices can – for certain cooperation problems such as Display Mapping – be represented by a global quality measure that is independent of the specific makeup of an ensemble. Any ensemble that maximizes this quality measure will exhibit coherence with respect to the user needs represented by this quality measure.

- The maximization of the coherence realized by an ensemble can be achieved by a distributed optimization process that requires only local knowledge of every device in the ensemble. A device only needs to be able to assess its own contribution to the solution provided by the ensemble.

Complete distribution and locality are inevitable requirements created by the dynamic nature of ad-hoc ensembles.

This approach is applicable to other aspects of coherent ensemble behavior as well – for instance, optimizing illumination.

Some additional aspects are worth mentioning:

- In order for this approach to be applicable in the real world, q has to represent the user expectations faithfully. Developing a suitable quality measure will require significant user studies. With respect to display mapping, a study is presented in the next section.

- Currently, the DGRASP algorithm seems to be a better approach (providing a higher global quality on average) than an auction-based mechanism. However, the auction-based mechanism uses much less communication, hinting at a significantly better scaling capability. It would need further investigation with respect to designing a better auction mechanism as well as with respect to reducing the communication overhead of DGRASP.

Also, we need to understand how to better control the main factors in an ensemble's composition that drive the complexity of the optimization problem.

- Is this all worth the effort? I.e., will the user notice, if we just achieve 80% quality rather than 95%? – Yes, because already small deviations from the global optimum result in a different display mapping, immediately noticeable to the user and violating his expectation. Users might be tempted to correct the system manually, which can require more effort (changing all mappings manually) than saved by the system – the well known "obtrusive paper clip assistance" syndrome.

6.8 Combining DGRASP and Planning

During this chapter I introduced DGRASP as a method to generate a strategy that achieves indirect goals for the user, goals that define an optimal ensemble behavior (see 2.4.4 for the example goal and the resulting plan). The reason to use an optimization algorithm was that AI planning is not powerful enough to solve such kinds of problems. However, if we look exactly at the result that is delivered by the DGRASP algorithm, we can see that this is not the actual plan (strategy) that we were looking for. Actually, it is only a translation from an optimization goal (description of optimal ensemble behavior) into an achievement goal (description of environment state).

6.8.1 Goal Refinement - Goal Deliberation

Optimization goals are such where the system has no exact knowledge of the environment state that would fulfill the intention of the user. For this type of goal we need a goal refinement. The calculation of the optimization function leads to the concrete goal, *i.e.* the environment state.

If we look at the example of Table 6.1, we see that we get the following result from DGRASP:

DGRASP result: $\{y1 \mapsto s1, y2 \mapsto s3\}, \{dA \mapsto \{y1\}, dC \mapsto \{y2\}\}$

This is the mapping that displays all documents in the best possible way. So, what DGRASP actually does is to translate this indirect goal:

Goal: $DisplayMapping = \exists \textbf{Document} \in perceivableMedia$
Metric: $q(m, m_0) = \alpha\ q_s(m) + \beta\ q_t(m, m_0) + \gamma\ q_p(m)$

which denotes that there should exist at least one document that is perceivable, whereby the actual display mapping should be optimized based on the metric q, into this direct goal:

Goal: $render(\textbf{DisplayMapping}) =$
$\textbf{Projector}_1\ projectsOnto\ \textbf{Screen}_1\ \wedge\ \textbf{Projector}_2\ projectsOnto\ \textbf{Screen}_3\ \wedge$
$\textbf{Document}_A\ renderedAt\ \textbf{Display}_1\ \wedge\ \textbf{Document}_C\ renderedAt\ \textbf{Display}_3$

This direct goal (achievement goal) is the concrete environment state that we looked for. The planning component that I have described in Chapter 5 is then responsible to find the actual actions (plan) that delivers the desired environment state:

Partial plan:

1. Open motor screen 1.

2. Turn on the video projector 1.

3. Bring the document A to display on video projector 1.

    (a) Find document A and copy it to computer X.

    (b) Start display application on computer X.

    (c) Switch the crossbar: *input* to computer X, *output* to projector 1.

    (d) Turn on projector 1.

    (e) Set the projector input to VGA (connected to crossbar).

4. etc.

After the execution of this sequential plan, the goal is fulfilled. We can see that in the case of optimization goals, we have a two-stage approach. Now we need to have a look at how the system decides if the planning approach of Chapter 5 or the approach of Chapter 6 is in charge of dealing with the respective goals.

6.8.2 SODA-POP's Selection Mechanism

In the event that a goal is emitted into the goal-channel, SODA-POP's message handling and agent selection strategy (see sections 4.4.4 and 4.6.3) is responsible to choose the components that are able to handle the goal. All components that can process goals and are therefore subscribed to the goal-channel, provide information about their ability to handle the given goal.

In the case of the Display Mapping goal, the planning component of Chapter 5 would respond with a low fidelity value, because it can handle the goal somehow, but is not able to deal with the non-linear metric q. All the components that have the DGRASP algorithm for the Display Mapping goal implemented (*e.g.*, Projectors, Screens) will respond with a high fidelity value that they can handle this goal as a part of the algorithm. The goal channel would then decide to assign this goal to all the components that can handle DGRASP. These components will then apply the illustrated DGRASP algorithm (see Section 6.6.6) and will deliver the refined goal as an achievement goal. This goal will be emitted again to the goal channel, starting the next step of this two-stage goal refinement approach. This time the planning component will receive the goal, because it possesses the highest fidelity value to handle this goal. The planning component will then generate the appropriate plan.

6.9 Evaluation of q

The motivation of this thesis was to show that ambient intelligence environments are **realizable, appropriate,** and **useful.** I have shown in the last sections that certain important aspects are realizable. We now need to investigate if such systems are a benefit for the user.

The goal of Ambient Intelligence is a future in which intelligent environments are easy to build and pleasing to use. But what is useful, usable, appropriate, and what do people actually want? The research community is only beginning to answer these questions, because ambient intelligence systems haven't evolved beyond a prototype status yet.

How well a technical system meets the needs of the users depends on the ability of system designers to understand and meet the requirements and expectations of the users[14]. To assess a technical system, it is a common approach to use evaluation techniques.

For traditional desktop applications, usability testing consists of 3 main metrics (ISO 9241-11): (I) Efficiency (amount of time taken to complete a task), (II) Effectiveness (percentage of that task that users are able to complete with and without assistance), and (III) Satisfaction (user's ratings of their interactions with the application).

Is it the same for ubiquitous computing systems? The principle methods can be borrowed and the same criteria can be used, but there are differences between desktop applications and UbiComp. Traditional desktop applications are based on the concept of one user per application. The typical environment is a workplace with the user seated at a desk. Competition for the user's attention is assumed to be low and the user is aware of the capabilities of the system. In ubiquitous computing settings we can assume more than one user per application and the users may not know the available devices or appliances. Furthermore, the users may need to compete for the available recources. UbiComp systems can be sensor-based, gesture-based, can have multiple users, or mobile scenarios. In this setting unusual user behavior may cause a wrong reaction of the environment. Hence, adapted and alternative methods are needed. A good overview of the challenges of ubiquitous evaluation can be found e.g. in [177, 178]. Scholtz and Consolvo proposed a framework for evaluating ubiquitous computing [179]. However, this framework is rather fine grained and not all aspects are applicable for general UbiComp systems. According to my interpretation of the state of the art, the following aspects are possible criteria for UbiComp evaluation:

Core methods for UbiComp systems: (I) Measuring the user experience of the system. (II)

---

[14] The definition of q was my attempt to meet the requirements of the users for the display mapping problem.

Recording attitudes and opinions about the system at various times. (III) Asking people to respond, explain (think aloud, joint exploration) while using the system. (IV) Observing actual use of the system. (V) Sampling and logging behavior when using the system.

Other measures: (I) Adoption/drop out rate. (II) How many people used it once and never again? (III) Amount of information a person is willing to divulge to the system. (IV) Users opinions about the system. (e.g., trustworthy, ineffective, impressive)? (V) User's understanding of the system.

Methods to use: (I) Interviews. (II) Questionnaires. (III) Observations via video in lab (given scenario). (IV) Observations via video in-situ. (V) Expert critique using interaction design principles. (VI) Experiments. (VII) Logging of interactions with system. (VIII) Experience sampling data over time.

Multiple display environments are relatively new and there are no real evaluations of such systems, especially not for a scenario of automatic display assignment. A related topic is for example ambient display environments (see *e.g.* [180]). However, ambient displays are at the periphery of the user's attention and so not directly comparable to the intended scenarios of MDEs.

Due to the lack of comparable MDE scenarios in the literature, I compared the automatic display assignment to a manual assignment of documents to displays. As main metrics the time taken to complete a task and the number of interactions with the system were used. These measures can also give a hint about the cognitive load of the users when using different systems. Additionally the users were observed while using the system to assess aspects of system use not measurable, like enjoyment or stress level.

To assess the user acceptance, I used the technology acceptance model (TAM). TAM was developed by Davis [181] to explain computer-usage behavior. It is an information systems theory that models how users come to accept and use a technology. The model suggests that when users are presented with a new technology, a number of factors influence their decision about how and when they will use it, primarily:

Perceived usefulness – "The degree to which a person believes that using a particular system would enhance his or her job performance".

Perceived ease-of-use – "The degree to which a person believes that using a particular system would be free from effort". [181]

Optimization as Source of the Assistance Strategy

The technology acceptance model was the basis of the questionnaires that were used to estimate the user satisfaction.

In the following I will describe the experiment I have used for assessing the performance of an automatic display assignment based on q in comparison to a manual assignment.

6.9.1 Overview

The objective of my evaluation is to answer the following questions with respect to automatic display mapping in general and the definition of q specifically:

- Is it possible to predict and automatically generate a good document display mapping that would satisfy a reasonable subset of users? Are the configurations produced by the algorithm actually useful and sensible to users in multi-display environments? What benefits does automatic content distribution offer over manual distribution?

- Is it possible to do automatic content distribution in a way that users find usable, intuitive, understandable, and satisfying? How does this compare to existing techniques for assigning content to displays?

- Is it possible to develop a universal approach, or do different application domains, situations, and contexts require different assignment strategies (or even a pure manual mechanism)?

In this evaluation, I focus on an experimental study whose objective was to assess the effectiveness of an automatic display assignment in comparison to a manual assignment in a multi-user, multi-display environment.

The evaluations are based on two experiments:

- Calibration experiment: The objective of the calibration experiment was to verify that a multiple display environment is able to improve performance in comparison to a single display environment. (This experiment – for which the outcome can be considered as obvious – was conducted as safety measure against a seriously flawed experimental setup.)

- Evaluation experiment: The objective of this experiment is to measure the impact of manual vs. automatic display assignment on the performance of a team in solving a semi-cooperative assignment. In semi-cooperative tasks, the need for cooperation and joint use of information is not evident from the start, but rather arises while working on

Chapter 6

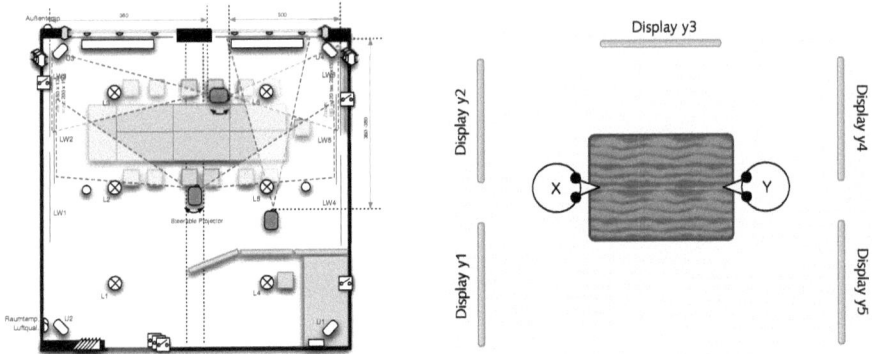

Figure 6.16: Smart Appliance Lab, equipment examples (left), experimental setup (right)

the task. I think that this kind of aspect pertains to many team processes, specifically in multidisciplinary teams.

Both experiments were carried out in our Smart Appliance Lab. This environment provides six projection based public displays, arranged in two pairs at three sides of the room that were used for the experiments (see Fig. 6.16, left)[15].

6.9.2 Calibration Experiment

Goal and Hypothesis

The objective of this experiment was to establish that multiple display environments improve the performance over single display environments. Specifically, we wanted to make sure that this performance improvement is valid for the type of tasks intended for the following evaluation experiment.

Procedure

The subjects were given the task of finding the differences between two similar pictures[16] (Fig. 6.17). Subjects in group A were given a single display (which could present only one

---
[15] Other infrastructure available in the Smart Appliance Lab – such as steerable projectors, additional motor screens, UbiSense-based location tracking, remote-controlled lighting and HVAC, etc.
[16] Source: Gregory, Richard L.: Eye and Brain – the Psychology of Seeing, Oxford University Press, 1998

Optimization as Source of the Assistance Strategy

Figure 6.17: Calibration experiment pictures, source: Oxford University Press

picture at a time), subjects in group B were given two displays, so they could compare both pictures side by side. We measured the time it took the participants to complete each task.

Results

Although only a few participants per group took part in the evaluation, the result was clear. The group with the option to use two displays was able to solve the task in distinctly shorter time. Also the post-experiment questionnaire showed that all participants would prefer a multi-display environment over a single-display environment for this kind of task. This result is not very surprising and confirms my hypothesis.

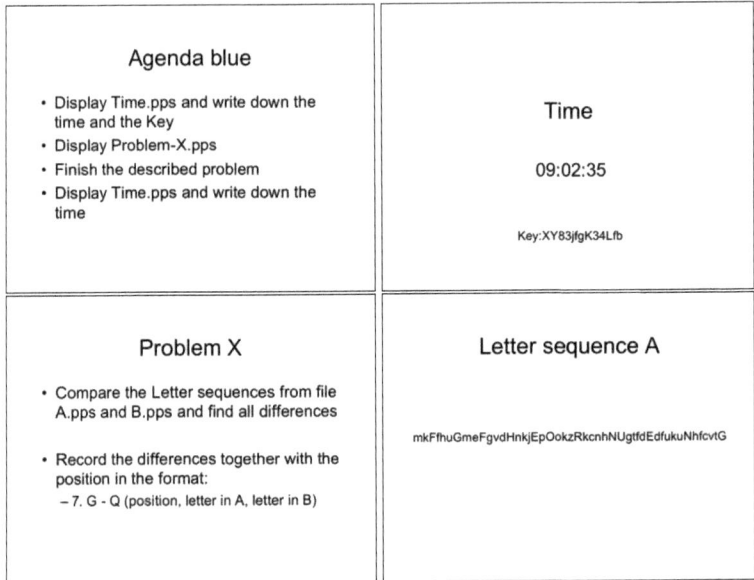

Figure 6.18: Problem documents, from top left: `Agenda`, `Time`, `Problem-X`, `A`

6.9.3 Evaluation Experiment – Setup

Goal and Hypothesis

The objective of this experiment was to compare the effect of manual and automatic display assignment on task performance. My hypotheses is that automatic assignment enables teams to solve their tasks in a shorter time, with less conflicts between team members, and with greater satisfaction.

Procedure

In order to test my hypothesis, I chose an experimental design that allowed us to measure both objective performance data and subjective user satisfaction.

In the experiment, two-person teams had to solve a semi-cooperative set of comparison tasks as fast as possible. The two team members, X and Y, were given different agendas, each containing the description of an individual comparison. For X the task was to compare two documents

Optimization as Source of the Assistance Strategy

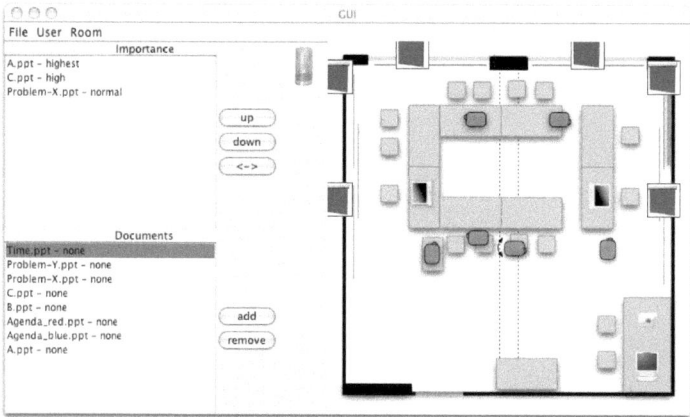

Figure 6.19: GUI for document importance and document-display assignment

A and B, for Y the task was to compare A and C. The task was a simple letter comparison, counting the number of differences in the two letter sequences contained in A and B resp. A and C. In addition, X and Y had to report time information and a random key from another document Time. The seemingly unrelated tasks for X and Y were linked into a cooperative task through the shared documents A and Time – see Fig. 6.18 for the documents.

The seating arrangement used for a team is shown in Fig. 6.16, right. Note that there are two pairs of displays exclusively visible to X and Y, respectively, and one display visible to both X and Y. For the experiments, every participant was given a simple user interface for document assignment. Manual assignment of a document to a display-surface is done through simple "drag & drop" (Fig. 6.19, right). For automatic assignment, the user just associates an importance value with the documents (Fig. 6.19, left). The optimal document-display assignment is then computed using the goal function q.

As the agendas and task descriptions were mutually unknown, the sharing had to be discovered through a conflict in the manual assignment group. (In order to enforce resource conflicts in this simple setting, each document could only be displayed on one display at a time.)

Finally, the teams were assigned to two equally sized groups, A and M. The teams had to solve two sets of comparison tasks in sequence, with a short break after the first set. Group A had to solve the first set using automatic assignment and the second set with manual assignment. Group M had to solve the first set with manual, the second set with automatic assignment.

In the evaluation of the results, we will call the first set "Initial Test" and the second "After Training", respectively.

Summary of experimental design

Group A:	
First Task Set (Initial Test)	Second Task Set (After Training)
Automatic	Manual

Group M:	
First Task Set (Initial Test)	Second Task Set (After Training)
Manual	Automatic

For each experiment, we recorded the time required for completing the task, the number of interactions with the provided user interfaces, and the solution correctness (percentage of letter differences found). After each task set, the subjects were asked to answer a questionnaire regarding user satisfaction. After both task sets, the subjects were asked to complete a final questionnaire regarding the comparison of the automatic and the manual assignment.

Note that a goal of the experimental design was to (I) explicitly provoke conflicts between the team members regarding the use of the available display space and (II) to enforce substantial changes in the set of documents currently important for a user. Clearly, display assignment becomes an issue only, if more relevant documents than displays are available (specifically, if different users have different sets of relevant documents), and once the set of currently relevant documents changes dynamically. In order to achieve these effects with a manageable and reproducible experimental setup, we had to settle with a somewhat artificial experimental design. However, the results we have achieved with this setup are independent from the specific trial task. They are valid in any situation that involves multiple-user and multiple-display scenarios with inherent conflicts and/or dynamics between the team members' sets of relevant documents.

The main task of the experiment (comparing letter sequences) was purposely one that could be solved in a short time. It was important that the actual task is easy and fast to solve in order to limit the influence of different participants, as it was the system we wanted to test, not the participants. The part of solving the task must be small compared to the time of dealing (interacting) with the system. Otherwise the differences in using the system (AA vs. MA) would vanish in the variance of solving the task. Additionally, it was important to have a reasonable overall time requirement for the whole procedure (experiments + questionnaires), because all participants were volunteers.

Optimization as Source of the Assistance Strategy

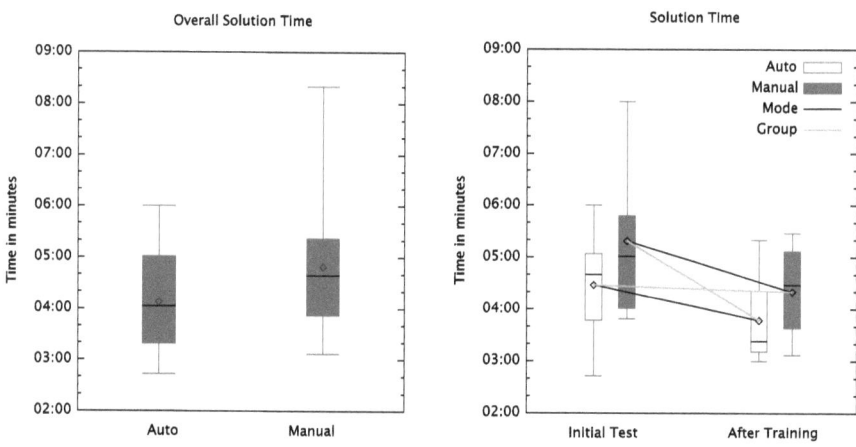

Figure 6.20: Boxplots of solution time vs. mode, overall (left) and per task set (right)

Participants

24 voluntary subjects (19 male and 5 female) were recruited from colleagues and students of our department and the local university. The participants were between the ages of 20 and 41, had at least one year of a Bachelor degree and were used to computer systems. The participants were randomly grouped into 12 teams, from which 6 were randomly assigned to group A, the other ones to group M.

6.9.4 Results

Overview

In the analysis of the experimental data, we have focused on my first research question: is an automatic display assignment able to assist users in solving tasks in multi-display environments in a shorter time and with less interactions than conventional manual assignment?

On average all subjects needed 4:28 min to complete one set of a comparison task. When the teams were using automatic assignment, the average time was 4:08 min, while they required an average time of 4:49 min using manual assignment. The overall average number of interactions was 11.8, where the subjects needed 8.5 interactions on average with automatic and 15 interactions on average with manual assignment. The average solution correctness was 95%,

163

for both manual and automatic assignment.

This indicates that the automatic assignment is superior to manual assignment, regarding time and interactions (a brief statistical validation for this claim is given further below).

An overview of the collected data is shown in the boxplots in Fig. 6.20, 6.21, and 6.22[17]. In these plots, "mode" refers to the display assignment mode (manual vs. automatic). In the per-task-set plots, grey lines connect the mean values of the two consecutive task sets of a group (Group A or Group M), black lines connect consecutive task sets using the same assignment mode. So, the boxes in Fig. 6.20, right, have the following interpretation:

- Bottom left unfilled box: Group A, first set using automatic assignment ("Initial Test").
- Top left filled box: Group M, first set using manual assignment ("Initial Test").
- Top right, filled box: Group A, second set using manual assignment ("After Training").
- Bottom right unfilled box: Group M, second set using automatic assignment ("After Training").

Interpretation

As can be seen in Fig. 6.20, right, for both task sets the solution time is shorter when using automatic assignment. In addition, Group M was able to solve the task substantially faster in the second set (i.e., when switching from manual to automatic assignment), whereby Group A was not able to improve performance in the second set (i.e., switching from automatic to manual assignment). The number of interactions (Fig. 6.21) is smaller for the automatic method in both sets. Interestingly, the interaction counts within a mode are almost identical in both sets. There was no training effect. This indicates that the training (due to solving similar task in both sets) had no influence on usage of the system infrastructure. The training effect was limited to solving the key problem of comparing the letter sequences.

In the manual assignment mode, both groups initially had no idea that they needed to share documents. So they unwittingly "stole" the shared documents from each others "private" displays. It took a couple of interactions until the participants realized that they needed to cooperate and to assign some of the documents to a display visible to both users. This process of realization and negotiation was the reason for confusion and delay (manifesting itself in the

---

[17]These boxplots show the minimum and maximum values, the 25% and 75% percentiles, the median (horizontal bar inside the box), and the mean (small circle inside the box).

Optimization as Source of the Assistance Strategy

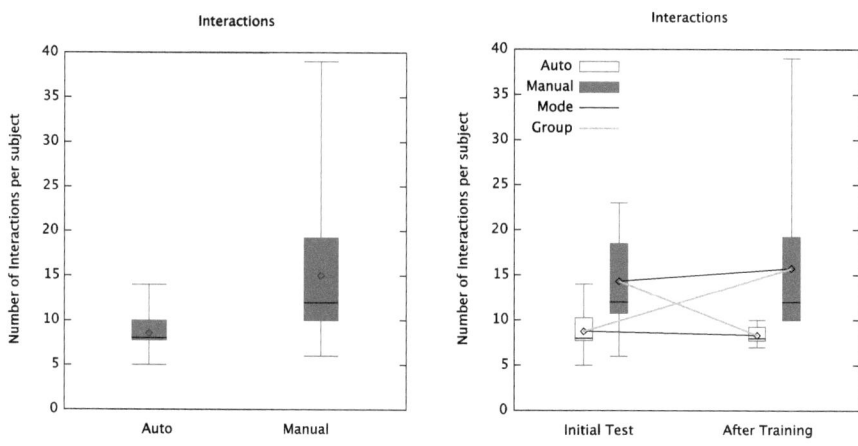

Figure 6.21: Boxplots of interaction count vs. mode, overall (left) and per task set (right)

higher solution time and interaction counts required in the manual mode). Interestingly, even Group A did not realize that they had to share documents in the manual task set (second task set for Group A), although they might have been able to discover this fact in the first task set.

In the automatic assignment mode no such conflicts did arise as the system automatically displayed shared documents on a shared screen. If we use the number of interactions as indicator of occurred conflicts, the data shows that with the automatic mode the number of conflicts is considerably smaller than in the manual mode. A detailed survey of the log files showed that documents which had to be shared, very frequently were reassigned in the manual mode. This proves the presumption that resolving conflicts by social negotiation is – in some situations – inferior to a computer supported negotiation, which can be solved by an automatic assignment using a global quality function such as q.

User Satisfaction

The questionnaires were used for answering my second hypothesis: is automatic display assignment able to improve user satisfaction?

For the questionnaires, I used parts of the technology acceptance model (TAM) [181]. I included the following items, each to be answered on a scale from 1 (strongly disagree) to 5 (strongly agree):

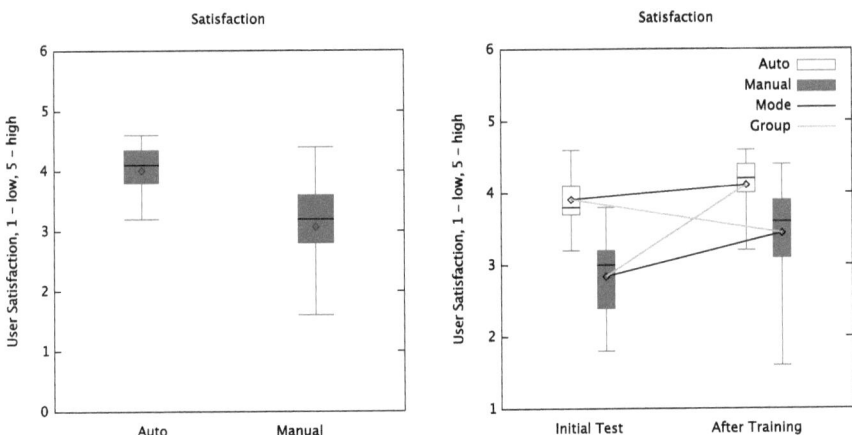

Figure 6.22: Boxplots of user satisfaction vs. mode, overall (left) and per task set (right)

- The system is easy to use.
- The system helps in solving the task efficiently.
- It is easy to cooperate with the team partner.
- The system helps in solving team conflicts.
- I felt comfortable in using the system.

The final questionnaire had the same items, but with the request to compare both approaches, automatic and manual assignment, on a scale from 1 (manual assignment strongly preferred) to 5 (automatic assignment strongly preferred).

The detailed results of the questionnaire are given in Table 6.5. The average user satisfaction for the automatic assignment is 4.0, it is 3.1 for the manual assignment. The comparison value is 3.8, which is 0.8 in favorite for the auto mode (3.0 would be the neutral value), which could be interpreted as a 40% preference of the automatic system (a value of 5.0 would indicate a 100% preference). Also worth noting are the values for the "conflict" items: Users tend to quite strongly agree with the statement that the automatic system helps in solving team conflicts, while they tend to quite strongly disagree that the manual system helps.

The distribution of the user satisfaction data (using per-questionnaire averages) is shown in Fig. 6.22. The overall user satisfaction is higher in the auto mode, for both task sets. In

Table 6.5: Questionnaire Summary
A = Automatic, M = Manual, 1 = strongly disagree, 5 = strongly agree.
C = Comparison, 1 = Manual strongly preferred, 5 = Automatic strongly preferred

Item	Group A			Group M			All Participants		
	A	M	C	A	M	C	A	M	C
Ease of use	3.9	4.3	3.3	4.2	3.5	4.1	4.0	3.9	3.7
Efficiency	4.1	3.9	3.2	4.2	3.0	4.3	4.1	3.5	3.7
Cooperation	3.7	3.4	3.8	4.0	2.6	4.1	3.9	3.0	4.0
Conflicts	4.2	1.5	4.5	4.1	1.7	4.4	4.1	1.6	4.4
Comfort	3.6	3.7	2.6	4.1	3.1	3.7	3.9	3.4	3.2
Average	3.9	3.4	3.5	4.1	2.8	4.1	4.0	3.1	3.8

addition, user satisfaction *decreases* within a *group* when switching from auto to manual, while it *increases* when switching from manual to auto. Interestingly, the user satisfaction relatively increases in the second set for both *modes*, auto and manual. A possible reason for this might be that if the subjects know the task, the cognitive load is lower, which leads to less stress and a higher satisfaction.

The correlation of the subjective user satisfaction with the objective data from the log files confirm my hypothesis that the automatic display assignment is superior to the manual assignment in multi-user, multi-display situations with conflicting and dynamic document sets.

Statistical Validation (t-test)

For assessing the statistical validity of the results for solution time t, interaction count i, and overall satisfaction s, I have used a one-sided t-test (assuming unknown and not necessarily equal variances for the automatic and the manual test results) [182]. The null hypothesis in each case was that the manual method is at least as good as the automatic method. The alternative hypothesis in each case is that automatic assignment is superior to manual assignment.

The results of test are given below. As can be seen, for all values the null hypothesis can be rejected. For solution time, the result is statistically significant, for interaction count and overall satisfaction it is even highly significant.

H_0	H_1	H_0 rejected at level
$t_{man} \leq t_{auto}$	$t_{man} > t_{auto}$	2.5%
$i_{man} \leq i_{auto}$	$i_{man} > i_{auto}$	0.5%
$s_{man} \geq s_{auto}$	$s_{man} < s_{auto}$	0.5%

Therefore I conclude that automatic assignment for multi-user and multi-display situations is superior to manual assignment.

A different question is how much better automatic assignment is. Clearly, the statistically reliable *minimal* improvement is smaller than the difference between the average values. Here, we have the following results:

value	minimal improvement	level
solution time	15 sec.	10%
interaction count	4	10%
overall satisfaction	0.57	10%

Due to the comparatively small sample size, the significance level is somewhat weak (5% would be preferable). However, a larger sample size should allow to make stronger statements here, also regarding the size of the minimal improvement.

Also, the independence assumptions for the samples for automatic and manual assignment are somewhat problematic: the 48 samples (24 manual, 24 automatic) have been taken from the same 24 subjects (although each subject has contributed just one automatic and one manual sample). We do not think that this has a significant impact on our claims – it too will be resolved by increasing the sample size.

(I admit that an "improvement of 0.57 in overall satisfaction" is somewhat difficult to interpret.)

User Comments and other Observations

In the questionnaire the users were also asked to express their impressions of the systems in a free form. The statements of the participants are summarized in the following list.

- Automatic Assigment (AA)
    - The transition between two mappings should be better visualized.
    - Assistance requires rethinking of known system behavior, but is rewarding.
    - AA is more relaxing and comfortable, but a small orientation phase is needed after redistribution of the documents.
    - The relocation of a document in case of a resource conflict was pleasant, but an animation should visualize the direction.

- Additional manual relocation of documents is desirable[18].
- It remains perhaps unknown that the users work as a team.
- Time saving through AA was sometimes limited, because of unexpected relocation of the documents.
- Some participants didn't like it that the computer had the control, even if the AA provided an objectively better result.

- Manual Assignment (MA)
  - Many documents and many displays are confusing and causing cognitive load.
  - Manual assignment requires contemplation and concentration.
  - The "stealing" of shared documents was very annoying.
  - The communication and negotiation of a display assignment that satisfied both users was difficult.

- Comparison
  - Information if different users need the same document would be good.
  - Display shortage should be visualized in the GUI.
  - AA is more efficient, MA is more fun. MA is more intuitive.
  - Participant from group A: The pleasantly ease of use of the AA was not perceived until using the manual system.
  - To have control of what will be displayed at which display is more pleasant, however in the case of a conflict it is a drawback compared to the AA.

Other observations from a bystanders point of view that were not stated by the participants in the questionnaires are the following.

In the MA setting, two users didn't come to the conclusion that they could use a shared display in case of a resource conflict. They negotiated to use the documents one after the other on their "private" displays. Another participant simply turned around and looked at the "private" display of the other user to resolve the resource conflict. Two participants almost got in a fight, because they constantly "stole" the shared document from each other[19]. They just didn't come to the solution to use the shared display and their negotiations failed because of the competing task and the high stress level.

---

[18] This feature was disabled during the experiments.

[19] In Fig. 6.21, left you can see the high number of interactions of these two participants as an outlier.

6.9.5 Section Summary

In this section, I have discussed the problem of assisting teams in effectively using multi-display environments for working together. The user studies show that – at least for specific scenarios – an automatic display assignment based on the above definition of q is at least as good as a manual assignment (in fact, it is even better). Therefore, it proves that it is *possible* to provide automatic assistance for the user.

My experimental work indicates that there is indeed a noticeable effect of display assignment methods on team performance, at least for semi-cooperative tasks. An automatic display assignment (I) improves the team effectiveness (measured in time to complete a task), (II) reduces the level of conflict in the team (i.e., the number of arguments about resource use), and (III) improves the individual user experience and satisfaction.

Providing automated assistance in using multi-display environments is based on the hypothesis that there are situations where an automatism streamlines and simplifies the social negotiation processes required for agreeing on the use of limited resources in a team of users. Other aspects such as understandability of the computed assignment and its compatibility with user expectations have to be measured. The same holds for an assessment of the usability of automatic display assignment in other team situations.

To summarize, although there are many open questions, I have shown that automatic display assignment provides a measurable benefit in multi-display environments, at least in some situations. Future investigations will have to show whether this benefit offers the universality and significance required to generally incorporate it into such environments.

6.10 Excursus: Goal function as Benchmark:

As different software infrastructures emerge, criteria are required by which the potential and efficiency of different solutions can be compared. Clearly, user trials - the ubiquitous evaluation strategy for pervasive computing applications - are not a viable approach in this case: the users of system software are application designers. Doing extensive user trials with highly trained experts is prohibitively expensive.

Therefore, it seems desirable to identify comparison criteria that can be evaluated at a formal level, using a standardized set of example problems - a set of benchmarks.

It may be interesting to use explicit definitions of optimal behavior as a means for creating such benchmarks. So, as already outlined above, different approaches to computing display mappings could be compared with respect to their ability to approximate q_{max} (or a more refined "theory of an optimal display mapping").

6.11 Chapter Summary

In Section 2.4.4 we have seen that certain kind of goals in Smart Environments are optimization goals. In this chapter I have introduced the Display Mapping problem as an example of such goals. For this special problem, a goal function q was defined that provides a precise definition of a *globally optimal* display mapping in a multiple display environment.

To optimize the goal function, the distributed algorithm DGRASP was presented that requires only *local knowledge* at each participating device and that is applicable to arbitrary objective functions.

The evaluation of the implemented solution has shown that automated assistance is a benefit for the users.

For a more elaborate conclusion, see the section summaries 6.5.4, 6.7.2, and 6.9.5.

Additional note: In this chapter I have argued that we need a fully decentralized approach to optimize q, even though I have chosen to use a central planning component in the approach of Chapter 5. The arguments that lead to a central planning component can be found in Section 5.10. One important rationale to choose a reasoning approach for user assistance is the solution quality that the system is able to deliver. I mentioned that a colleague of mine is currently implementing a fully decentralized planning approach. However, the average solution quality of that system is about 80% compared to the optimum. I'm sure that the users will not tolerate such deviations from an optimal assistance, hence my choice of a central planner.

Chapter 7

Conclusion

Users are often overwhelmed by the functionality of modern infotainment appliances and instrumented environments. Smart environments promise to provide a new level of assistance and support, by *reacting* to the activities of users, in a way that *assists* the users in achieving *their objectives* in this environment. We have seen that we need to rely on the paradigm of ubiquitous computing to create such environments. We can't rely on manually configured static environments, because people continuously want to add new devices to enhance their homes and it is a severe cost factor for institutional operators of professional meeting rooms. An ever growing proportion of the physical infrastructure of our everyday life will consist of smart appliances. An effective realization of smart environments therefore inherently requires to address the challenge of self-organization and spontaneous cooperation for ad hoc ensembles of smart appliances. I argue that a possible solution should be based on the fundamental concept of goal based interaction, because this enables an ad hoc ensemble to generate strategies that accomplish the goal of the user, instead to be dependent on predefined or learned strategies.

This thesis describes how we can deal with the problems of *invisible computer* and *dynamic infrastructures* if we rely on *explicit goals* to allow the smart ensemble to cooperate spontaneously on behalf of the user's needs. To make goal based interaction possible we need to have an explicit state model of the environment. This is the foundation for the formulation of explicit goals. The analysis of the application domain revealed that we have to support at least two kinds of goals in smart environments, (i) direct goals (the description of the environment state) and (ii) indirect goals (the definition of an optimal ensemble behavior). Direct goals can be supported by the illustrated planning approach and indirect goals – which often describe an optimization problem – can be managed with the distributed algorithm DGRASP. Finally, a user evaluation has proved that the proposed kind of assistance is useful for the user.

7.1 Final example

To illustrate the main features of my approach – the unified framework for goal-based interaction with smart environments – I will use a final example that incorporates the individual aspects of the separated chapter of my thesis. Remember the smart meeting room scenario of Section 1.2.1. The following scenario takes place in the presented room, which is well equipped with sensors, devices and appliances that are useful for a smart meeting room. All individual components are forming an ensemble by using the proposed architecture, based on the topology of goal-based interaction and the middleware SODA-POP. The self-organization is achieved by the given set of channels that completely cover the essential message processing behavior for any appliance in the application domain.

The introduced users, Carmen, Annette, and Maria enter the room for the appointed meeting and bring their notebooks and a mobile beamer. The new devices join the ensemble by connecting to the defined interfaces (see Fig. A.2).

Carmen stands up and goes to a wall in the room. The intention analysis infers (based on the agenda) that she wants to present document A at screen 6. The intention analysis emits that (direct) goal (**Document**$_A$ $diplayedAt$ **Screen**$_6$ $\wedge$ $brightnessAt$ **Screen**$_6$ = low) to the goal channel and the subscribed transducers compete about that goal with their ability to fulfill this goal. The planning component of Chapter 5 wins this competition – based on the agent selection algorithm of Section 4.6.3 (channel conflict resolution strategy) – and is selected, because it offers the highest values of importance and fidelity for both parts of the goal. Based on the semantic self-description of the available components (projectors, lamps, etc.) – provided as PDDL operators that model the functionality – the planning component is able to create an action sequence (executed via the action channel by the scheduler) that displays the document on screen 6 with a low illumination at that screen.

Now, during a discussion, also Annette and Maria have documents that are important for all participants, what they indicate by giving their documents a high importance for all users by using a GUI. The intention analyses recognizes that a new *Display Mapping* is needed and emits that (indirect) goal ($\exists$**Document** $\in perceivableMedia$) with q as metric to the goal channel. Again, all subscribed components announce their ability to handle this goal. In this case, devices like the projectors or screens submit that they can take part to find a solution and the channel decides to delegate the task to all components that can handle the display mapping

Conclusion

with DGRASP. With this distributed optimization algorithm, the involved components find the best best display mapping:
($\mathbf{Projector}_1$ $projectsOnto$ $\mathbf{Screen}_1$ ∧ $\mathbf{Document}_C$ $renderedAt$ $\mathbf{Display}_1$ ...), which as a result is a new direct goal at the goal channel. This new goal will be handled like before and the planning assistant finds an optimal action sequence that accomplishes this goal. Note, that we can define this goal refinement step with DGRASP as a channel cooperation strategy of SODA-POP.

This example shows that the presented approach is able to account for the two identified aspects of self-organization, architectonic and operational integration.

7.2 Summary of the results

The main identified requirements for future intelligents systems were that 1) Smart Environments will have to be composed from individual components that have to assemble themselves into a coherently acting ensemble, and that 2) we need appliances that cooperate spontaneously and that are able to autonomously generate strategies for assisting the user. The presented framework, *i.e.*, the combination of the architecture and the middleware SODA-POP, AI Planning, and DGRASP are able to support these requirements.

The presented multi-agent architecture supports multimodal interaction with technical infrastructures of the everyday life. The underlying middleware mechanisms, the SODA-POP model, provides the essential communication patterns of a data-flow based multi-component architecture that can be used for the creation of Smart Environments.

The SODA-POP model contains the following properties: 1) Support data-flow based event processing topologies. 2) Support conventional remote procedure calls. 3) Support self-organization of system components. 4) Support decentralized problem decomposition and conflict resolution. 5) Support dynamic extension by new components.

The self-organization is achieved by two means in SODA-POP: 1) Identifying the set of channels that completely cover the essential message processing behavior for any appliance in the prospective application domain. 2) Developing suitable channel strategies that effectively provide a distributed coordination mechanism tailored to the functionality, which is anticipated for the listening components. Then, based on the standard channel set, *e.g.*, as outlined in Fig. 4.2, any device is able to integrate itself autonomously into an ensemble, and any set of devices can spontaneously form an ensemble.

The displayed architectural concept, which makes it possible to integrate classical Artificial Intelligence technology - such as planning and scheduling - into the domain of networked consumer appliances, showed how we can support goal-based assistance with dynamic environments. AI Planning is an efficient concept for the dynamic generation of sequential plans for the realization of achievement goals. This is based on an explicit modeling of the semantics of device operations as "precondition / effect" rules, which are defined over an environment ontology. It was shown that PDDL is a very expressive language for a variety of planning applications and that it is an applicable representation language for the modeling of planning problems in Smart Environments.

Due to the fact that AI Planners are not able to solve hard non-linear problems, it was needed to add a goal refinement step that translates optimization goals into achievement goals. To handle optimization goals, the distributed algorithm DGRASP was developed that is able to approximate the global optimum of an optimization task through local interactions of dynamic device ensembles. DGRASP is based on the GRASP framework and is able to solve NP-hard combinatorial optimization problems, like the quadratic assignment problem, a class of problems that the example problem of Chapter 6 belongs to.

With the display mapping problem I have discussed the problem of assisting teams in effectively using multi-display environments for working together. This served as an example for addressing the question whether it is possible to find well-defined quality criteria for automatic assistance in Smart Environments.

The proposed goal function q that provides a precise definition of a globally optimal display mapping in a multiple display environment, showed that some aspects of a globally coherent behavior of a dynamic ensemble of ubicomp devices can be treated as optimization problems.

The user evaluation revealed that – at least for specific scenarios – an automatic display assignment based on q can be at least as good as a manual assignment. Therefore, it proves that it is possible to successfully identify a set of quality criteria for automatic assistance. For the display mapping problem I have even been able to show that automatic assignment enables teams to solve their tasks in a shorter time, with less conflicts between team members, and with greater satisfaction.

7.3 Outlook

The presented solutions support only a part of the user requirements for future intelligent environments. It will be necessary to dedicate further research to support all requirements that were identified for example by the AMIGO project (see Section 1.2.2). However, the implementation of the concepts of this thesis have shown that Ambient Intelligence is realizable and the evaluation experiment has shown that it can be appropriate and useful.

The presented approach of goal-based interaction is a two-stage design, where at the first stage the system components recognize the intention of the user, and at the second stage the system components generate a strategy that fulfills the needs of the user. This thesis completely left aside the first stage, but of course intention analysis is an important research topic that is already very active.

The strategy generation approach of this thesis is based on a semantic self description of the available devices. This self description must comply to a common ontology. However, a widely excepted ontology for the definition of environment states has not yet emerged. The development of such an ontology will be an important task for the future. Also it is necessary that usability experts identify and define the goals (based on the environment ontology) that are typical in Smart Environments. Especially for indirect goals (optimal ensemble behavior) future research is needed.

The strategy generation approach of Chapter 5 uses centralized planning for decentralized plans. In Section 5.10 I illustrate the reasoning for that, but future systems should try to avoid central components and to develop decentralized planning. However, the choice of a reasoning approach for user assistance depends also on the solution quality that the system is able to deliver. If the assistance of the system is violating the expectations of the user and forcing him to correct the system manually, he will dislike the system. It will be necessary to determine with an user evaluation what deviations from the global optimum are accepted by the user.

Verdict

I do not expect the solution proposal I have outlined to be the only possibility. However, I hope that I have convinced the reader that there is at least one possible and sufficiently concrete approach towards solving the substantial challenges of dynamic ensembles, which are raised by the proliferation of ubiquitous computing technology.

It makes clear that the topics raised here are just a small fraction of the problems and challenges that have to be addressed in order to make ubiquitous computing as invisible and intuitive as it is called for in the well known visions. Enabling truly spontaneous and smart cooperation between ubiquitous multimedia appliances will remain a major challenge for future research.

7.4 Acknowledgements

I am grateful to all the people who helped me in conducting this thesis. Especially I would like to express profound gratitude to my advisor, Prof. Dr. Thomas Kirste, for his invaluable support, encouragement, supervision and useful suggestions throughout my research and the work on this thesis. His moral support and continuous guidance enabled me to complete my work successfully.

I am also highly thankful to Prof. Dr. Birgitta König-Ries and Prof. Dr. Klaus Schmid for their valuable suggestions and feedback. Thanks go to my colleagues Petra, Martin, Christiane, Albert, Christoph, and Sebastian for their inspiring advices and the fruitful collaboration. Thanks go also to the students who contributed valuable implementations.

I want to thank my parents and my family for their understanding, encouragement and support when it was most required. This work could not have been done without you.

I thank the experimental subjects for their participation in the usability evaluation and the colleagues of the Chair of Organisational and Business Psychology, Institute of Business Administration, Faculty of Business and Social Sciences of the Rostock University for their help in planning the experiment.

This work was partially supported by the German Ministry of Education and Research under the grant signature 01 IL 904 G 0, the Landesforschungsförderprogramm of the LMB Mecklenburg-Vorpommern and the DFG Graduiertenkolleg MuSAMA.

Bibliography

[1] *IEEE Intelligent Systems*, vol. 14 (2). Piscataway, NJ, USA: IEEE Educational Activities Department. March 1999.

[2] M. Weiser, "The computer for the 21st century," *Scientific American*, vol. 3, no. 265, pp. 94–104, 1991.

[3] M. Satyanarayanan, "Pervasive computing: vision and challenges," *Personal Communications, IEEE [see also IEEE Wireless Communications]*, vol. 8, no. 4, pp. 10–17, 2001.

[4] E. Aarts, "Ambient intelligence: A multimedia perspective," *IEEE Multimedia*, vol. 11, no. 1, pp. 12–19, 2004.

[5] K. Schmid, "Ambient intelligence," *KI - Zeitschrift Künstliche Intelligenz, special issue on Ambient Intelligence*, vol. 21, no. 2, pp. 5–9, 2007.

[6] B. Brummitt, B. Meyers, J. Krumm, A. Kern, and S. Shafer, "Technologies for Intelligent Environments," in *Proc. Handheld and Ubiquitous Computing.*, (Springer), 2000.

[7] D. Cook, M. Huber, K. Gopalratnam, and M. Youngblood, "Learning to Control a Smart Home Environment," in *Innovative Applications of Artificial Intelligence*, 2003.

[8] G. Abowd, A. Bobick, I. Essa, E. Mynatt, and W. Rogers, "The aware home: Developing technologies for successful aging," in *Proceedings of AAAI Workshop and Automation as a Care Giver*, Held in conjunction with American Association of Artificial Intelligence (AAAI) Conference 2002, (Edmonton, Alberta, Canada), AAAI, 2002.

[9] G. Herzog and N. Reithinger, "The SmartKom architecture: A framework for multimodal dialogue systems," in *SmartKom: Foundations of Multimodal Dialogue Systems* (W. Wahlster, ed.), pp. 55–70, Berlin, Heidelberg: Springer, 2006.

[10] N. Gershenfeld, R. Krikorian, and D. Cohen, "The internet of things," *Scientific American*, vol. 291, no. 4, pp. 46–51, 2004.

[11] D. Norman, "The Invisible Computer." MIT Press, 1998.

[12] "The Disappearing Computer Initiative." IST- Workprogramme 2003-2004-FET.

[13] D. Cook and S. Das, *Smart Environments: Technology, Protocols and Applications (Wiley Series on Parallel and Distributed Computing)*. Wiley-Interscience, 2004.

[14] S. K. Das, M. Conti, and B. Shirazi, *PERVASIVE AND MOBILE COMPUTING*. ISSN: 1574-1192: ELSEVIER, 2005.

[15] K. Ducatel, M. Bogdanowicz, F. Scapolo, J. Leijten, and J.-C. Burgelman, "Scenarios for ambient intelligence in 2010," tech. rep., IST Advisory Group Report, European Commission, February 2001.

[16] "Embassi, scenario private household." project document phhINP020GRU01, A-PHH working group, April 2000.

[17] C. Röcker, M. D. Janse, N. Portolan, and N. Streitz, "User requirements for intelligent home environments: a scenario-driven approach and empirical cross-cultural study," in *sOc-EUSAI '05: Proceedings of the 2005 joint conference on Smart objects and ambient intelligence*, (New York, NY, USA), pp. 111–116, ACM, 2005.

[18] "Amigo project." [online] <http://www.amigo-project.org>, (Accessed: June, 2008).

[19] I. A. G. Report, "Ambient intelligence: From vision to reality," tech. rep., European Commission, 2003.

[20] T. Heider and C. Reiße, "A survey of ambient intelligence projects regarding sources of strategy for coherent intelligent behavior," in *Towards Ambient Intelligence: Methods for Cooperating Ensembles in Ubiquitous Environments (AIM-CU), as Workshop of the 30th German Conference on Artificial Intelligence (KI-2007)*, September 2007.

[21] T. Heider and T. Kirste, "Architecture considerations for interoperable multi-modal assistant systems," in *Proceedings of the 9th International Workshop on Interactive Systems. Design, Specification, and Verification*, (London, UK), pp. 253–268, Springer-Verlag, June 2002.

BIBLIOGRAPHY

[22] T. Heider and T. Kirste, "Multimodal appliance cooperation based on explicit goals: concepts & potentials," in *sOc-EUSAI '05: Proceedings of the 2005 joint conference on Smart objects and ambient intelligence*, (New York, NY, USA), pp. 271–276, ACM Press, 2005.

[23] T. Heider and T. Kirste, "Supporting goal-based interaction with dynamic intelligent environments," in *Proceedings of the 15th European Conference on Artificial Intelligence Intelligence*, (Lyon, France), pp. 596–600, July 2002.

[24] T. Heider, "Goal-oriented assistance for extended multimedia systems and dynamic technical infrastructures," in *7th IASTED International Conference on Internet and Multimedia Systems and Applications 2003*, (Honolulu, USA), August 2003.

[25] T. Heider, M. Giersich, and T. Kirste, "Resource Optimization in Multi-Display Environments with Distributed GRASP," in *Proceedings of the First International Conference on Ambient Intelligence Developments (AmI.d'06)*, (Sophia Antipolis, France), pp. 60 – 76, Springer, September 19 - 22 2006.

[26] T. Heider and T. Kirste, "Automatic vs. manual multi-display configuration: A study of user performance in a semi-cooperative task setting," in *The 21st BCS HCI Group conference (HCI 2007)*, (Lancaster, UK), September 2007.

[27] T. Heider and T. Kirste, "Evaluating the effect of automatic display management on user performance in a Smart Meeting Room," in *3. Konferenz Mobile und Ubiquitäre Informationssysteme (MMS 2008)*, (München), Feb 26 - 28 2008.

[28] "DynAMITE - "Dynamic Adaptive Multimodal IT Ensembles"." [online] <http://www.dynamite-project.org>, (Accessed: December, 2008).

[29] M. Hellenschmidt and T. Kirste, "A generic topology for ambient intelligence," in *Proc. of the Second European Symposium on Ambient Intelligence (EUSAI 2004)*, (Eindhoven), November 8 – 10.

[30] "PERSONA - "PERceptive Spaces prOmoting iNdependent Aging"." [online] <http://www.aal-persona.org/>, (Accessed: March, 2009).

[31] A. Fides-Valero, M. Freddi, F. Furfari, and M.-R. Tazari, "The persona framework for supporting context-awareness in open distributed systems," in *AmI '08: Proceedings of the European Conference on Ambient Intelligence*, (Berlin, Heidelberg), pp. 91–108, Springer-Verlag, 2008.

[32] M. Hellenschmidt, "Software-Infrastruktur und Entwicklungsumgebung für selbstorganisierende multimediale Ensembles in Ambient-Intelligence-Umgebungen." Dissertation, TU Darmstadt, 2007.

[33] "MuSAMA - "Multimodal Smart Appliance Ensembles for Mobile Applications"." [online] <http://www.informatik.uni-rostock.de/musama.html>, (Accessed: December, 2008).

[34] D. L. Martin, A. J. Cheyer, and D. B. Moran, "The Open Agent Architecture: a framework for building distributed software systems," *Applied Artificial Intelligence*, vol. 13, no. 1/2, pp. 91–128, 1999.

[35] A. S. Rao and M. P. Georgeff, "Modeling rational agents within a bdi-architecture," in *Proceedings of the 2nd International Conference on Principles of Knowledge Representation and Reasoning (KR'91)* (J. Allen, R. Fikes, and E. Sandewall, eds.), pp. 473–484, Morgan Kaufmann publishers Inc.: San Mateo, CA, USA, 1991.

[36] M. Winikoff, L. Padgham, and J. Harland, "Simplifying the development of intelligent agents," in *AI2001: Advances in Artificial Intelligence. 14th Australian Joint Conference on Artificial Intelligence*, pp. 557–568, Springer, LNAI, 2001.

[37] M. Winikoff, L. Padgham, J. Harland, and J. Thangarajah, "Declarative & procedural goals in intelligent agent systems," in *In Proceedings of the Eighth International Conference on Principles of Knowledge Representation and Reasoning (KR2002*, pp. 470–481, 2002.

[38] J. R. Cooperstock, S. S. Fels, W. Buxton, and K. C. Smith, "Reactive environments – throwing away your keyboard and mouse.," *Communications ACM*, vol. 40, pp. 65–73, Sept. 1997.

[39] D. Franklin, J. Budzik, and K. Hammond, "Plan-based interfaces: Keeping track of user tasks and acting to cooperate," in *Intelligent User Interfaces (IUI'2002)*, (San Francisco, California, USA), January 13–16 2002.

[40] B. Brumitt, B. Meyers, J. Krumm, A. Kern, and S. Shafer, "EasyLiving: Technologies for intelligent environments," in *Proc. Handheld and Ubiqitous Computing, 2nd International Symposium*, pp. 12–29, Sep 2000.

[41] M. Mozer, "The neural network house: An environment that adapts to its inhabitants," in *Proc. Am. Assoc. Artificial Intelligence Spring Symp. Intelligent Environments*, (AAAI Press), 1998.

[42] M. H. Coen, "Design principles for intelligent environments," in *15th National Conference on Artificial Intelligence (AAAI'98)*, 1998.

[43] N. Hanssens, A. Kulkarni, R. Tuchida, and T. Horton, "Building agent-based intelligent workspaces," in *ABA Conference Proceedings*, June 2002.

[44] T. Herfet, T. Kirste, and M. Schnaider, "EMBASSI: multimodal assistance for infotainment and service infrastructures," *Computers & Graphics*, vol. 25, no. 4, pp. 581–592, 2001.

[45] R. Wasinger, W. Wahlster, E. Aarts, and J. L. Encarnação, "The anthropomorphized product shelf: Symmetric multimodal interaction with instrumented environments," in *Chapter in: True Visions: The Emergence of Ambient Intelligence*, Springer-Verlag, 2006.

[46] P. Markopoulos, B. E. R. de Ruyter, P. Saini, and A. J. N. van Breemen, "Case study: bringing social intelligence into home dialogue systems.," *Interactions*, vol. 12, no. 4, pp. 37–44, 2005.

[47] B. Johanson, A. Fox, and T. Winograd, "The interactive workspaces project: Experiences with ubiquitous computing rooms," *IEEE Pervasive Computing*, vol. 1, no. 2, pp. 67–74, 2002.

[48] American Association for Artificial Intelligence, "Smart rooms, smart houses & household appliances." [online] <http://www.aaai.org/AITopics/html/rooms.html>, (Accessed: May, 2008).

[49] C. O. H. Jensen, O. H. Jensen, O. H. Jensen, and R. Milner, "Bigraphs and mobile processes (revised)," tech. rep., 2004.

[50] A. van Lamsweerde, "Goal-oriented requirements engineering: A guided tour," in *RE '01: Proceedings of the 5th IEEE International Symposium on Requirements Engineering*, (Washington, DC, USA), p. 249, IEEE Computer Society, 2001.

[51] J. Mylopoulos, L. Chung, and E. Yu, "From object-oriented to goal-oriented requirements analysis," *Commun. ACM*, vol. 42, no. 1, pp. 31–37, 1999.

[52] A. Dardenne, A. V. Lamsweerde, and S. Fickas, "Goal-directed requirements acquisition," in *Science of Computer Programming*, pp. 3–50, 1993.

[53] F. M. Donini, M. Lenzerini, D. Nardi, and A. Schaerf, "Reasoning in description logics," Brewka, G. (ed.), *Foundations of Knowledge Representation*, pp. 191–236, 1996.

[54] Y. Forkl, M. Klarner, B. Ludwig, E. M. B.-U. Service-assistenz, and S. T. German, "Discourse and application modeling for dialogue systems," in *Proc. KI-2001 Workshop on Applications of Description Logics, TU Wien, CEUR Proceedings*, pp. 200–1, 2001.

[55] M. Giersich and T. Kirste, "Effects of Agendas on Model-based Intention Inference of Cooperative Teams," in *Proceedings of CollaborateCom2007 - The 3rd International Conference on Collaborative Computing: Networking, Applications and Worksharing*, (White Plains, NY, USA), IEEE Xplore, November 12 – 15 2007.

[56] T. Sheridan, "Task analysis, task allocation and supervisory control.," in *Handbook of Human-Computer Interaction* (M. Helander, T. Landauer, and V. Prabhu, eds.), pp. 159–173, Amsterdam: Elsevier Science Publishers, 2nd ed., 1998.

[57] H. Wandke, "Assistance in human-machine interaction: a conceptual framework and a proposal for a taxonomy," *Theoretical Issues in Ergonomics Science*, vol. 6, pp. 129–155, March-April 2005.

[58] J. Nitschke and H. Wandke, "Guideas. guidance for developing assistance. humboldt spektrum,," *Humboldt Spektrum*, no. 1, pp. 34 – 38, 2002.

[59] M. Sengpiel, "Mentale modelle zum wohnzimmer der zukunft, ein vergleich verschiedener user interfaces mittels wizard of oz technik. diploma thesis," Master's thesis, FU Berlin, Germany, 2004.

[60] A. A. N. Shirehjini, "A multidimensional classification model for the interaction in reactive media rooms," in *HCI (3)*, pp. 431–439, 2007.

[61] Y. Forkl, B. Ludwig, and K. Bücher, "Dialogue management in the embassi realm - using description logics to reason about ontology concepts," in *Proceedings of IMC2000 (Intelligent Interactive Assistance and Mobile Multimedia Computing)*, (Rostock), November 9 - 10 2000.

[62] M. Giersich and T. Heider, "Team Assistance in Smart Meeting Rooms," in *Ubicomp 2007 Workshop on Embodied Meeting Support: Mobile, Tangible, Senseable Interaction in Smart Environments*, (Innsbruck, Austria), September 16 2007.

[63] B. Brumitt and S. Shafer, "Better living through geometry," *Personal and Ubiquitous Computing*, vol. 5, pp. 42–45, Feb 2001.

[64] M. H. Coen, B. Phillips, N. Warshawsky, L. Weisman, S. Peters, and P. Finin, "Meeting the computational needs of intelligent environments: The metaglue system," in *Proceedings of MANSE'99*, (Dublin, Ireland), 1999.

[65] M. H. Coen, "Building brains for rooms: Designing distributed software agents," in *AAAI/IAAI*, pp. 971–977, 1997.

[66] R. A. Brooks, "A robust layered control system for a mobile robot," pp. 2–27, 1990.

[67] V. Lesser, M. Atighetchi, B. Benyo, B. Horling, A. Raja, R. Vincent, T. Wagner, P. Xuan, and S. X. Zhang, "A Multi-Agent System for Intelligent Environment Control," computer science technical report, University of Massachusetts, January 1999.

[68] V. Lesser, K. Decker, T. Wagner, N. Carver, A. Garvey, B. Horling, D. Neiman, R. Podorozhny, M. NagendraPrasad, A. Raja, R. Vincent, P. Xuan, and X. Zhang, "Evolution of the GPGP/TAEMS Domain-Independent Coordination Framework," *Autonomous Agents and Multi-Agent Systems*, vol. 9, pp. 87–143, July 2004.

[69] S. Russell and P. Norvig, *Artificial Intelligence: A Modern Approach*. Prentice-Hall, Englewood Cliffs, NJ, 2nd edition ed., 2003.

[70] D. Franklin, "Cooperating with people: the intelligent classroom," in *AAAI/IAAI*, pp. 555–560, 1998.

[71] B. Bouchard, S. Giroux, and A. Bouzouane, "A smart home agent for plan recognition..," in *Canadian Conference on AI*, pp. 25–36, 2006.

[72] S. K. Das, D. J. Cook, A. Bhattacharya, E. O. H. III, and T.-Y. Lin, "The role of prediction algorithms in the MavHome smart home architecture," *IEEE Wireless Communications*, vol. 9, pp. 77–84, Dec. 2002.

[73] M. C. Mozer, "Lessons from an adaptive home," *Smart Environments: Technology, Protocols, and Applications*, pp. 273–298, 2005.

[74] E. Tawil and H. Hagras, "An adaptive genetic-based architecture for the on-line coordination of fuzzy embedded agents with multiple objectives and constraints," in *Proceedings of the IEEE International Symposium on Evolving Fuzzy Systems*, (Lake District, UK), pp. 169–175, 2006.

[75] M. Vallée, F. Ramparany, and L. Vercouter, "Flexible composition of smart device services," in *The 2005 International Conference on Pervasive Systems and Computing (PSC-05)*, (Las Vegas, USA), Jun 27-30 2005.

[76] V. Issarny, D. Sacchetti, F. Tartanoglu, F. Sailhan, R. Chibout, N. Levy, and A. Talamona, "Developing ambient intelligence systems: A solution based on web services," *Automated Software Engg.*, vol. 12, no. 1, pp. 101–137, 2005.

[77] U. Küster, B. König-Ries, M. Stern, and M. Klein, "Diane: an integrated approach to automated service discovery, matchmaking and composition," in *WWW '07: Proceedings of the 16th international conference on World Wide Web*, (New York, NY, USA), pp. 1033–1042, ACM Press, 2007.

[78] B. König-Ries, P. Obreiter, and M. Klein, "Effektive und effiziente Dienstsuche und -nutzung in Ad-hoc-Netzen.," tech. rep., Progress report for the second phase of the DIANE-Project withing DFG SPP 1140., March 2006.

[79] J. a. P. Sousa and D. Garlan, "Aura: an architectural framework for user mobility in ubiquitous computing environments," in *Software Architecture: System Design, Development, and Maintenance (Proceedings of the 3rd Working IEEE/IFIP Conference on Software Architecture)* (J. Bosch, M. Gentleman, C. Hofmeister, and J. Kuusela, eds.), pp. 29–43, Kluwer Academic Publishers, 25-31 August 2002.

[80] C. Endres, A. Butz, and A. MacWilliams, "A survey of software infrastructures and frameworks for ubiquitous computing.," *Mobile Information Systems*, vol. 1, no. 1, pp. 41–80, 2005.

[81] C. Endres, "Towards a software architecture for device management in instrumented environments," in *Doctoral Colloquium at Ubicomp, Seattle, Oct. 12-15th 2003. Adjunct Proceedings*, (Seattle), pp. 245–246, 2003.

[82] M. Roman, C. Hess, R. Cerqueira, A. Ranganathan, R. H. Campbell, and K. Nahrstedt, "A middleware infrastructure for active spaces," *IEEE Pervasive Computing*, vol. 01, no. 4, pp. 74–83, 2002.

[83] H. Chen, F. Perich, D. Chakraborty, T. Finin, and A. Joshi, "Intelligent Agents Meet Semantic Web in a Smart Meeting Room," in *Proceedings of the Third International Joint Conference on Autonomous Agents and Multi Agent Systems (AAMAS 2004)*, (New York City, NY), July 2004.

[84] P. R. Cohen and H. J. Levesque, "Teamwork," Tech. Rep. 504, Menlo Park, CA, 1991.

[85] M. Brenner, "Planning for multiagent environments: From individual perceptions to coordinated execution," in *Workshop on Multiagent Planning and Scheduling*, (ICAPS 2005, Monterey, USA), 2005.

BIBLIOGRAPHY

[86] R. C. Eberhart, Y. Shi, and J. Kennedy, *Swarm Intelligence (The Morgan Kaufmann Series in Artificial Intelligence)*. Morgan Kaufmann, March 2001.

[87] D. Servat and A. Drogoul, "Combining amorphous computing and reactive agent-based systems: a paradigm for pervasive intelligence?," in *AAMAS '02: Proceedings of the first international joint conference on Autonomous agents and multiagent systems*, (New York, NY, USA), pp. 441–448, ACM Press, 2002.

[88] P. Maes, "Situated agents can have goals," in *Designing Autonomous Agents* (P. Maes, ed.), pp. 49–70, MIT Press, 1990.

[89] K. Dorer, "Behavior networks for continuous domains using situation-dependent motivations," in *IJCAI*, pp. 1233–1238, 1999.

[90] V. Decugis and J. Ferber, "An extension of Maes' action selection mechanism for animats," in *Proceedings of the fifth international conference on simulation of adaptive behavior on From animals to animats 5*, (Cambridge, MA, USA), pp. 153–158, MIT Press, 1998.

[91] D. Singleton, "An evolvable approach to the Maes action selection mechanism," tech. rep., 2002.

[92] D. Jung and A. Zelinsky, "An architecture for distributed cooperative planning in a behaviour-based multi-robot system," *Journal of Robotics and Autonomous Systems*, vol. 26, pp. 149–174, 1999.

[93] SRI International AI Center, "The Open Agent Architecture." [online] <http://www.ai.sri.com/ oaa/>, (Accessed: June, 2008).

[94] "Corba: Common object request broker architecture, the object management group (omg)." [online] <http://www.omg.org>, (Accessed: December, 2008).

[95] "Kqml - the knowledge query and manipulation language." [online] <http://www.cs.umbc.edu/kqml>, (Accessed: December, 2008).

[96] "Fipa - foundation for intelligent physical agents." [online] <http://www.fipa.org/repository/standardspecs.html>, (Accessed: December, 2008).

[97] S. Seneff, E. Hurley, R. Lau, C. Pao, P. Schmid, and V. Zue, "Galaxy-II: A Reference Architecture for Conversational System Development," in *ICSLP 98*, (Sydney, Australia), Nov. 1998.

[98] MITRE corporation, "Galaxy communicator." [online] <http://groups.csail.mit.edu/sls/technologies/galaxy.shtml>, (Accessed: December, 2008).

[99] G. D. Abowd and K. N. Truong, "Inca: A software infrastructure to facilitate the construction and evolution of ubiquitous capture & access applications," 2004.

[100] P. Tandler, "Software infrastructure for ubiquitous computing environments: Supporting synchronous collaboration with heterogeneous devices," in *UbiComp '01: Proceedings of the 3rd international conference on Ubiquitous Computing*, (London, UK), pp. 96–115, Springer-Verlag, 2001.

[101] T. Herfet and T. Kirste, "Embassi – multimodal assistance for infotainment and service infrastructures.," in *Proc. International Status Conference Lead Projects Human-Computer-Interaction*, (Saarbrücken), pp. 35–44, BMBF, October 26-27 2001.

[102] J. D. Foley and A. Van Dam, *Fundamentals of interactive computer graphics*. Reading, MA: Addison-Wesley, 1982.

[103] D. Smith, J. Frank, and A. Jonsson, "Bridging the Gap Between Planning and Scheduling," *Knowledge Engineering Review*, vol. 15, no. 1, 2000.

[104] L. Bass, R. Little, R. Pellegrino, S. Reed, S. Seacord, S. Sheppard, and M. Szezur, "The ARCH model: Seeheim revisitied," in *Papers presented at the User Interface Developers' Workshop*, (Seeheim, Germany), 1991.

[105] C. Kolski and E. Le Strugeon, "A Review of Intelligent Human-Machine Interfaces in the Light of the ARCH Model," *International Journal of Human-Computer Interaction*, vol. 10, no. 3, pp. 193–231, 1998.

[106] T. Kirste, "A communication model for data-flow based distributed agent systems," Tech. Rep. 01i0011-FIGDR, Fraunhofer IGD Rostock, Dec. 2001.

[107] D. Gelernter, *Mirror Worlds*. New York: Oxford University Press, 1993.

[108] D. G. Schwartz, *Cooperating Heterogeneous Systems*. Dordrecht: Kluwer Academic Publishers, 1995.

[109] S. P. Jones and J. H. (editors), "Haskell 98: A non-strict, purely functional language," tech. rep., February 1999. [online] <http://haskell.org/definition/haskell98-report.pdf>, (Accessed: December, 2008).

BIBLIOGRAPHY

[110] HAVi, Inc., "The HAVi Specification – Specification of the Home Audio/Video Interoperability (HAVi) Architecture – Version 1.1." [online] <www.havi.org>, (Accessed: June, 2008), May 2001.

[111] Sun Microsystems, Inc., "Jini Technology Core Platform Specification – Version 1.1." www.jini.org, Oct. 2000.

[112] W. Clocksin and S. Mellish, "Programming in prolog," *Springer*, 1987.

[113] D. A. Turner, "Miranda: A non-strict functional language with polymorphic types," in *Proceedings IFIP International Conference on Functional Programming Languages and Computer Architectures, Nancy, France* (J. Jouannaud, ed.), vol. 201, pp. 1–16, Sept. 1985.

[114] T. Kirste, "A proposal for an opinion-based agent selection algorithm," Tech Report Technical Report 02i021-FIGDR, Fraunhofer Institute for Computer Graphics Rostock, Germany, 2002.

[115] E. Guttman, "Autoconfiguration for ip networking: Enabling local communication," *IEEE Internet Computing*, vol. 5, pp. 81–86, 2001.

[116] N. J. Nilsson, *Principles of artificial intelligence*. San Francisco, CA, USA: Morgan Kaufmann Publishers Inc., 1980.

[117] D. Nau and M. Ghallab, "Measuring the performance of automated planning systems." Performance Metrics for Intelligent Systems Workshop (PerMIS '04), 2004.

[118] D. Nau, M. Ghallab, and P. Traverso, *Automated Planning: Theory & Practice*. San Francisco, CA, USA: Morgan Kaufmann Publishers Inc., 2004.

[119] R. E. Fikes and N. J. Nilsson, "Strips: A new approach to the application of theorem proving to problem solving," *Artificial Intelligence*, vol. 2, pp. 189–208, 1971.

[120] E. Pednault, "ADL and the State-Transition Model of Action," *J. Logic Computat.*, vol. 4, no. 5, pp. 467–512, 1994.

[121] A. Barrett, D. Christianson, M. Friedman, C. Kwok, K. Golden, S. Penberthy, Y. Sun, and D. Weld, "UCPOP Users Manual," Tech. Rep. 93-09-06d, University of Washington, Dept. of Computer Science and Engineering, Nov. 1995.

[122] J. Blythe, J. G. Carbonell, O. Etzioni, Y. Gil, R. Joseph, D. Kahn, C. Knoblock, S. Minton, A. Perez, S. Reilly, M. Veloso, and X. Wang, "Prodigy 4.0: The manual and tutorial," tech. rep., Pittsburgh, PA, USA, 1992.

[123] K. Erol, J. Hendler, and D. S. Nau, "Umcp: A sound and complete procedure for hierarchical task-network planning," pp. 249–254, 1994.

[124] J. Hoffmann, "Extending FF to numerical state variables," in *Proceedings of the 15th European Conference on Artificial Intelligence (ECAI-02)*, (Lyon, France), pp. 571–575, July 2002.

[125] C. Bäckström, "Computational aspects of reordering plans," *Journal of Artificial Intelligence Research*, vol. 9, pp. 99–137, 1998.

[126] AIPS-98 Planning Competition Committee, "PDDL – The Planning Domain Definition Language," Tech Report CVC TR-98-003/DCS TR-1165, Yale Center for Computanional Vision and Control, Oct. 1998.

[127] M. Fox and D. Long, "PDDL2.1: An Extension to PDDL for Expressing Temporal Planning Domains," tech. rep., University of Durham, UK, Oct. 2001.

[128] S. Edelkamp and J. Hoffmann, "Pddl2.2: The language for the classical part of the 4th international planning competition," in *Proceedings of the 4th International Planning Competition (IPC'04)*, January 2004.

[129] A. Gerevini and D. Long, "Plan constraints and preferences in pddl3 - the language of the fifth international planning competition," tech. rep., University of Brescia, Italy, 2005.

[130] D. E. Wilkins, *Practical planning: extending the classical AI planning paradigm*. San Francisco, CA, USA: Morgan Kaufmann Publishers Inc., 1988.

[131] "IPC 2002, International Planning Competition." [online] <http://planning.cis.strath.ac.uk/competition/>, (Accessed: September, 2008).

[132] A. Gerevini, I. Serina, A. Saetti, and S. Spinoni, "Local search techniques for temporal planning in lpg," in *ICAPS*, pp. 62–72, 2003.

[133] S. Edelkamp, "Taming numbers and durations in the model checking integrated planning system," *Journal of Artificial Intelligence Research*, vol. 20, pp. 195–238, 2003.

[134] K. Erol, J. Hendler, and D. S. Nau, "Complexity results for htn planning," in *Annals of Mathematics and Artificial Intelligence*, pp. 69–93, 1996.

BIBLIOGRAPHY

[135] D. Wu, B. Parsia, E. Sirin, J. Hendler, and D. Nau, "Automating daml-s web services composition using shop2," in *In Proceedings of 2nd International Semantic Web Conference (ISWC2003, 2003.*

[136] D. Nau, O. Ilghami, U. Kuter, J. W. Murdock, D. Wu, and F. Yaman, "Shop2: An htn planning system," *Journal of Artificial Intelligence Research*, vol. 20, pp. 379–404, 2003.

[137] "OWL Web Ontology Language, Use Cases and Requirements, W3C Recommendation," 10 February 2004. [online] <http://www.w3.org/TR/webont-req/>, (Accessed: December, 2008).

[138] P. Wang, Z. Jin, and L. Liu, "On constructing environment ontology for semantic web services," in *Knowledge Science, Engineering and Management, First International Conference, KSEM 2006, Guilin, China, August 5-8, 2006*, Lecture Notes in Computer Science, pp. 490–503, Springer, 2006.

[139] "Val, the automatic validation tool for pddl, including pddl3 and pddl+." [online] http://planning.cis.strath.ac.uk/VAL/, (Accessed: June, 2008).

[140] M. Helmert, "New complexity results for classical planning benchmarks," in *Proceedings of ICAPS 2006*, pp. 52–61, 2006.

[141] T. L. Mccluskey, "Pddl: A language with a purpose?," in *Proceedings of the ICAPS-03 workshop on PDDL, International Conference on Automated Planning and Scheduling (ICAPS03)*, 2003.

[142] F. Amigoni, N. Gatti, C. Pinciroli, and M. Roveri, "What planner for ambient intelligent applications?," *IEEE Transactions on Systems, Man and Cybernetics - Part A*, vol. 35, no. 1, pp. 7–21, 2005.

[143] U. Saif, H. Pham, J. M. Paluska, J. Waterman, C. Terman, and S. War, "A case for goal-oriented programming semantics," (Seattle, USA), Oct 2003.

[144] H. Lieberman and J. Espinosa, "A goal-oriented interface to consumer electronics using planning and commonsense reasoning," in *IUI '06: Proceedings of the 11th international conference on Intelligent user interfaces*, (New York, NY, USA), pp. 226–233, ACM Press, 2006.

[145] C. Reisse and T. Kirste, "A Distributed Action Selection Mechanism for Device Cooperation in Smart Environments." Proceedings of Intelligent Environments 2008, Seattle, USA, July 21-22, 2008.

191

[146] R. Want, G. Borriello, T. Pering, and K. I. Farkas, "Disappearing hardware," *IEEE Pervasive Computing*, vol. 1, no. 1, pp. 36–47, 2002.

[147] A. Waibel, T. Schultz, M. Bett, M. Denecke, R. Malkin, I. Rogina, R. Stiefelhagen, and J. Yang, "Smart: the smart meeting room task at isl," in *in Acoustics, Speech, and Signal Processing (ICASSP '03). 2003: IEEE*, pp. 752–755, 2003.

[148] N. Charif and J. McKenna, "Tracking the activity of participants in a meeting," *Mach. Vision Appl.*, vol. 17, no. 2, pp. 83–93, 2006.

[149] M. Weiser, "Some computer science issues in ubiquitous computing," *Communications of the ACM*, vol. 36, pp. 75–84, July 1993.

[150] A. Ferscha, G. Kortuem, and A. Krüger, "Workshop on ubiquitous display environments," in *Proc. Ubicomp 2004*, (Nottingham, England), Sep 7 2004.

[151] M. B. et al., "Usable ubiquitous computing in next generation conference rooms: design, architecture and evaluation," in *Ubicomp Workshop 2006*, (Newport Beach, CA, USA), Sep 17 2006.

[152] P. Chiu, Q. Liu, J. S. Boreczky, J. Foote, D. Kimber, S. Lertsithichai, and C. Liao, "Manipulating and annotating slides in a multi-display environment.," in *Human-Computer Interaction INTERACT '03: IFIP TC13 International Conference on Human-Computer Interaction*, 2003.

[153] B. Johanson, G. Hutchins, T. Winograd, and M. Stone, "Pointright: Experience with flexible input redirection in interactive workspaces," in *Proc. ACM Conference on User Interface and Software Technology (UIST2002)*, (Paris, France), pp. 227–234, 2002.

[154] M. R. Morris, K. Ryall, C. Shen, C. Forlines, and F. Vernier, "Beyond social protocols: multi-user coordination policies for co-located groupware," in *CSCW '04: Proceedings of the 2004 ACM conference on Computer supported cooperative work*, (New York, NY, USA), pp. 262–265, ACM Press, 2004.

[155] R. Badi, S. Bae, J. M. Moore, K. Meintanis, A. Zacchi, H. Hsieh, F. Shipman, and C. C. Marshall, "Recognizing user interest and document value from reading and organizing activities in document triage," in *IUI '06: Proceedings of the 11th international conference on Intelligent user interfaces*, (New York, NY, USA), pp. 218–225, ACM, 2006.

[156] M. Claypool, P. Le, M. Waseda, and D. Brown, "Implicit interest indicators," in *In Intelligent User Interfaces*, pp. 33–40, 2001.

BIBLIOGRAPHY

[157] C. Pinhanez, "The Everywhere Displays Projector: A Device to Create Ubiquitous Graphical Interfaces," in *Proc. of Ubiquitous Computing 2001 (Ubicomp'01)*, (Atlanta, USA), Sept. 2001.

[158] D. Molyneaux and G. Kortuem, "Ubiquitous displays in dynamic environments: Issues and opportunities," in *Ubicomp 2004 Workshop on Ubiquitous Display Environments* [150].

[159] T. A. Feo and M. G. C. Resende, "Greedy randomized adaptive search procedures," *Journal of Global Optimization*, vol. 6, pp. 109–133, 1995.

[160] C. Blum and A. Roli, "Metaheuristics in combinatorial optimization: Overview and conceptual comparison," *ACM Computing Surveys*, vol. 35, pp. 268–308, September 2003.

[161] P. Modi, W. Shen, M. Tambe, and M. Yokoo, "Adopt: Asynchronous distributed constraint optimization with quality guarantees.," in *Artificial Intelligence Journal(AIJ)*, vol. 161, pp. 149–180, 2005.

[162] G. M. P. O'Hare and N. R. Jennings, eds., *Foundations of distributed artificial intelligence*. New York, NY, USA: John Wiley & Sons, Inc., 1996.

[163] E. H. Durfee, "Distributed problem solving and planning," pp. 118–149, 2001.

[164] M. Wooldridge, *Introduction to MultiAgent Systems*. John Wiley & Sons, June 2002.

[165] M. Yokoo, E. H. Durfee, T. Ishida, and K. Kuwabara, "The distributed constraint satisfaction problem: Formalization and algorithms," *IEEE Transactions on Knowledge and Data Engineering*, vol. 10, no. 5, pp. 673–685, 1998.

[166] T. Koopmans and M. Beckman, "Assignment problems and the location of economic activities.," *Econometric 25*, pp. 53–76, 1957.

[167] S. Sahni and T. Gonzalez, "P-complete approximation problems," *J. ACM*, vol. 23, no. 3, pp. 555–565, 1976.

[168] P. M. Pardalos, F. Rendl, and H. Wolkowicz, "The quadratic assignment problem: A survey and recent developments," in *In Proceedings of the DIMACS Workshop on Quadratic Assignment Problems, volume 16 of DIMACS Series in Discrete Mathematics and Theoretical Computer Science*, pp. 1–42, American Mathematical Society, 1994.

[169] C. W. Commander, "A survey of the quadratic assignment problem, with applications," *Morehead Electronic Journal of Applicable Mathematics*, 2005.

[170] L. S. Pitsoulis and M. G. C. Resende, "Greedy randomized adaptive search procedures," in *Handbook of Applied Optimization* (P. M. Pardalos and M. G. C. Resende, eds.), pp. 168–183, Oxford University Press, 2002.

[171] P. Festa, P. Pardalos, M. Resende, and C. Ribeiro, "Randomized heuristics for the max-cut problem," 2002.

[172] L. de Assumpcao Drummond, L. Vianna, M. da Silva, and L. Ochi, "Distributed parallel metaheuristics based on grasp and vns for solving the traveling purchaser problem," in *ICPADS '02: Proceedings of the 9th International Conference on Parallel and Distributed Systems*, (Washington, DC, USA), p. 257, IEEE Computer Society, 2002.

[173] R. Schwartz and S. Kraus, "Bidding mechanisms for data allocation in multi-agent environments," in *Agent Theories, Architectures, and Languages*, pp. 61–75, 1997.

[174] S. Kraus, *Strategic Negotiation in Multiagent Environments*. MIT Press, 2001.

[175] R. Grube, "Verteilte Zuordnung von Informationen zu Darstellungsflächen im Kontext eines Smart Meeting Rooms." Studienarbeit, 2006.

[176] W. Vickrey, "Counterspeculation, auctions, and competitive sealed tenders," *The Journal of Finance*, vol. 16, no. 1, pp. 8–37, 1961.

[177] S. Carter and J. Mankoff, "Challenges for ubicomp evaluation," Tech. Rep. UCB/CSD-04-1331, EECS Department, University of California, Berkeley, Jun 2004.

[178] S. Consolvo, L. Arnstein, and B. R. Franza, "User study techniques in the design and evaluation of a ubicomp environment," in *UbiComp '02: Proceedings of the 4th international conference on Ubiquitous Computing*, (London, UK), pp. 73–90, Springer-Verlag, 2002.

[179] J. Scholtz and S. Consolvo, "Toward a framework for evaluating ubiquitous computing applications," *IEEE Pervasive Computing*, vol. 3, pp. 82–88, April 2004.

[180] J. Mankoff, A. K. Dey, G. Hsieh, J. Kientz, S. Lederer, and M. Ames, "Heuristic evaluation of ambient displays," in *CHI '03: Proceedings of the SIGCHI conference on Human factors in computing systems*, (New York, NY, USA), pp. 169–176, ACM, 2003.

[181] F. D. Davis, "Perceived usefulness, perceived ease of use, and user acceptance of information technology," vol. 13:3, pp. 319–340, MIS Quarterly, Sep 1989.

[182] L. Fahrmeir, R. Künstler, I. Pigeot, and G. Tutz, *Statistik*. Berlin: Springer, 6. überarb. a. ed., 2007.

Appendix A

AI Planning Documents

A.1 Example operator file

```
; generated by module Planner

;;;;;;;;;;;;;;;;;;;;;;;;;;;;;;;;;;;;;;;;;;;;;;;;;;;;;;;;;;;;
;;; Embassi domain
;;;;;;;;;;;;;;;;;;;;;;;;;;;;;;;;;;;;;;;;;;;;;;;;;;;;;;;;;;;;

(define (domain embassi-domain)

(:requirements :strips :equality :fluents :typing :adl :universal-preconditions )

(:types device string)

(:predicates (IMAGEVIEWER ?x) (RENDERING ?x) (IMAGEZOOMEDIN) (IMAGEZOOMEDOUT)
 (ZOOMEDIN ?x) (ZOOMEDOUT ?x) (IMAGEHIDDEN) (AUDIOPLAYER ?x)
 (AUDIOMIXER ?x) (INCREASEDVOLUME) (DECREASEDVOLUME)
 (CURRENTMIXERCHANNEL ?x)
 (Opened ?x) (Closed ?x) (TurnedOn ?x) (TurnedOff ?x)
 (SETDIMMER ?x) (DIMMERGOALBRIGHTNESS ?x) (STOPRENDERING)
 (ALITTLEBRIGHTER ?x) (ALITTLEDARKER ?x)(ALOTBRIGHTER ?x)
 (ALOTDARKER ?x) (AVLocationIdValue ?x ?y)
 (RenderAudio) (warmer) (cooler) (brighter) (darker)
 (higher-ambient_brightness) (calc) (open ?x - device)
 (shutter ?x - device) (lamp ?x - device) (eib-dimmer ?x - device)
 (ventilator ?x - device) (on ?x - device) (sony-xmp3 ?x - device)
 (AVProgramm ?x) (hasFileID ?x) (hasNoFile ?x) (playing ?x))

(:functions (Costs) (percent ?x))


(:action SON-MP3-query-PREP
:parameters (?d - device ?AVProg)
:precondition (and (sony-xmp3 ?d) (AVProgramm ?AVProg)
                (not (hasFileID ?d)) (not (hasNoFile ?d)))
:effect (RenderAudio))

(:action SON-MP3-Play
:parameters (?d - device ?fileID)
:precondition (and (not (playing ?d)) (sony-xmp3 ?d)
                (hasFileID ?d) (AVLocationIdValue ?d ?fileID))
:effect (and (RenderAudio) (playing ?d)))

(:action SON-MP3-Stop
```

i

```
    :parameters (?d - device)
    :precondition (and (playing ?d) (sony-xmp3 ?d))
    :effect (and (STOPRENDERING) (not (playing ?d))))

(:action LOE-EIB-ShutterUp
    :parameters (?s - device)
    :precondition (and (not (open ?s)) (shutter ?s) (not (Closed ?s)))
    :effect (and (Opened ?s) (open ?s) (increase (costs) 19) (brighter)))

(:action LOE-EIB-ShutterDown
    :parameters (?s - device)
    :precondition (and (open ?s) (shutter ?s) (not (Opened ?s)))
    :effect (and (Closed ?s) (not (open ?s)) (increase (costs) 21) (darker)))

(:action LOE-VENTILATOR-SWITCHON
    :parameters (?v - device)
    :precondition (and (not (on ?v)) (ventilator ?v) (not (TurnedOff ?v)))
    :effect (and (TurnedOn ?v) (on ?v) (increase (costs) 1) (cooler)))

(:action LOE-VENTILATOR-SWITCHOFF
    :parameters (?v - device)
    :precondition (and (on ?v) (ventilator ?v) (not (TurnedOn ?v)))
    :effect (and (TurnedOff ?v) (not (on ?v)) (increase (costs) 1) (warmer)))

(:action LOE-LAMP-SwitchOff
    :parameters (?lamp - device)
    :precondition (and (on ?lamp) (lamp ?lamp) (not (TurnedOn ?lamp)))
    :effect (and (TurnedOff ?lamp) (not (on ?lamp)) (darker) (increase (costs) 20)))

(:action LOE-LAMP-SwitchOn
    :parameters (?lamp - device)
    :precondition (and (not (on ?lamp)) (lamp ?lamp) (not (TurnedOff ?lamp)))
    :effect (and (TurnedOn ?lamp) (on ?lamp) (brighter) (increase (costs) 20)))

(:action LOE-LAMP-ALITTLEBRIGHTER
:parameters (?dimmer - device)
:precondition (and (lamp ?dimmer) (or (= (percent ?dimmer) 0)
            (> (percent ?dimmer) 0)) (< (percent ?dimmer) 100))
:effect (and (increase (costs) 5)(ALITTLEBRIGHTER ?dimmer)))

(:action LOE-LAMP-ALOTBRIGHTER
:parameters (?dimmer - device)
:precondition (and (lamp ?dimmer) (or (= (percent ?dimmer) 0)
            (> (percent ?dimmer) 0)) (< (percent ?dimmer) 100))
:effect (and (increase (costs) 10) (ALOTBRIGHTER ?dimmer)))

(:action LOE-LAMP-ALITTLEDARKER
:parameters (?dimmer - device)
:precondition (and (lamp ?dimmer) (> (percent ?dimmer) 5))
:effect (and (increase (costs) 5) (ALITTLEDARKER ?dimmer)))

(:action LOE-LAMP-ALOTDARKER
:parameters (?dimmer - device)
:precondition (and (lamp ?dimmer) (> (percent ?dimmer) 5))
:effect (and (increase (costs) 10) (ALOTDARKER ?dimmer)))

(:action LOE-LAMP-DIMABSOLUTE
:parameters (?dimmer - device ?val)
:precondition (and (DIMMERGOALBRIGHTNESS ?val)
         (or (= (percent ?dimmer) 0) (> (percent ?dimmer)0)))
:effect (and (increase (costs) 10) (SETDIMMER ?dimmer)))

(:action IGD-IMAGEVIEWER-HIDE
:parameters (?viewer - device)
:precondition (and (IMAGEVIEWER ?viewer) (RENDERING ?viewer))
:effect (and (increase (costs) 10) (IMAGEHIDDEN) (STOPRENDERING)))

(:action IGD-IMAGEVIEWER-ZOOMIN
:parameters (?viewer - device)
:precondition (and (IMAGEVIEWER ?viewer) (RENDERING ?viewer))
```

AI Planning Documents

```
:effect (and (increase (costs) 10) (ZOOMEDIN ?viewer) (IMAGEZOOMEDIN)))

(:action IGD-IMAGEVIEWER-ZOOMOUT
:parameters (?viewer - device)
:precondition (and (IMAGEVIEWER ?viewer) (RENDERING ?viewer))
:effect (and (increase (costs) 10) (ZOOMEDOUT ?viewer) (IMAGEZOOMEDOUT)))

(:action IGD-MP3-STOP
:parameters (?player - device)
:precondition (and (AUDIOPLAYER ?player) (RENDERING ?player))
:effect (and (STOPRENDERING) (not (RENDERING ?player))))

(:action IGD-AMIXER-INCREASEVOLUME
:parameters (?mixer - device ?channel)
:precondition (and (CURRENTMIXERCHANNEL ?channel) (AUDIOMIXER ?mixer))
:effect (INCREASEDVOLUME))

(:action IGD-AMIXER-DECREASEVOLUME
:parameters (?mixer - device ?channel)
:precondition (and (CURRENTMIXERCHANNEL ?channel) (AUDIOMIXER ?mixer))
:effect (DECREASEDVOLUME))

)
```

A.2   Environment Ontology extract

```xml
<?xml version='1.0' encoding='ISO-8859-1'?>
<!--DAML+OIL Language, version 03/2001, generated by OntoEdit v2.0, ontoprise GmbH-->
<rdf:RDF xmlns:rdf="http://www.w3.org/1999/02/22-rdf-syntax-ns#"
xmlns:rdfs="http://www.w3.org/2000/01/rdf-schema#"
xmlns:daml="http://www.daml.org/2001/03/daml+oil#"
xmlns="http://www.embassi.de/ontology#">

    <daml:Ontology rdf:about="">
        <daml:versionInfo>
            $ http://www.embassi.de/ontology $
        </daml:versionInfo>
        <rdfs:comment>
            An ontology created by OntoEdit
        </rdfs:comment>
        <daml:imports rdf:resource="http://www.daml.org/2001/03/daml+oil"/>
    </daml:Ontology>
    <rdfs:Class rdf:ID="environmentState">
        <rdfs:comment xml:lang="de">
            Variablen der Umgebungszustaende.
            Version 0.5
        </rdfs:comment>
    </rdfs:Class>

    <rdfs:Class rdf:ID="setOfPerceivableMedia">
        <rdfs:subClassOf rdf:resource="#environmentState"/>
    </rdfs:Class>

    <rdfs:Class rdf:ID="setOfRenderedMedia">
        <rdfs:subClassOf rdf:resource="#environmentState"/>
    </rdfs:Class>

    <rdfs:Class rdf:ID="ambientBrightness">
        <rdfs:subClassOf rdf:resource="#environmentState"/>
        <rdfs:comment xml:lang="de">
            Helligkeit im Raum
        </rdfs:comment>
    </rdfs:Class>

    <rdfs:Class rdf:ID="ambientNoise">
        <rdfs:subClassOf rdf:resource="#environmentState"/>
```

```xml
        <rdfs:comment xml:lang="de">
            Umgebungslautstaerke;
            (Summe aller Geraeusche)
        </rdfs:comment>
</rdfs:Class>

<rdfs:Class rdf:ID="ambientTemperature">
    <rdfs:subClassOf rdf:resource="#environmentState"/>
    <rdfs:comment xml:lang="de">
        Raumtemperatur
    </rdfs:comment>
</rdfs:Class>

<rdfs:Class rdf:ID="setOfLocalMedia">
    <rdfs:subClassOf rdf:resource="#environmentState"/>
</rdfs:Class>

<rdfs:Class rdf:ID="setOfAvailableDevices">
    <rdfs:subClassOf rdf:resource="#environmentState"/>
</rdfs:Class>

<rdfs:Class rdf:ID="consumedResources">
    <rdfs:subClassOf rdf:resource="#environmentState"/>
</rdfs:Class>

<rdfs:Class rdf:ID="mediumQuality">
    <rdfs:subClassOf rdf:resource="#environmentState"/>
    <rdfs:comment xml:lang="de">
        Technische Qualitaet des Medium.
    </rdfs:comment>
</rdfs:Class>

<rdfs:Class rdf:ID="renderedMediumQuality">
    <rdfs:subClassOf rdf:resource="#environmentState"/>
</rdfs:Class>

<rdfs:Class rdf:ID="percievableMediumQuality">
    <rdfs:subClassOf rdf:resource="#environmentState"/>
    <rdfs:comment xml:lang="de">
        Theoretische wahrnehmbare Qualitaet der Wiedergabe eines Mediums.
    </rdfs:comment>
</rdfs:Class>

<rdfs:Class rdf:ID="percievedMediumQuality">
    <rdfs:subClassOf rdf:resource="#environmentState"/>
    <rdfs:comment xml:lang="de">
        Tatsaechliche Qualitaet der Wahrnehmung eines Mediums. Z.B. der Fernseher steht 5m entfernt.
    </rdfs:comment>
</rdfs:Class>

<rdfs:Class rdf:ID="userLocation">
    <rdfs:subClassOf rdf:resource="#environmentState"/>
    <rdfs:comment xml:lang="de">
        Aufenthaltsort des Nutzers.
    </rdfs:comment>
</rdfs:Class>

<rdfs:Class rdf:ID="Audio">
    <rdfs:subClassOf rdf:resource="#environmentState"/>
</rdfs:Class>

<rdfs:Class rdf:ID="balance">
    <rdfs:subClassOf rdf:resource="#Audio"/>
    <rdfs:comment xml:lang="de">
        A-B
    </rdfs:comment>
</rdfs:Class>

<rdfs:Class rdf:ID="volume">
    <rdfs:subClassOf rdf:resource="#Audio"/>
```

```xml
        <rdfs:comment xml:lang="de">
            Audio Lautst0rke
        </rdfs:comment>
    </rdfs:Class>

    <rdfs:Class rdf:ID="equalizer">
        <rdfs:subClassOf rdf:resource="#Audio"/>
        <rdfs:comment xml:lang="de">
            L(f)
        </rdfs:comment>
    </rdfs:Class>

    <rdfs:Class rdf:ID="renderMode">
        <rdfs:subClassOf rdf:resource="#environmentState"/>
        <rdfs:comment xml:lang="de">
            Mode der Wiedergabe (Audio, Video, etc.)
        </rdfs:comment>
    </rdfs:Class>

    <rdfs:Class rdf:ID="ambientDraught">
        <rdfs:subClassOf rdf:resource="#environmentState"/>
        <rdfs:comment xml:lang="de">
            Variable fuer Zugluft.
            Verursacht z.B. durch Ventilator.
        </rdfs:comment>
    </rdfs:Class>

    <rdfs:Class rdf:ID="renderLocation">
        <rdfs:subClassOf rdf:resource="#environmentState"/>
        <rdfs:comment xml:lang="de">
            Ort der Wiedergabe.
        </rdfs:comment>
    </rdfs:Class>

    <rdfs:Class rdf:ID="sourceMediumQuality">
        <rdfs:subClassOf rdf:resource="#environmentState"/>
    </rdfs:Class>

    <rdfs:Class rdf:ID="ambientHumidity">
        <rdfs:subClassOf rdf:resource="#environmentState"/>
    </rdfs:Class>

    <rdf:Property rdf:ID="RootRelation"/>

    <rdf:Property rdf:ID="hasEnvironmentState"/>

</rdf:RDF>
```

A.3 Dynamic Strategy Planning

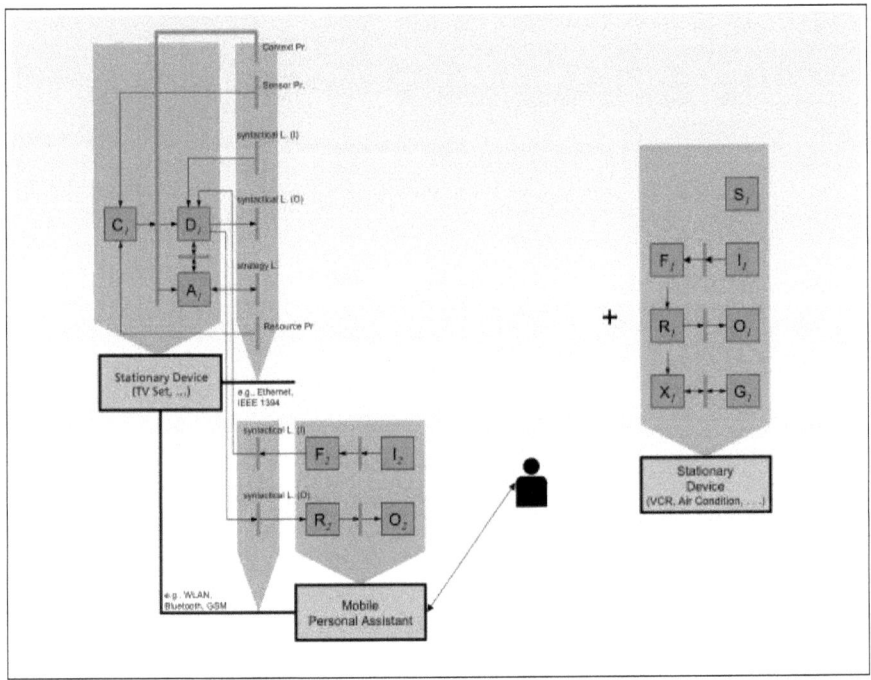

Figure A.1: A new device is added to the ensemble.

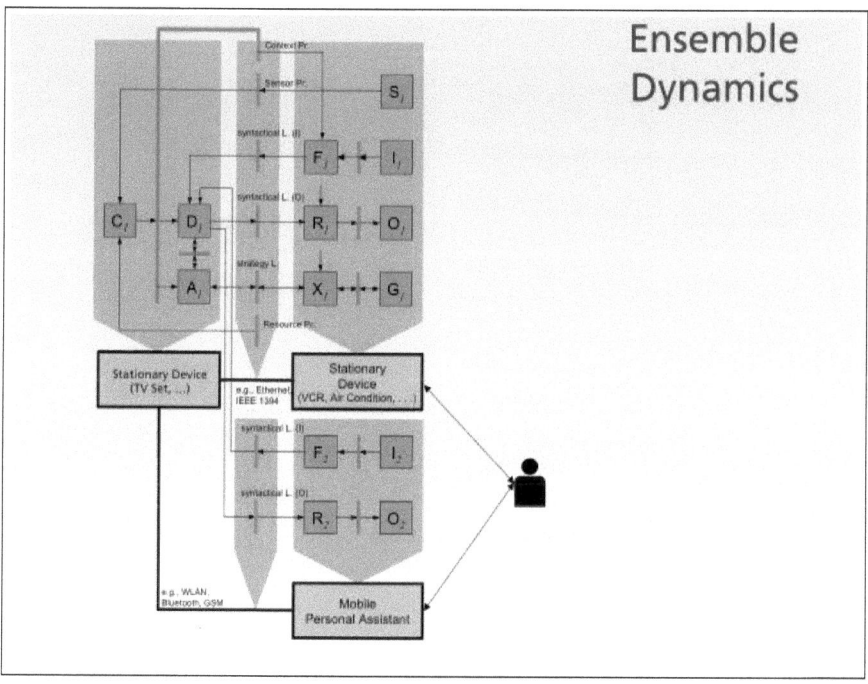

Figure A.2: The new device joins the ensemble by connecting to the defined interfaces within the topology of the architecture.

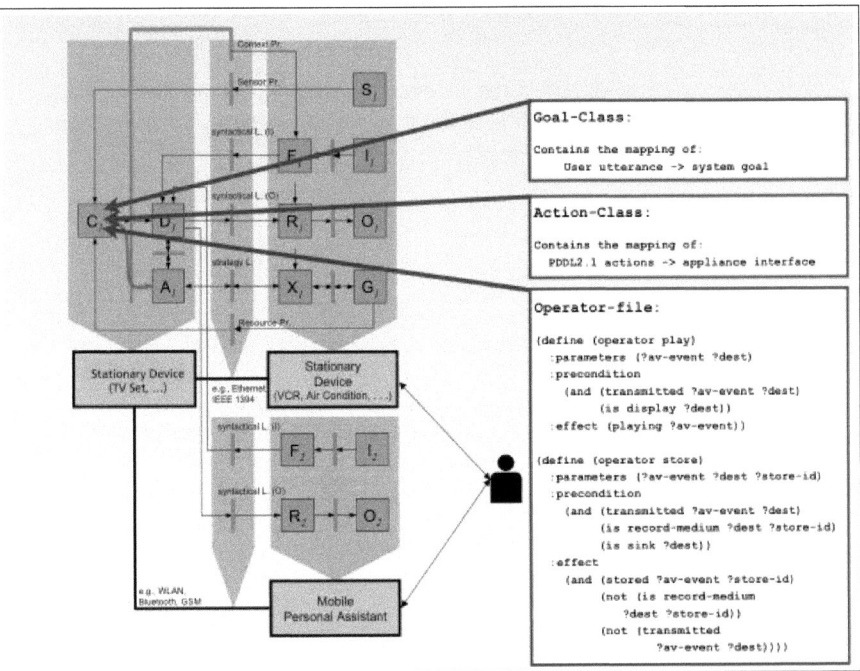

Figure A.3: The new device gives a description of its capabilities that is the basis for a seamless integration in the ensemble.

AI Planning Documents

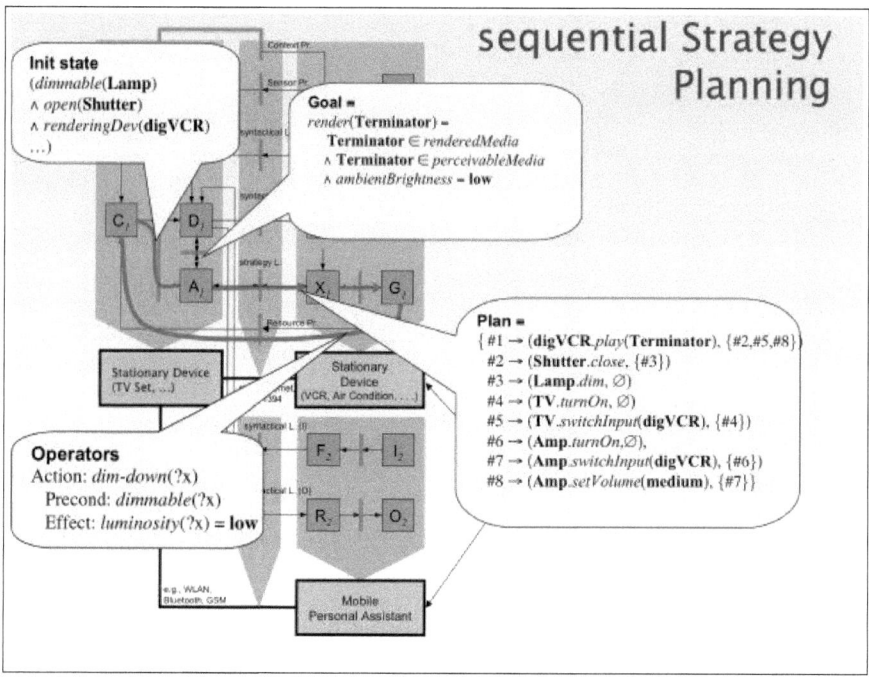

Figure A.4: With the description (operators) of all connected devices, the planning component is able to generate device comprehensive strategies that fulfill the goal of the user.

ix

Appendix B

Test rooms for optimization algorithms

On the next pages the test room configurations are displayed, that were used to test the optimization strategies of Section 6.7. The test rooms were defined as a xml-structure and were visualized by a developed testing application for validity checking only. That is why it is only a simple graphical representation.

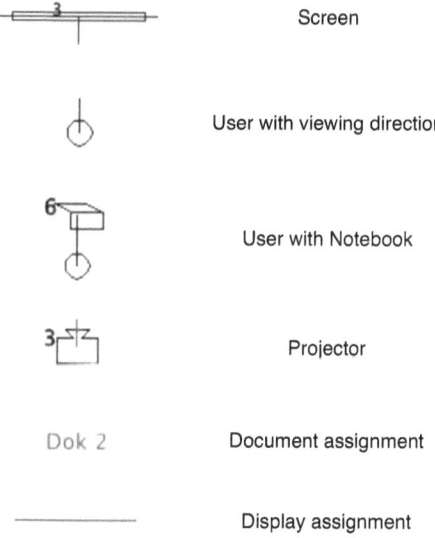

Figure B.1: Keys for the testroom pictures

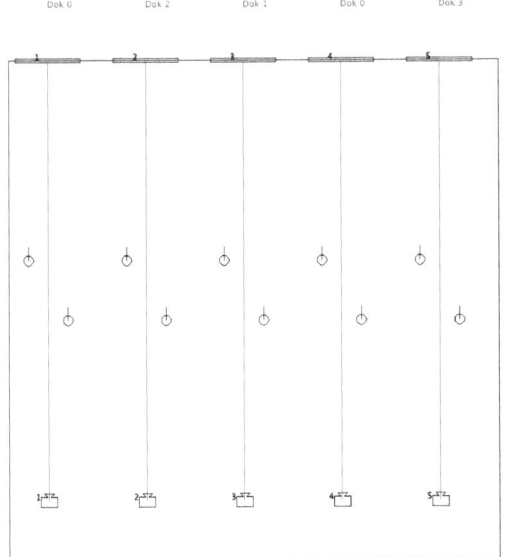

Figure B.2: Testroom 1

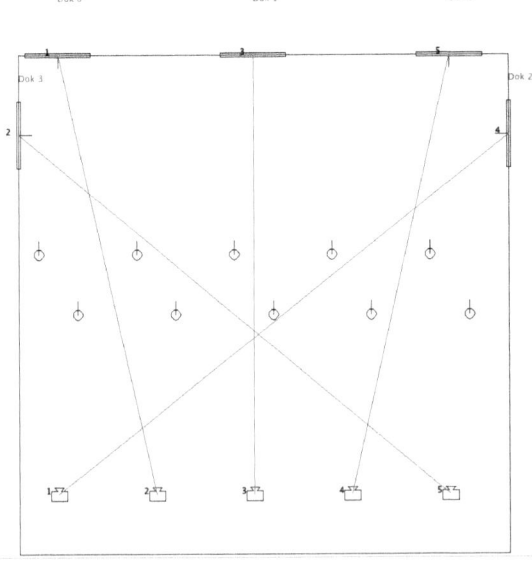

Figure B.3: Testroom 2

Test rooms for optimization algorithms

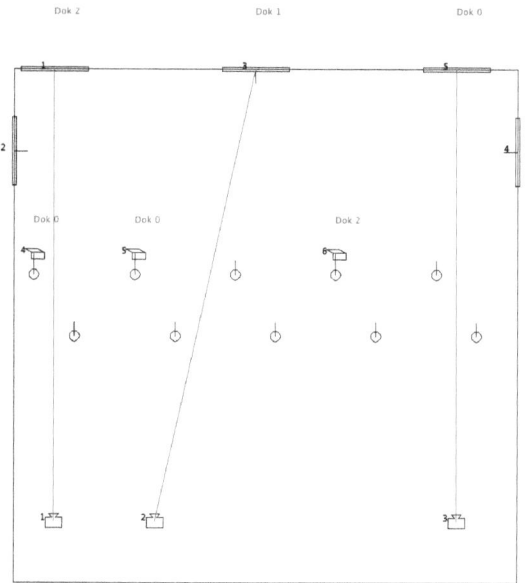

Figure B.4: Testroom 3

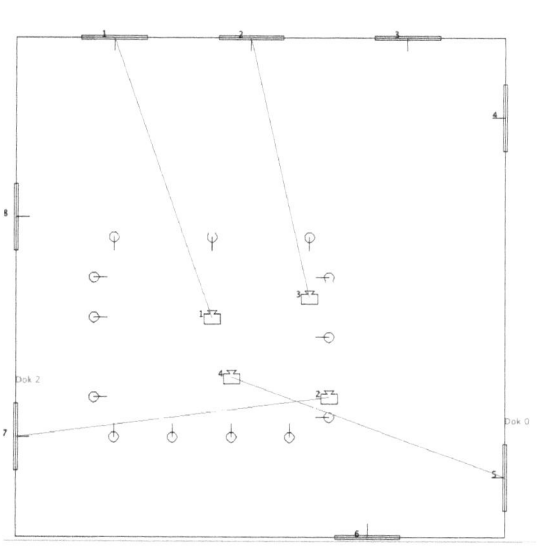

Figure B.5: Testroom 4

xiii

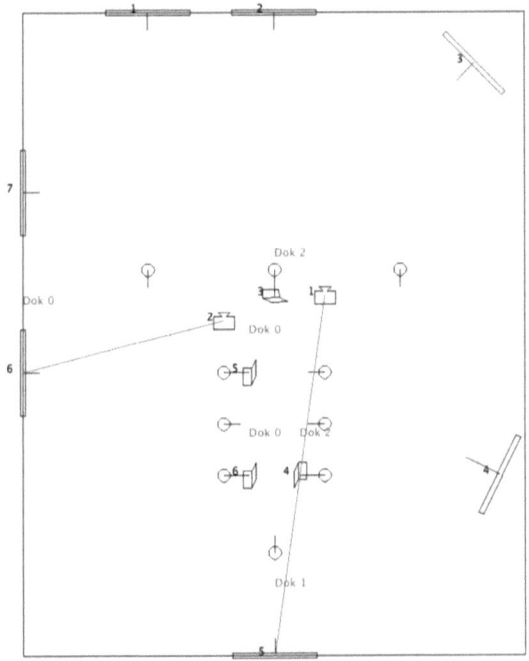

Figure B.6: Testroom 5

Test rooms for optimization algorithms

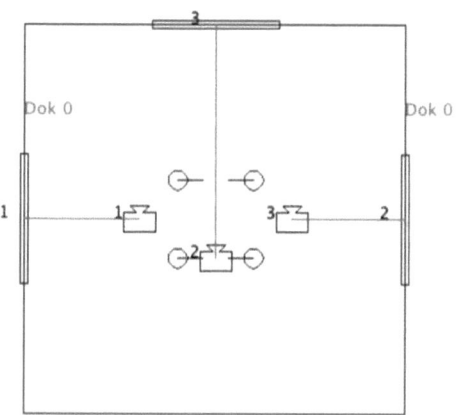

Figure B.7: Testroom 6

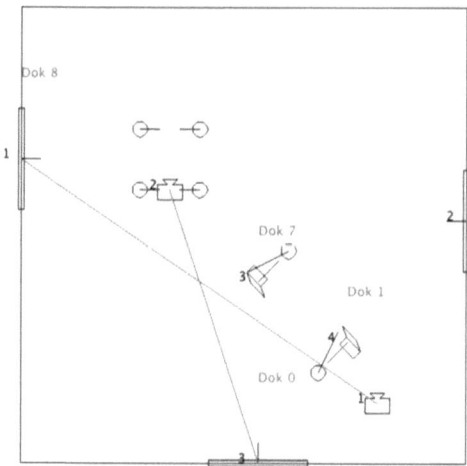

Figure B.8: Testroom 7

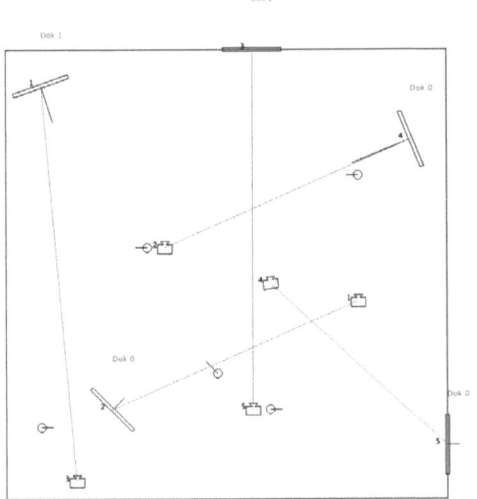

Figure B.9: Testroom 8

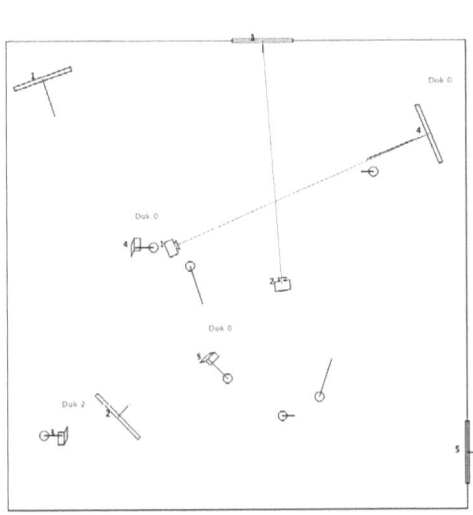

Figure B.10: Testroom 9

Test rooms for optimization algorithms

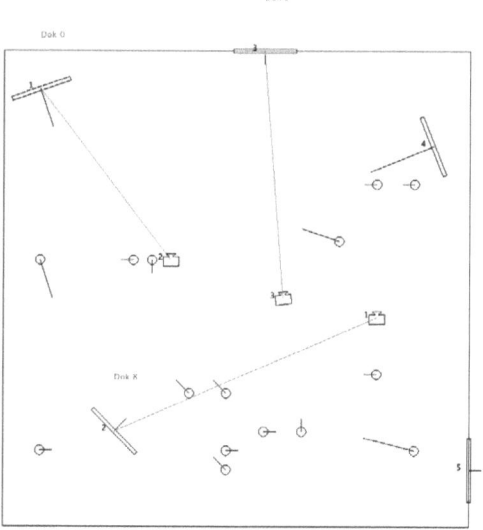

Figure B.11: Testroom 10

Die VDM Verlagsservicegesellschaft sucht für wissenschaftliche Verlage abgeschlossene und herausragende

Dissertationen, Habilitationen, Diplomarbeiten, Master Theses, Magisterarbeiten usw.

für die kostenlose Publikation als Fachbuch.

Sie verfügen über eine Arbeit, die hohen inhaltlichen und formalen Ansprüchen genügt, und haben Interesse an einer honorarvergüteten Publikation?

Dann senden Sie bitte erste Informationen über sich und Ihre Arbeit per Email an *info@vdm-vsg.de*.

Sie erhalten kurzfristig unser Feedback!

VDM Verlagsservicegesellschaft mbH
Dudweiler Landstr. 99
D - 66123 Saarbrücken
www.vdm-vsg.de

Telefon +49 681 3720 174
Fax +49 681 3720 1749

Die VDM Verlagsservicegesellschaft mbH vertritt

Printed by Books on Demand GmbH, Norderstedt / Germany